The Spur

The
CH SPURGEON
collection

The
CH SPURGEON
collection

Psalms

EMERALD HOUSE

BELFAST
NORTHERN IRELAND **GREENVILLE**
SOUTH CAROLINA

CONTENTS

I

"A PECULIAR PEOPLE"

"But know that the Lord hath set apart him that is godly
for himself: the Lord will hear when I call unto him."—
Psalm iv. 3.

IF you read this Psalm through, you will notice that, when
David wrote it, he had been pestered and troubled by certain
ungodly men who had made a mock of that which was his
greatest delight. They had turned his glory into shame, and
had proved that they loved folly and falsehood; so he said to
them, "O ye sons of men, how long will ye turn my glory into
shame? How long will ye love vanity, and seek after leasing,"
—or, "lying?" In order that he might stop them from angering
him, he reminded them of two great facts: "But know,"—said
he,—understand, do not doubt it, rest assured of it, "know that
Jehovah hath set apart him that is godly for himself: Jehovah
will hear when I call unto him." Why did David want these
men to know those two facts?

Well, first, that they might cease to oppose him; for, if they
did but know that the man whom they mocked at was really a
child of God, set apart by the Most High by a divine choice to
be his own peculiarly favoured one, surely, they would not go
on with their persecution. Those who put Christ to death did it
in ignorance, "for had they known, they would not have
crucified the Lord of glory." And we are persuaded that there
are many men who now oppose the servant of God, who would
not do so if they did but know really that he was a servant of
God, and that God looked upon him with delight. Therefore
David, to stop the cruel mockings of his persecutors, said to
them, "Know that Jehovah hath set apart him that is godly for
himself: Jehovah will hear when I call unto him."

He may also have had a still better motive, and I think that
he had,—namely, to draw these men towards his God. There is
no better way of taking flies than with honey, and no better
way of getting men to Christ than by drawing them to him by

7

a display of the privileges and advantages which belong to a godly life. "Know, then," said he, "you who are saying, 'Who will show us any good?' and who are seeking after mere vanities that never can satisfy you,—know ye that in true religion there is to be found that which will delight you, and which will give you rest and peace. Know this, 'that Jehovah hath set apart him that is godly for himself.'"

First, then, let us notice A PECULIAR CHARACTER: "him that is godly."

On reading the Psalm, it is very clear that this is *a man misunderstood*, or, *not understood on earth*. The ungodly cannot comprehend the godly; they scoff at them, they turn their glory into shame because they themselves love vanity and seek after lying. The godly man is not understood by the people among whom he dwells; God has made him to be a stranger and a foreigner in their midst. They who are born twice have a life which cannot be comprehended by those who are only born once. Those who have received the Spirit of God have a new spirit within them which is so singular that the carnal mind cannot perceive what it is. Spiritual things must be spiritually discerned. When a man has become a new creature in Christ Jesus, the old creatures round about him cannot make head or tail of him. They look at him, they see him actuated by motives which they cannot understand, they see that he is kept in check by forces which they do not acknowledge, that he is constrained by energies of which they are not partakers, and that he looks for a something which they do not desire; so the Christian becomes in a measure like to Christ himself, of whom the poet sings,—

> "*The Jewish world knew not their King,*
> *God's everlasting Son.*"

"Therefore the world knoweth us not, because it knew him not." "You are a very peculiar person," said one to a Christian. "I thank you for that testimony," answered the Christian; "for that is what I desire to be, as Peter says, 'Ye are a chosen generation, a royal priesthood, an holy nation, a peculiar people.'" "Ah!" said the other, "but there is a strangeness about you that I do not like; I feel sometimes that I cannot endure your company." "I thank you again," replied the

Christian, "for you only fulfil our Lord's words, 'Because ye are not of the world, but I have chosen you out of the world, therefore the world hateth you.'" Yes, dear friends, it is so; and if you never strike the worldling as being a strange person, if you never get the mocking laughter of the ungodly, if they never slander you, if you never detect any difference between yourself and them, and they never discover any between themselves and you, it must be because you are not a genuine child of God. "Marvel not, my brethren, if the world hate you. We know that we have passed from death unto life, because we love the brethren;" but the worldling does not understand the peculiar character of the godly, or delight in it.

But notice that, according to our text, this peculiar character is *understood in heaven*. God knows what godliness is, for he has created it, he sustains it, he is pledged to perfect it, and his delight is in it. What matters it whether you are understood by your fellow-men or not, so long as you are understood by God? If that secret prayer of yours is known to him, seek not to have it known to anyone besides. If your conscientious motive be discerned in heaven, mind not though it be denounced on earth. If your designs—the great principles that sway you,—are such as you dare plead in the great day of judgment, you need not stop to plead them before a jesting, jeering generation. Be godly, and fear not; and, if you be misrepresented, remember that, should your character be dead and buried among men, there will be "a resurrection of reputations" as well as of bodies. "Then shall the righteous shine forth as the sun in the kingdom of their Father."

What does the text mean when it mentions "him that is godly"? Well, it means, first, *a God-fearing man*. There are many who have not the fear of God before their eyes. Whether there be a God or not, is a matter of small consideration to them; they do not care which way the discussion terminates, for God is not in all their thoughts; and as long as he is not there, it does not matter to them whether he is anywhere. There are some who are not afraid of the terrors of God even with regard to the world to come; at any rate, they flatter themselves that they shall die at ease even if they live in wickedness; and, for the present, they even dare to defy the Most High. They have been heard—and our blood has chilled as we have heard them,—they have been heard to invoke condemnation from his hand as they have blasphemed his holy name. The godly man is one who fears God; he would not take God's name in vain, he would not wilfully violate God's law, he would not do anything that would grieve the Most High; and when he does so through infirmity, or sudden temptation, he is himself grieved that he should have grieved his God, for the fear of the Lord is upon him. He would not wish to stand at the judgment-bar of God, to be judged according to his works, apart from Jesus Christ his Lord; he would dread such a thing. The name of God,—the person of God,—the character of God,—these are matters of holy awe with him, his soul is filled with hallowed trembling while he thinks thereon; and everything that has to do with God is sacred to him. Heaven is no trifle, and hell is no trifle to him; the Book of God is no fable to him, the day of God is hallowed by him, and the Church of God is dear to him, for he is a God-fearing man. Often would he have done this or that, but he said, with Nehemiah, "So did not I, because of the fear of God."

But, advancing another step, a godly man is *a God-trusting man.* He is one who has learned to entrust his soul to the hands of God as unto a faithful Creator, one who has trusted his sin with God, beholding it laid upon the Divine Substitute. He has trusted his eternity with God; he believes that he shall die the death of the righteous, and that his last end shall be like his. He is resting in the living God, he trusts God about the present, he takes his troubles to God; aye, and if the day opens without trouble, he will not enter upon it without taking his day to God, nor will he fall asleep without committing his night to God. He trusts in God for little things, saying, "Give us this day our daily bread." He trusts in God for great things, saying, "Lead us not into temptation, but deliver us from evil."

Then advance still further, and understand the word "godly" as meaning *a God-loving man.* A godly man loves God; he is one whose heart has gone out after God. He loves his dear ones here below; but his God he loves more than all of them. He loves them in God, and loves God the more for giving them to him; but God himself has become his great object of delight. I am sure that he is a saved man who can follow David in saying, "God my exceeding joy." When one comes to joy in God, it is a sure evidence of godliness. The hypocrite has no delight in God; he may have a delight in the outward parade of religion, or in the name of godliness, possibly he has a delight in the bliss of heaven which he sometimes hopes that he may enjoy; but in God himself he has no delight; whereas, to the true believer, God is heaven. "Delight thyself also in the Lord," says David; and the genuine believer does so. He can say of his God,—

> "Thou art the sea of love,
> Where all my pleasures roll;
> The circle where my passions move,
> The centre of my soul."

And, assuredly, he is a godly man who is *a God-knowing man.* He does not merely fear and trust and love God but he has come into personal acquaintance with God. The other day, I saw a book entitled, "Is God knowable?" Well, that is a question that can be answered by some of us; we can say, "We know him; we have spoken to him, and he has spoken to us. Our spirit has come into actual contact with the Divine Spirit. We do not need anybody to prove this truth to us, for it is a matter of faith, nay, of joyous, ecstatic, delicious experience.

"My God, it is a fact that I have touched thee, and that thou hast touched me,—that I have spoken to thee, and that thou hast spoken unto me,—and it is that fact which has for ever made me glad." O beloved, if you know not God, what do you know? How are you a child of God if you do not know your Father? How are you saved if you do not know your Saviour? How can you come to the table to remember him whom you never knew? And must you not expect to hear him say at the last, "Depart from me; I never knew you"? If we know him, we are known of him; the two things go together, and are much the same; but, if we know him not, then he knows us not in the sense of acquaintance and of love.

Once more, a godly man is *a God-like man.* We reach this point, you see, by steps,—the man is God-fearing, God-trusting, God-loving, God-knowing, and then God-like. Can a man be like to God? Ah, me! what a wide discrepancy there must always be between God and the best of men! We are unlike God even in our likeness to him; he who is most like God is only like him as a dew-drop is like the sea, or as a glow-worm is like the sun. Yet grace does make us like God in righteousness, and true holiness, and especially in love. Has the Holy Spirit taught thee to love even those that hate thee? Hast thou a love that leaps out, like the waters from the smitten rock, that every thirsty one may drink? Wouldst thou fain love the poorest and the most depraved into the wealth and glory of thy Master's love? Dost thou love even those that render thee no love in return, as he did who gave his life for his enemies? Then art thou to that extent made like God. And dost thou choose that which is good? Dost thou delight thyself in peace? Dost thou seek after that which is pure? Art thou ever gladdened with that which is kind and just? Then art thou like thy Father who is in heaven, thou art a godly man, and this text is for you: "Know that the Lord hath set apart him that is godly for himself."

This leads me to dwell with pleasure upon A PECULIAR HONOUR which has been conferred upon this peculiar character: "The Lord hath set apart him that is godly for himself."

You see, then, that *God discerns godliness in men.* There is a great deal of dross in all of us, but God spies whatever gold there may be; if there be any gold in the ore, God preserves the lump because of the precious metal that is in it. I know that you are not perfect. Perhaps you are at this moment grieving over a great fault; if so, I am glad you have the godliness that makes you grieve over sin. I know that you are not what you want to be, or wish to be, or ought to be. Still, you do fear the Lord, and you do trust him, and you do love him. Now, the Lord can spy all that out, and he knows about the good that is in you. He casts your sin behind his back, but that which is of his own grace he sets apart for himself, and he sets you apart for himself because of the good which is in you. I do like to notice, in Scripture, that, although God's people are described as a very faulty people, and although the Lord is never tender towards sin, yet he is always very gentle towards them. If there is any good point about them, he brings it out, and he is most gracious to them; and his love casts a mantle over a thousand of their mistakes and errors. If God's people mentioned in the Old and New Testaments had all been perfect, I should have despaired; but, because they seem to have just the kind of faults that I grieve over in myself, I do not feel any more lenient toward my faults, but I do have the more hope that I also am among those whom the Lord sets apart for himself because they are godly.

Know yet further that *God makes those who are really godly to differ from the world.* He will not let them be like the world. Some of them try to be so, but they must not. And the world sometimes gets the victory over them for a time, and makes them like itself; but they soon get out of its power. Poor Samson told the secret of his great strength, and the Philistines cut off all that long hair of his which used to hang down his back till he seemed to be like a wild man of the woods. The Nazarite told his secret, and then they clipped away his hair, and set him to grind in the mill when they had put out his eyes. They should have had a razor drawn over his head every morning, but they forgot to do that; and when his hair had grown again, he pulled the temple down upon his enemies, and in his last moments won a glorious victory for his nation.

If the devil ever does cut the Nazarite locks of a true child of God, they will grow again in time; they must grow again, and they grow when the devil is not noticing them, and then the old strength of grace comes back again. I have known a child of God fall, like Peter did, when he denied his Master. Yet, when the locks of his consecration had grown again, in a short time there was Peter preaching a sermon that brought three thousand to Christ; and the devil had not made much of a gain of Peter after all, when once he came back to his Lord. But, oh, what a mercy it is to be kept so as never to lose those locks of consecration! Oh, that we may differ from the world in a thousand respects, so that we may go through it as Mr. Bunyan pictures his pilgrim going through Vanity Fair! "Buy, buy, buy," the merchants cried, but he did not buy any of their wares; and when they pressed him very hard, he said, "We buy the truth, and sell it not." All he had to do was to go through the fair; and that is what you and I have to do. Let us go through the world as those who are in it but not of it, the Lord always, by his grace, making us to differ from other men.

Further, the Lord sets apart him that is godly for himself, *by dealing with his people differently from others.* I fancy that I hear somebody say, "I stoutly deny that." Well, deny away if you like, for, apparently, the Lord does not deal with his people differently from what he does with others, and it says, even in Scripture, "All things come alike to all: there is one event to the righteous and the wicked." Here is a man of God, but the Sabeans steal his oxen and his asses, the Chaldeans carry away his camels, the fire of God burns up his sheep and his servants, and his children are destroyed by a great wind from the wilderness. Yes, yes; but read the whole of Job's story, and see that, when God turns his captivity, and gives him twice as much as he had before, and enables him to gain a great victory over the devil, after all, God did not deal with Job as he dealt with others. "Oh!" says another, "but whom the Lord loveth, he chasteneth." Yes, and that is one of the ways in which he differs in his dealings with them and with others; for, sometimes, he does not chasten the ungodly, but lets them have no trouble in their lives, and no pangs in their death. He lets them have as much pleasure as they can have, for what they get here is all they ever will have; whereas he chastens his own people for their present and eternal good. There is never exactly the same providence to the ungodly as to the godly. There is a difference somewhere, there is a difference in the end if nowhere else, for to you and to me, as God's people, "all things work together for good;" but they do not work together for good to the ungodly.

So God does make a difference between the godly and the rest of mankind; and there is one peculiar point of difference, he has set them apart for himself. For what purpose? That they may be his friends, and *that he may converse with them.* God does not usually come to this earth to talk with kings and princes;—the greatest king is but a brother-worm like the rest of us;—but God has often been here to converse and commune with his poor people. If men are godly, whether they are rich or poor, God has fellowship with them. It does seem wonderful to me that God should so often be unknown in his own world. The great majority of his creatures never hear his voice, and never give a response to his call; but the godly, when they hear the voice of their God saying to them, "Seek ye my face," cry out at once, "Thy face, Lord, will we seek." There are thousands at this moment speaking with God, but all of them are godly people; and God is speaking to them. The Holy Spirit is holding high intercourse with many of the sons and daughters of Adam, but only with those who are godly.

Moreover, God has also set apart him that is godly *that he may use him.* If you are a godly man, God will make you his own servant, and he will send you on his errands, and he will be with you all the while. He will employ you to carry messages of comfort, messages of warning, messages of invitation, to those who need them. If you are godly, God will use you. He will not use dirty vessels; but when we are clean, washed by his own hand in the cleansing fountain, then he will use us for his own purposes. We say to God, "Take my lips, my eyes, my ears, my feet, my whole being; reserve me for thyself." That is exactly what the Lord has done with the godly.

Know this, beloved, for, *at the last, God will own you as his.* Before astonished worlds, when ungodly men shall not dare to lift up their faces, God will own you in that day as belonging to him if you are godly. Your righteousness shall come forth as the light, and your judgment as the noon-day, for God has made you his own, and set a hedge about you, and none shall destroy you, or separate you from his Son.

Now I must speak briefly of A PECULIAR PRIVILEGE: "The Lord will hear when I call unto him."

This means, first, *"He will grant me an audience;* he will hear what I have to say." There were certain princes of Media and Persia who had the right to come to the king whenever they pleased. Such is the right of all the godly; whensoever you desire to speak with God, God is waiting to hear you. Oh, what a privilege is this! There are none of us who could go to see earthly kings and queens whenever we liked. We should have to be properly introduced, and go through all manner of forms and ceremonies; but through the one Mediator between God and men, we have the right at any moment of the day or night to have an audience with the King of kings and Lord of lords.

It means, next, *"The Lord will not only hear, but he will answer me."* Answer is intended in the word "hear": "The Lord will hear when I call unto him." Ask what ye will, O ye children of the King, and it shall be done unto you; ask him not merely for the half of his kingdom, but for the whole of it, and you shall have it. "No good thing will he withhold from them that walk uprightly." "He that spared not his own Son, but delivered him up for us all, how shall he not with him also freely give us all things?"

I am not going to preach about that part of my subject, I only want just to apply it. Many of you, dear brethren and sisters, desire to commune at the Lord's table; yet I hear one say, "I feel so dull, I do not know whether I dare come to the table. I seem as if I was dead, and I cannot get out of this cold, lethargic state." Let me whisper this message in your ear, "The Lord will hear you when you call unto him." Now, then, pray, "Lord, quicken me." You need not be dull, you need not be lethargic; up with you, for you have wings! Ask the Lord to help you to stretch them out, that you may rise superior to everything earth-born and grovelling, up into communion with the Most High.

"Ah!" sighs another, "but I feel so desponding, I am as heavy as lead. If I were thrown up, I should fall down again. I have so many doubts, I have such a sinking of spirit, that I often question whether I am a child of God at all." Now listen to our text: "The Lord will hear when I call unto him." Call unto him, "Lord, bring my soul out of prison! Lord, appear to thy poor servant!"

Try it now, believing and expecting that the Lord will hear you. You see, he has set you apart for himself, you belong to him, you are his treasure, his jewel, the signet on his finger, the delight of his heart, your name is graven on the palms of his hands; do you think he wishes you to be in this miserable state? Oh, no; he has sent the Comforter to deal with just such as you are! One Person of the Divine Trinity has undertaken the office of comforting the people of God; therefore he must want you to be happy and comfortable.

But I hear a brother say, "I have a great trouble on me, I have sustained a very heavy, a very serious loss in my business." Another says, "I have lost a dear child, and there is another loved one sickening." "Ah!" cries one, "if you were to step into my house, you would find it like the wards of a hospital; everybody in it seems to be ill. 'I am the man that hath seen affliction.'" Are you, dear brother? Then you are the very man who ought to pray, and to say, "The Lord will hear when I call unto him." He will either take your trouble away, or else make you glad that it ever came. He will either take your burden off, or else he will give you a strong back to bear it. You know, the deeper your troubles, the louder shall be your song at the last; and God will get more glory out of you by a life of trial than if you had a smooth path all the way. Come, then, call unto him: "The Lord will hear when I call unto him."

"Ah!" says one, "but my trouble is that I want to have my children converted." Then, pray for them, pray for them. "Oh, but it is my husband who is not a Christian!" says another. Then, pray for him. "I have prayed," says one. Pray on, dear sister, and the Lord will hear you. "I am afraid my husband will not be saved." Well, you must not be afraid, but say with David, "The Lord will hear when I call unto him." "Ah!" says another, "but I have to go back to-morrow into business, and I shall have to work with so many ungodly men, my life is one long struggle." Well, never mind about that to-night; it is not Monday yet. Let us get Monday's grace when Monday comes; and let us now enjoy ourselves as we repeat this precious text, "The Lord will hear when I call unto him." He will either stop those wicked men's mouths, or else he will open yours. He will give you the right word by way of reply, or else he will not let them say anything that needs a reply. Only tell the Lord about them. "The Lord will hear when I call unto him." Call unto him now, and he will hear and answer you.

II

UNANSWERED PRAYER

"O my God, I cry in the daytime, but thou hearest not; and in the night-season, and am not silent."—Psalm 22:2.

IT is very clear to everyone who reads this Psalm that these are not so much the words of David as they are the words of David's Son and David's Lord, our blessed Master. He prayed with strong crying and tears; he came before his Father's throne with supplications, and for a long time it seemed as if he would have no answer. It did appear as if God had utterly forsaken him, and that his enemies might persecute and take him.

Now, wherefore was the Saviour permitted to pass through so sad an experience? How was it that he, whose lightest word is prevailing with heaven, that he who pleads with Divine authority this day in his continual intercession, was permitted, when here below, to cry, and cry, and cry again, and yet to receive no comforting answer? Was it not mainly for this reason, that *he was making an atonement for us*, and he was not heard because *we as sinners did not deserve to be heard*? He was not heard, that we might be heard. The ear of God was closed against him for a season, that it might never be closed against us: that for ever the mourner's cry might find a way to the heart of God, because the cry of Jesus was for a while shut out from mercy's gate. He stood the surety for our sins, and was numbered with the transgressors: upon him the Lord laid the iniquity of all his people, and therefore being the sinner's representative, he could not for a while be heard.

There was also, no doubt, another reason, namely, *that he might be a faithful High-Priest having sympathy with his people in all their woes.* As this not being heard in prayer, or being unanswered for a while, is one of the greatest troubles which can fall upon the Christian, and fall it does, the Saviour had to pass through that trouble, too, that so it might be said of him :—

18

"In every pang that rends the heart,
The Man of Sorrows bore his part."

When I fear that I have not been heard in prayer, I can now look upon my Saviour and say:—

"He takes me through no darker rooms
Than he went through before."

He can now have a tender, touching sympathy with us, because he has been tempted in all points like as we are.

Was it not also, once more, in our Saviour's case, *with a view to display the wondrous faith, fidelity, and trustfulness of the obedient Son of God?* Having been found in fashion as a man, he humbled himself, and became obedient to his Father's will. Now, obedience is not perceived until it is tried, and faith is not known to be firm and strong until it is put to the test and exercised. Through what an ordeal did this pure gold pass! It was put into the crucible and thrust into the hottest coals; all glowing with a white heat, they were heaped upon him, and yet no dross was found in him. His faith never staggered; his confidence in his God never degenerated into suspicion, and never turned aside into unbelief. It is, "*My* God! *my* God!" even when he is forsaken. It is, "*My* God and *my* strength" even when he is poured out like water, and all his bones are out of joint.

In this thing he not only sympathises with us, you see, but *he sets us an example.* We must overcome, as he did, through faith. "This is the victory which overcometh the world, even your faith"; and if we can copy this great High-Priest of our profession, who endured such contradiction of sinners against himself—if we can copy him so as to be neither faint in our minds, nor turn from our Master's work—we shall triumph even as he overcame.

But my chief object in considering this theme is not so much to speak of the Saviour's trial, as to address myself to those of our number who may even now be passing through the same experience as our Lord.

In the first place, the text—without any enquiry into the cause of unanswered prayer, seems to give: A GENERAL GUIDE FOR OUR CONDUCT.

Supposing that we have been seeking some blessing from God for many months, and have not obtained it; whether it be a personal blessing, or on behalf of others, what ought to be our conduct under such a trial as that, the trial of a long delay, or an apparent refusal? The text, it is clear, teaches us that *we must not cease to trust God.* "O my God." Oh! that appropriating word! It is not, perhaps, "My Father." The spirit of adoption is not here so much, as the spirit of reverent trustfulness, but still there is the hold-fast word still—"O *my* God." Christian, never be tempted to give up your hold upon your only strength, upon your solitary hope. Under no conceivable circumstances, ever give place for an instant to the dark thought that God is not true and faithful to his promises. Though you should have seven years of unanswered prayer, yet suggest any other reason to your mind than one which would dishonour him. Say, with the Saviour in this Psalm, "But thou art holy." Settle that in your mind. Oh! never suffer the faintest breath of suspicion to come upon the fair fame of the Most High, for he doth not deserve it. He *is* true; he *is* faithful. In this apparently worst of all cases, he did deliver his Son, and come to the rescue in due time. In all other cases he has done the same and I pray you never to distrust your God, never cast a slur upon his integrity. Oh! believe him to be good and true! You may not know why it is that he deals so strangely with you, but oh! never think that he is unfaithful for an instant, or that he has broken his word. Continue still to trust him.

Once again, as we are never to cease to trust, so we are *never to cease to pray.* The text is very express upon this point. "I cry in the daytime, but thou hearest not: and in the night-seasons I am not silent." Never cease your prayers. No time is ill for prayer. The glare of daylight should not tempt you to cease; and the gloom of midnight should not make you stop your cries. I know it is one of Satan's chief objects to make the Christian cease praying, for if he could but once make us put up the weapon of all-prayer, he would easily vanquish us and take us for his prey. But so long as we continue to cry to the Most High, Satan knows he cannot devour the very weakest lamb of the flock. Prayer, mighty prayer, will yet prevail if it hath but time.

And while you never cease from your trust, nor from your prayer, *grow more earnest in both.* Let your faith be still more resolved to give up all dependence anywhere but upon God, and let your cry grow more and more vehement. It is not every knock at mercy's gate that will open it; he who would prevail must handle the knocker well, and dash it down again, and again, and again. As the old Puritan says, "Cold prayers ask for a denial, but it is red-hot prayers which prevail." Bring your prayers as some ancient battering-ram, against the gate of heaven, and force it open with a sacred violence, "for the kingdom of heaven suffereth violence, and the violent take it by storm." He that would prevail with God must take care that all his strength be thrust into his prayers.

And yet again, *cease not to hope.* The New Zealander has a word for hope which signifies "the swimming-thought"; because when all other thoughts are drowned, hope still swims. She lifts her head out of the foamy waves, with her tresses all trailing, but sees the blue heaven above her, and hopes, as that is there. So if thou hast prayed never so long, yet hope on. "Hope thou in God, for I shall yet praise him, who is the strength of my life, and my portion for ever." As long as there is a place of prayer, and a promise of an answer, no believer ought to give way to despair.

"Go again," said Elijah to his servant seven times. It must have been weary work to the prophet to have to wait so long. He did not stand up once and pray to God as on Carmel, and then instantly came down the fire to continue the sacrifice; but again and again, and, getting more humble in posture, with his face between his knees, he beseeches the Lord, not for fire, which was an unusual thing, but for water, which is the common boon of the skies. And yet, though he pleads for that which the Lord himself had promised, yet it did not at once come, and when his servant came back, four, five, six times, the answer was still the same; there was no sign of rain, but the brazen heavens looked down on an earth which was parched as if in an oven. "Go again!" said the prophet, and at the seventh time lo! there appeared the cloud like unto a man's hand, and this cloud was the sure forerunner of the deluge and storm. Christian, go again seven times. Nay, I will venture to say seventy times seven, for God *must* keep his promise. Heaven and earth may pass away, but not one jot or tittle of Jehovah's word can fail. "The grass withereth, the flower thereof fadeth away, but the word of our God endureth for ever." Do you plead that enduring word? Let no dark thoughts drive you to despair. Continue to trust; continue to pray; increase in your fervency, and in the hope that the blessing will yet come. It did come to the Saviour. The morning broke upon his midnight after all. Never tide ebbed out so far as in the Saviour's case, when the great stretches of misery and sorrow were visible where once God's love had rolled in mighty floods; but when the time came it began to turn, and see how it hath turned now in mighty floods of matchless joy. The love of God has come back to our once suffering Saviour, and there upon the eternal throne he sits, the Man, the Crucified, who bowed his head under mountains of almighty wrath, which broke in huge billows, and covered his soul. Be of good courage, Christian! Hope on, poor soul, and hope on for ever.

We now go on to a second point, and shall enquire into: THE CAUSES OF UNANSWERED PRAYER.

We shall, perhaps, on this theme, get a few special directions which may be available in particular cases. There are some of us who are not often troubled about unanswered prayer: on the contrary, our own experience is such that the existence of a God who hears his people's cry is reduced to an absolute, mathematical certainty.

I have no more doubt about this than about my own existence, not because I can see it clearly and understand it perfectly, nor because, with a blind credulity, I submit myself to the Bible as being the infallible revelation of God. But because I have had real dealings with God, have tried and proved his promises to be true, and have found out that, according to my faith, it has been done unto me in a thousand instances. This is truth that those who have learned to live in the spirit-world, and to talk with God, understand and know as plainly as they understand and know that when a child speaketh to its father, its father granteth its request. It has become to many believers, not at all a matter to be argued or talked of by way of dispute. They *know* that they have fellowship with the Father, and with his Son, Jesus Christ, and their prayers are answered. But occasionally, to all believers, I suppose, there will come staggering moments, when they scarcely know how to reply to their doubts, because certain of their prayers have not been answered.

It may possibly happen that the cause of unanswered prayer may many times lie *in something connected with sin*. Do you not think that unanswered prayers are often a Fatherly chastisement for our offences? The Saviour, in that wonderful chapter where he tells out his love to us, says, "If ye keep my commandments, ye shall abide in my love," and then he notes, as a special favour, if a man abide in his love, and keep his commandments, he "shall ask what he will, and it shall be done unto him." Now, it seems to me to be only reasonable that if I will not do what God wills, God will refuse to do what I will: that if he asks me a certain duty, and I refuse it, when I ask him for a certain privilege or favour, it is not unkind, but, on the other hand, most wise and kind, that he should say, "No: my child, no: if thou wilt not listen to my tender command, it is kind to refuse thee thy desire until thou dost repent and obey."

Perhaps this is the way in which, too, are visited upon God's people, *some neglects of ordinances*. "He that knoweth his Master's will and doeth it not, the same shall be beaten with many stripes"; and one of these stripes may surely be our non-success in prayer. It may be also temporal affliction, but probably this is one of the main ways in which the Master inflicts the stripes upon his children. They are negligent of his commands, and he says, "Then thou shalt tarry awhile; I will not yet grant thee what thou seekest; but when thou comest to a better mind, and art more scrupulous and tender in the fulfilling of my commands, then thy longings shall be satisfied."

It may occur, too, that this delay may be a sort of *disclosure* to us as to wherein our sin lieth. Sin sometimes lieth in a Christian unrepented of, because he only dimly realises that it is there. Hear what Job declares: "Are the consolations of God small with thee? Is there any secret thing with thee?" That is to say, if thou lovest selfish ease and feeble comforting, if thou dost not prevail with God in prayer, is there some secret sin in thee which keepeth back the blessing? God doth, as it were, say to us, "Search and look." Unanswered prayer should be to every Christian a search-warrant, and he should begin to examine himself to see whether there be not something harboured within which is contrary to the will of God. Oh! believer, this is not a hard work for thee to do, surely, but it is a very necessary one. Search thyself, and breathe the prayer, "Search me, O God, and try me, and know my ways, and see if there be any evil way in me, and lead me in the way everlasting."

Sometimes there may be great sin in the prayer itself. Are not our greatest sins often connected with our holiest things? We must be aware of our prayers. There is such a thing as polluting the mercy-seat. Remember what became of Nadab and Abihu, who offered strange fire before the Lord. Beware, Christian, beware; thou mayest sin against God in the prayer-chamber, as well as thou canst in the market; and thou mayest offend on thy knees, as well as when thou art in thy business. Have a care, for how canst thou hope that a prayer thus stained with sin can ever succeed, unless thou bringest it to the blood to have it purged and cleansed from all defiling before it mounts to the throne of grace?

And I do sometimes fear, too, that our prayers do not speed, because the thing asked for, though as we think good for us, is *asked for from a wrong motive*. If, for instance, a Christian minister asks that he may win souls in order that he may gain reputation and fame as a useful and successful evangelist for his Master, he will probably not be heard, for he asks from an unworthy motive. If I seek to be useful merely that I may be known to be a useful man or woman, I am really seeking my own honour, and can I expect God to minister to, and pamper that? I must take care, then, that even when I ask for a good thing, I ask it for the purest of reasons, namely, for God's glory. Oh! what washing even our prayers need! What cleansing, what purging!

But we go on to notice that non-success in prayer *may sometimes be the result of ignorance*.

I think persons often offer *very ignorant prayers indeed*. I am sure I have good evidence that some do. There is scarcely ever a week passes in which I do not receive intelligence from different persons who are on the verge of bankruptcy, or deeply in debt, that they have prayed to God about it, and that they have been guided to write to me to get them out of their difficulties, and to pay their debts. Now, I am always perfectly willing to do so as soon as ever I am directed expressly by God himself, but I shall not receive the direction at second-hand. As soon as I receive it myself—and I think it is only fair that I should receive it, as well as they—I shall be quite willing to be obedient to his direction, provided, too, the funds are in hand, which does not often happen. But folks must be very foolish to suppose that, because they ask God that such and such a debt may be paid by miraculous means, it will certainly be done.

I have a right to ask for anything which God has promised me, but if I go beyond the range of the Divine promises, I also go beyond the range of assured and confident expectation. The promises are very large and very wide, but when one gets a fancy in his head, he must not suppose that God is there, in his fancy. I have known some fanatical persons who thought they could live by faith. They were going to preach the Gospel, having no gifts whatever for preaching. They were going to be missionaries in a district having no more gift to be missionaries than horses in a plough. But they thought they were destined to do it, and therefore they tried to live by faith, and when they had been nearly half-starved, then they complained against the goodness, and abandoned the labour. Had God really inspired and sent them, he would have sustained and kept them, but if they go about it wilfully and stubbornly on their own account, they must be driven back to realise their own ignorance of the Divine will.

And then often-times we pray in a way *in which our prayers could not be heard consistent with the dignity of the Most High.* I love a holy familiarity with God, and I believe it to be commendable; but still, man is but man, while God is God, and, however familiar we may be with him in our hearts, still we must recollect the distance there is between the Most High and the most elevated and most beloved of his creatures, and we are not to speak as though it were in our power to do as we will and as we please. We must mind that we do not mistake the familiarity of communion for the impudence of presumption. We must be careful to distinguish between the two, for he who is taught of God, and waiteth upon him according to his own mind, will find, as a general rule, that he will not be long without an answer to his prayer.

Again, does it not often happen that there may be *reasons for delay lying in our own infirmity?*

Sometimes, if a mercy were to come to a believer immediately that he asked for it, it would come too soon, but God timeth it until it appears only at the right and best moment. Perhaps thou art not yet ready for the blessing. Thou hast asked for strong meat, but thou art but as yet a babe, and therefore thou art to be content with milk for a little while longer. Thou hast asked for a man's trials, and a man's privileges, and a man's work, but thou art as yet only a child growing up into manhood, and thy good Father will give thee what thou askest for, but he will give it thee in such a way as to make it not a burden to thee, but a boon. If it came now, it might involve responsibilities which thou couldest not overtake, but, coming by and bye, thou shalt be well prepared for it.

There are reasons, too, I doubt not, *which lie in our future,* why our prayers are not answered. Delays in prayer may turn out to be a sort of training school for us. Take the Apostle's instance. The "thorn in the flesh" was very painful, and though he was a chosen apostle, yet he had no answer. Thrice he cried, but still the "thorn in the flesh" was not removed. It was well that it was not, for Paul needed to be taught tenderness, in order that he might write those loving epistles of his, and therefore he received an answer of another sort, "My grace is sufficient for thee." Oh! Christian! if thou couldest get rid of the trouble in which thou now art, thou wouldest not be able to comfort poor mourners, as thou shalt yet do. Thou wouldest not be a full-grown, strong man, if thou hadst not these stern trials to develop thy manly vigour. Men do not learn to be intrepid sailors by staying on dry land. Thou art to put out to sea in the midst of the storm, that thou mayest learn how to manage and guide the vessel of thy soul. Thou art going through a rough drill, that thou mayest be a valiant and stalwart, a good soldier of Jesus Christ, for battles are yet to come, and grim foes yet to face: for thou hast many fightings between now and the blessed active ease of heaven.

Thou hast not yet won the crown, but thou wilt have to cut thy way inch by inch and foot by foot, and the Master is making thee an athlete, that wrestling with thine enemies thou mayest overcome. He is strengthening thy muscles and tendons, thews and sinews, by the arduous exercise of unanswered prayer, that thou mayest be finely useful in the future.

Still, yet again, perhaps the reason why prayer is not always quickly answered is this: a reason which no tongue can tell, but *which is inscrutable lying in the sovereign purposes and wisdom of God.*

Now, see! If I cannot tell why God doth not hear me, what must I say? I had better say naught, but put my finger on my lips and wait. Who am I that I should question him as to what he doeth! Who am I that I should arraign my Maker before my bar, and say unto him, "What doest thou?" Almighty Potter, thou hast a right to do as thou willest with thine own clay! We have learned to submit to thy will, not because we must, but because we love that will, feeling that thy will is the highest good of thy creatures, and the sublimest wisdom.

And now I conclude this point by saying that if the Christian, after looking into the matter, cannot find out a reason why he should not be answered, let him still expect that he shall be, and wait *still upon God*, remembering, however, that he may never be answered after his own fashion, but that he shall be answered after God's fashion.

And now, to conclude, I thought I would say a few words upon a very special case which may occur, and which may be here represented this evening. It is not the case of a Christian asking a boon for himself, but it is the case of *a sinner, conscious of his danger as a sinner, asking for mercy.*

Brethren and sisters, it was a very unhappy lot to have to seek the Lord, with such earnestness as I could command as a child for four or five years, with sighs, and cries, and entreaties, but to have no comfortable answer whatsoever, to be as one that chooses strangling rather than life, because of a sense of God's anger, in my soul, to desire reconciliation, to live in the midst of gospel light, and to hear the truth preached every Sabbath day, indeed every day in the week after a fashion, and yet not to discover the way to heaven. Now, sometimes it is not good advice to say to such a person, go on praying. It *is* good advice; I must correct myself there, but it is not the best advice in such a case. Soul, if thou hast been seeking mercy, and thou canst not find it, go on praying by all means; never relax that, but it is not by that that thou wilt ever get peace.

The business of thy soul is to listen to Christ's command, and his command is contained in the gospel, which gospel is not, "Go ye into all the world and tell every creature to pray," but it is, "He that believeth and is baptised shall be saved." Now, thy business is to pray, certainly, but thy first business is to believe. Thy prayers before thou believest have but little weight in them. Unbelieving prayers! Shall I call them prayers? Prayers without faith! They are birds without wings, and ships without sails, and beasts without legs. Prayers that have no faith in Christ in them are prayers without the blood on them: they are deeds without the signature, without the seal, without the stamp—they are impotent, illegal documents. Oh! if thou couldest but come as thou art, and look to Christ on the Cross! It is not thy prayers that can save thee: it is Christ's prayers and Christ's tears, and Christ's sufferings, and Christ's blood, and Christ's death. If thou trusteth to thy prayers, thou hast gone back again to the old beggarly elements of the law. Thou mightest as well trust to thy good works as to thy prayers, and to trust either will be to rest in "a refuge of lies." Thy hope, sinner, lies in the altogether gratuitous mercy of God, and that mercy only comes to those who rest in Jesus Christ alone, waiting patiently for him. Oh! that thou couldest but come just as thou art, and lay thyself at mercy's door, with such a word as this on thy lips:—

> "My hope is fixed on nothing else
> Than Jesus' blood and righteousness."

There are no doings of thine needed to complete the work. Nay! I venture to say, not even any praying of thine. Thy prayings and thy doings shall each occupy their proper place afterwards, and then they shall be essential in their way, but now, as a sinner, thy business is with the sinner's Saviour. If thou art enabled now to look completely out of self, and see all that thy flesh can do as dead and buried for ever in the grave of Christ, and as being naught and worse than naught, and if thou canst see Jesus, the mighty Saviour, distributing the gifts which he has received for men, even distributing them to the rebellious—if thou canst thus trust him, thou art saved.

As to you who have never looked before, I pray the Master

to open your blind eyes, and cause the scales to drop, so that you may look now, and, while you look, may see everything you want laid up for you in Jesus. Everything a sinner needs can be richly supplied by him, and then the sinner can go his way rejoicing and singing "Christ is all, and happy am I that I have sought and found him."

III

THE SAINTS' LOVE TO GOD

"O love the Lord, all ye his saints."—Psalm 31 : 23.

DO we, if we are called the saints of the Lord, need to be exhorted to love him? If we do, shame upon us! And we do, I am quite sure; so let us be ashamed and confounded that it should ever be needful to urge us to love our Lord. Why, after he has done so much for us, and manifested such wondrous love to such unworthy ones as we are, we ought to love him as naturally as sparks of fire ascend towards the sun, or as the waters of the river run towards the sea. It should be our second and higher nature evermore to love the Lord without the slightest prompting. What the law required, the Gospel should have wrought in us, namely, to love the Lord our God with all our heart, and with all our mind, and with all our soul, and with all our strength.

But, brethren and sisters, we do need this exhortation; we feel that we do. Well, then, let us take it home to ourselves, and let us hear it as though it had been spoken personally to each one of us who are the Lord's saints: "O love the Lord." Do nothing else just now; bid every other thought begone, and every other emotion, too.

Remember that the man, who here exhorts the saints to love their Lord, was one who had been enduring very sharp trials. This Psalm is, in many respects, a very sad one. If you will read it through, you will see that David had been afflicted by slanderous and other cruel enemies; and yet, while he was still suffering from their attacks, and also fearing that he was cut off from the Lord's presence, he yet said, "'O love the Lord, all ye his saints,' for my Lord is so good that I will speak well of him even when he smites me. He is such a gracious God that I can truly say, 'Though he slay me, yet will I trust in him.' Though he may smite me never so hard, yet still will I adore him, still will I bless and magnify his name as long as I have any being." If a tried child of God could talk like that, how ought we, who have comparatively few trials, to love the Lord!

So, first, let us remember that THIS EXHORTATION REFERS TO EACH PERSON OF THE DIVINE TRINITY.

We can never understand how Father, Son, and Holy Spirit can be three and yet one. We bless him that he is one, as Moses said, "Hear, O Israel: the Lord our God is one Lord;" yet we also bless him that Father, Son, and Holy Spirit, each in his separate personality, should be worshipped as God.

O then, ye saints, *love God the Father!* We sometimes meet with Christians who are so ignorant as scarcely to give the same degree of love to the Father as they give to the Son. They foolishly suppose that the Son has done something to make the Father love us. That is not the belief of any Spirit-taught children of God, for we say, with good John Kent,—

> "'Twas not to make Jehovah's love
> Towards the sinner flame,
> That Jesus, from his throne above,
> A suffering man became.
>
> "'Twas not the death which he endured,
> Nor all the pangs he bore,
> That God's eternal love procured,
> For God was love before."

It was because of his love that the Father gave his Son; it was not the Son who came to make that love possible. O Christians, love the Father, for he chose you! Or ever the earth was, the Father concentrated his love upon you, and gave you to Christ to be his portion and his reward. If you are this day, children of the great Father, it is because he has taken you out from among the rest of mankind, and has made you "heirs of God, and joint-heirs with Christ." It is the Father, too, who has given you the nature as well as the name and the position of children, for he "hath begotten us again unto a lively hope by the resurrection of Jesus Christ from the dead, to an inheritance incorruptible, and undefiled, and that fadeth not away," and he "hath made us meet to be partakers of the inheritance of the saints in light." For your election unto everlasting life, for your salvation by Christ Jesus, for your regeneration by the Holy Spirit, for your adoption into the family of God, "O love the Lord, all ye his saints." Let your soul swim as in a sea of love, and each one say, "My Father, my God, my own God, I love thee! My soul exults at the very thought of thy great love to me, which has made my love to thee possible!"

And then, O ye saints, *love God the Son!* I know that you do this also, for there is not a Peter amongst us, who, if Christ said to him, "Lovest thou me?" would not reply, "Lord, thou knowest all things: thou knowest that I love thee." How shall I speak of what God the Son has done for us? Think of the glory that he left, and of the shame that he endured, for our sakes. Picture him hanging at a woman's breast at Bethlehem, and afterwards hanging on a cross at Calvary. Let your eye lovingly gaze upon him in the weakness of his infancy, and then in the greater weakness of his death-agony, and remember that he suffered all this for you. For you the thorn-crown; for you the spittle on his cheeks; for you the plucking of his hair; for you the accursed lash that scourged his sacred shoulders; for you the nails, the sponge, the vinegar, the gall, the spear, the tomb,—all for you. "O love the Lord, all ye his saints," as ye think of his amazing love to you! I would almost ask you to come to those dear feet of his, and to do as the woman who was a sinner did,—to wash his feet with your tears, and to wipe them with the hairs of your head, while you might softly sing,—

> *"Love and grief my heart dividing,*
> *With my tears his feet I'll bathe,*
> *Constant still in faith abiding,*
> *Life deriving from his death."*

And then, O ye saints, I must not forget to dwell upon the thought that you must *love God the Holy Spirit!* Never let us forget him, or speak of him, as some do, as "it", for the Holy Spirit is not "it"; or talk of him as though he were a mere influence, for the Holy Ghost is divine, and is to be reverenced and loved equally with the Father and the Son. It was that blessed Spirit who quickened us when we were dead in trespasses and sins; it was he who illuminated us, and removed our darkness; and, since that time, it has been he who has taken of the things of Christ, and revealed them unto us. He has been our Comforter to cheer us, and our Instructor to teach us; and, most wonderful of all, he dwelleth in us. I have often said that I do not know which mystery to admire the more,—the incarnation of the Son of God, or the indwelling of the Holy Spirit. For Christ to take our nature upon him was, doubtless, marvellous condescension; but that only lasted for a little over thirty years; but the Holy Spirit comes and dwells, century after century, in successive generations of his people, abiding and working in the hearts of men. O ye saints, love the Lord the Spirit!

Then, in the second place, note that THIS EXHORTATION MAY BE UNDERSTOOD IN THE FULLEST CONCEIVABLE SENSE: "O love the Lord, all ye his saints."

You may pull up the sluices of your being, and let all your life-floods flow forth in this sacred stream, for you cannot love God too much. Some passions of our nature may be exaggerated; and, towards certain objects, they may be carried too far; but the heart, when it is turned towards God, can never be too warm, nor too excited, nor too firmly fixed on the divine object: "O love the Lord, all ye his saints."

Put the emphasis upon that sweet word, love,—*love the Lord as you cannot love anyone or anything else.* Husband, you love your wife; parent, you love your children; children, you love your parents; and all of you love your friends; and it is well that you do so. But you must spell all other love in little letters, but spell LOVE to God in the largest capitals you can find. Love him intensely, love the Lord, all ye his saints, without any limit to your love.

Next, *love him with a deep, abiding principle of love.* There is a certain kind of human love which burns very quickly, like brushwood, and then dies out. So, there are some Christians, who seem to love the Lord by fits and starts, when they get excited, or at certain special seasons; but I pray you, beloved, to let your love be a deep-seated and lasting fire. What if I compare it to the burning in the very heart of a volcano? It may not be always in eruption, but there is always a vehement heat within; and when it does burst forth, oh, what heavings there are, what seethings, what boilings, what flamings, and what torrents of lava all around! There must always be the fire at the heart, even when it is somewhat still and quiet.

Then, *love the Lord with an overwhelming emotion.* You will not always feel like that, and you need not wish to do so, because the human mind is not capable of continually feeling, to an overwhelming degree, the emotion of love to God. There may be a slackening of conscious emotion, for we have to go to our business, and to be occupied with many cares, and with thoughts that, necessarily, claim our attention; but we do not love the Lord any the less because we are not so conscious of our love as at other times. Still, you must have your times when you are conscious of the emotion of love to God. Set apart special seasons when you may pray the Lord to come to you in an unusual manner. On such occasions, you do not want to do anything but just love him, and give your soul full liberty to gaze upon the unspeakable beauties of your God. Oh, it is delightful to be utterly carried away with this emotion!

There are some of the saints of God who have found that this emotion has been too strong for them, and they have had to cry to the Lord, "Hold! hold! for I am but an earthen vessel; and if more of this amazing love be poured into me, I shall be unable to bear it." There have been very remarkable experiences with some of the saints when this sacred passion has completely overpowered them. They have been forgetful of all things else, and have seemed absent-minded and abstracted;— whether in the body, or out of the body, they could not tell. Well, beloved, indulge that emotion all you can. If you cannot get the highest degree of it, get as much of it as you can. Have the principle of love, and then ask the Lord to give you the emotion which arises from it. Yea, I would go still further, and join you in praying that our love to our God might come to be a very passion of the soul,—a passion that can never be satisfied until we get to him, and are with him for ever. That is the true love which grows so eager and impatient that it counts life a banishment so long as it is spent down here.

Having thus shown you that this exhortation is applicable to each Person of the Divine Trinity, and that it may be understood in the most emphatic sense, now let me say, in the third place, that IT HAS A THOUSAND ARGUMENTS TO ENFORCE IT.

The short time we have for this service will not allow me to mention many of these reasons; but this is my comfort,—that *a soul that truly loves God does not want any reasons for loving him.* We have an old proverb, which says that "love is blind;" and, certainly, love is never very argumentative. It overcomes a man so that he is completely carried away by it; and he, who really loves God, will feel that this supreme passion puts aside the necessity for cold reasoning. How could you, by logic, produce love even between two human beings? You may prove that you ought to love, but "ought to love" and "love" itself are two very different things. Where true love is, however, it finds a thousand arguments for its own increase.

This love, to which God's saints are exhorted, is in every way deserved. *Think of the excellence of his character whom you are bidden to love.* God is such a perfect being that I feel now that, altogether apart from anything he has done for me, I love him because he is so good, so just, so holy, so faithful, so true. There is not one of his attributes that is not exactly what it ought to be. If I look at his dear Son, I see that his character is so gloriously balanced that I wonder why even those who deny his Godhead do not worship such a character as his, for it is absolutely unique. When I think of the character of the ever-blessed Spirit,—his patience and his wisdom,—his tenderness and his love to us,—I cannot help loving him. Yes, beloved, we must love Father, Son, and Spirit, for never had human hearts such an object to love as the Divine Trinity in Unity.

If you will let your mind specially dwell upon God's great goodness, surely you must feel the throbbings of strong affection towards him. What is God? "God is love." That short word comprehends all. He is a great God, but he is as gracious as he is great. We might conceive of a god who was a great tyrant; but it was impossible that our God should be one. "The Lord is good to all: and his tender mercies are over all his works." He is as full of goodness as the sun is full of light, and as full of grace as the sea is full of water; and all that he has he delights to give out to others. It is his happiness and glory to make his creatures happy; and even when he is stern and terrible, it is only of necessity that he is so, because it cannot be for the good of the universe which he governs that sin should be lightly treated or suffered to go unpunished. God, my God, thou art altogether lovely; and where the heart is in a right condition, it must love thee.

I cannot walk the glades beneath the forest trees, and listen to the singing of the birds, and observe how even the insects in the grass leap up for very joy, without saying, "He is a blessed God, indeed, who has made such a beautiful world as this." Some men and women seem to think that this world was made for them, and they talk about flowers wasting their sweetness upon the desert air; but let them gaze upon the marvels of beauty in the fair woods; and let them look at the myriad ants which build their cities there. They appear to be happy enough in their way, and to be bringing some honour and glory to the God that made them, and this beautiful world in which they dwell.

Then think of the providence of God,—his providence to you especially. I cannot tell the various ways in which the Lord has led each one of you, but I can speak for myself. If there is any man, under heaven, who has reason to love the Lord for every step of the way in which he has been led, I am that man; but I hope there are many others here who could say just the same if I gave them the opportunity. Notwithstanding all your trials and troubles, has not the Lord been a good God to you? I have heard many strange things in the course of my life; but I have never heard one of the Lord's servants, when he came to die, regret that he had taken him for a Master; nor have I ever heard one of them rail at him because of even the heaviest blows of his hand; but, like Job, they have said, "The Lord gave, and the Lord hath taken away; blessed be the name of the Lord." Yes, as much blessed when he takes away as when he gives.

But, my brethren and sisters, if I call to your remembrance the great mystery of the atoning sacrifice of Christ,—if I only utter these words,—"Incarnation,—Substitution,—Justification,—Sanctification,—" without dwelling upon the great truths that they represent, surely they must awaken responsive echoes in your spirit, and, as far as your faith has grasped these precious things, you must feel that you have many weighty reasons why you should love the Lord.

I must pass on to remark that another reason for loving the Lord is that *it is such a pleasant and profitable exercise.* If David had said, "Dread the Lord's anger, fear the Lord as a slave fears the lash," that would have been a crushing, weakening, sorrowful message. That is not what you are bidden to do; but, "O love the Lord, all ye his saints." If it had merely been said, "Obey the Lord, whether you do it cheerfully or not; just do what you are told to do;"—well, that is a poor sort of religion that consists in a formal round of performances, and nothing more. If it had been said, "Submit to the Lord: you cannot do otherwise, for he is your Master;"—well, we should have been obliged to do it, but it would have been cold work, and there would have been no comfort to be derived from it. If it had been written, "Understand the Lord," we might have given up the task in despair, for how can the finite comprehend the Infinite? But when it is written, "O love the Lord,"—why, one of the most delightful exercises of the human heart is to love. Many, who have had no other sources of happiness, have found great joy in domestic love; and those who have been denied domestic love have found a sweet assuagement of their grief in the love of benevolence towards the poor. That heart may well be wretched that has no one to love. If you want to be happy, and to do the best thing that is possible in your whole life, love your God. When you want to have a season of ecstatic bliss, this is the way to it,—by the road of love to God, you will get to the purest, highest joys that can be known even in heaven itself. Now that you have this blessed secret communicated to you, make use of it, and love your God because it is such a pleasant and profitable exercise.

Let us love the Lord, next, *because it is so beneficial to do so.* The man who loves God is delivered from the tyranny of idols, and idols are great tyrants. Suppose you make an idol of your child; you have a tyrant directly. Suppose you make an idol of your money; there is not a more grim tyrant even in hell than Mammon is. Do you make an idol of other people's opinion of you? The poor galley slave, who is flogged at every stroke of the laborious oar, is free in comparison with the man who lives upon the breath of popularity, who craves the esteem of his fellow-men, and is afraid and trembles if they censure him. Whatever idol you have, you will be the slave of that idol; but if you love God, you are free. The love of God makes men true; and making them true, it also makes them bold; and making them bold, it makes them truly free.

Moreover, *to love God is the way to be cleansed from sin.* I mean, that the love of God always drives out the love of sin. The one, who really loves the Lord, when tempted to sin, cries, with Joseph, "How can I do this great wickedness, and sin against God?" Every act of sin arises out of the absence or the decline of the love of God; but perfect love to God leads to the perfect life with God.

Love to God will also strengthen you in the time of trial. Love will bear his will without repining, will endure bereavements, and the loss of worldly substance; and, even when the suffering saint lies panting on the bed of sickness, or on the bed of death, love will enable him to sing.

And, then, *love to God will also strengthen you for Service.* A man is strong to serve his God, spiritually, just in proportion as he loves God. Love laughs at what men call impossibilities. Perhaps someone here says, "I could never go abroad as a missionary, leaving my native land, and living amongst heathens." Brother, you could do it if you had love enough. Another says, "I could never spend my whole life in the back slums of London amongst the filthy and the ragged, trying to raise them up; I recoil from such work." Brother, you would not recoil from it, but you would rejoice in it, if you had more love. There is a power, in love to God, which makes that pleasant which, without love, would have been irksome and painful,—a power which makes a man bow down his shoulders to carry the cross, and then find the cross grow into a seraph's wings enabling him to mount up toward his God. Only love God more and you can do anything.

I might continue to give you reasons for loving the Lord, but I will only give you one more; that is, *it is most ennobling.* He who loves God is certainly akin to the holy angels, for this is what they do. He is also akin to glorified saints, for this is what they do. He is also akin to the Lord Jesus Christ himself, for this is what he does. The less love you have to God, the lower is your rank among his saints; and the more love you have to him, the higher is your rank.

"O LOVE THE LORD, ALL YE HIS SAINTS." Sit there, and feel that he loves you; sit there, and love him, and then say to yourself, "Now, if I *really do love the Lord, I must do something to prove it.*" Every now and then, I like to do something for the

Lord which I would not have anybody else know, for that would spoil it;—something which I do not do for you, nor for my wife and children, nor for myself, but purely and wholly for God. I think we ought to have something in our purse which is not to be given even for the winning of souls, or the relief of the poor, or the comfort of the sick;—though these are most important things, which must not be neglected;—but something which shall be for God alone. I like to think of that woman breaking the alabaster box, and pouring out the precious ointment upon the Lord Jesus Christ. There was Judas, the traitor, who shook his head, and said that it might have been sold for much, and given to the poor,—he being the representative of the poor, and intending to see that a portion of the money should remain adhering to his own palms; but the woman had no thought of pleasing Judas, or Peter, or anybody beside the Lord Jesus Christ, whom she loved so intensely.

Cannot you, beloved, select something which you can do out of love to him? What can I suggest to you? Is there some sin that still lurks within your heart? If so, hunt it out, and destroy it for Christ's sake. Fling down the gage of battle, and say that you will contend against the evil thing, in the name of God, with this as your war-cry, "For the love of Christ." You will get the mastery over it in that way; and when you have done that, is there not something that you could give distinctly to the Lord? Have you ever done that? If not, you have missed a very pure form of happiness; and I think that love to God suggests that we should sometimes do this, telling nobody about it, but keeping it entirely to ourselves. Cannot you also think of some service which you could render distinctly to God? It is a very wonderful thing that God should ever accept any service at our hands. It is thought to be a great act of condescension when a king or queen accepts a little wild flower from some country child, yet there is not much cause for wonder in that; but it is a marvellous condescension when God accepts the services even of cherubim and seraphim, and it is wonderful that he should be willing to accept anything from us. Is there not something, my sister, that you can do, over and above what you have been doing,—something, perhaps, which you do not quite like the thought of doing?

Shall I suggest something else? You know that there is

nothing which pleases our Lord more than when we try to be
like him. Have not you, fathers, been greatly pleased when
you have seen your little ones imitating your way of walking,
and your way of talking? Yes, and our Lord loves to see himself reproduced in us, even though it is in a very childlike way,
and more like a caricature than a true image. For instance, he
is very great at forgiving those who have offended him. Is there
somebody with whom you have been out at elbows for a while?
Then, for love of your Lord, seek out that somebody; I do not
know who it may be,—a former friend, perhaps,—possibly, a
child, or a brother. Seek him out; go and find him. "Oh,
well!" you say, "he must come half-way to meet me." No;
you go all the way, dear brother, for the love of Christ. You
would not do it for anybody else, but you can go all the way
for Christ's sake.

Then, is there somebody, who has never quarrelled with you,
but who is a very objectionable person, and a very ungodly
person, about whom you have always felt, "I should not like
to have anything to do with that person"? Yet, perhaps, God
means to bless a word from you to that man's salvation; will
you not try to bring him to Christ? You know that there are
many others who will look after the very pleasant people. We
are always glad to bring them with us to hear the sermon, and
we can talk to them about Christ, because, if they do not like
it, they will not say so, for they are so gentlemanly or so lady-
like. There are always plenty of people willing to go after them,
so will not you try to take up one of those hedgehog sort of
people that nobody else cares to handle? If he pricks your
hands, you can say, "Ah! my Lord was pierced far deeper
than this for my sake, and I am glad to bear the sharp cuts and
hard words for his sake; the more there are of them, the better
I like it, for I feel that I am bearing all for his sake." Well
now, try to do, for your Lord Jesus Christ, something which will
cost you much,—perhaps a good deal of pain, or the overcoming
of strong natural tendencies; and do it for his sake.

Perhaps you are called to suffer persecution for Christ's sake.
Well, I have told you this story before, but I will tell it to you
again. There was once a King's Son, who came down to a
country which ought to have been his home; but it was full of
traitors and rebels against him, who would not receive him.

They saw that he was their Prince, but they hated him; and, therefore, they heaped all sorts of insults upon him. They set him in the pillory, and pelted him with filth, and put him in prison. Now, there was, in that country, one loyal subject; and when he saw the Prince, he knew him, and went and stood by his side. He was close by him when the mob surged around him, and they hooted him as well as the Prince. When the Prince was put into prison, they pushed this man in with him to keep him company; and when they put the Prince in the pillory, this man also stood there, putting his own face, whenever he could, in front of the Prince's face, so as to catch the filth that was thrown at him. When a stain came upon the royal visage, he wiped it off with his handkerchief, and stood there in tears, entreating the wicked mob to let their Prince alone, and always interposing himself to receive any filthy garbage or stone that was aimed at the Prince. Years went by, and the Prince came to his throne, his enemies having been trodden under foot. He alone reigned supreme, and his courtiers thronged around him. You know that Prince, and who his courtiers are,—angels, and cherubim, and seraphim. And the Prince, looking among the throng, cried out, "Make way, angels; clear the road, cherubim; stand back, seraphim. Bring hither the man who was my companion in the prison and in the pillory. Come hither, my friend," said he; and he set him upon his own throne, and honoured him that day in the sight of the whole universe. Brother, is that man yourself? I charge you to let it be so, for the day shall come when you will be rewarded ten thousand times over for any little jests, and jeers, and sarcasms, and lies that men may have poured upon you because you were loyal to Christ.

IV

PRAYER, THE PROOF OF GODLINESS

"For this shall every one that is godly pray unto thee in a
time when thou mayest be found."—Psalm 32 : 6.

ALL men are not godly. Alas! the ungodly are the great
majority of the human race. And all men who are to some
extent godly are not equally godly. The man who fears God,
and desires truly to know him, has some little measure of godliness. The man who has begun to trust the Saviour whom God
has set forth as the great propitiation for sin, has a blessed
measure of godliness. The man, whose communion with God
is constant, whose earnest prayers and penitential tears are
often observed of the great Father, and who sighs after fuller
and deeper acquaintance with the Lord,—this man is godly in a
still higher sense. And he who, by continual fellowship with
God has become like him, upon whom the image of Christ has
been photographed, for he has looked on him so long, and
rejoiced in him so intensely,—he is *the* godly man. The man
who finds his God everywhere, who sees him in all the works of
his hands, the man who traces everything to God—whether it
be joyful or calamitous—the man who looks to God for everything, takes every suit to the throne of grace, and every
petition to the mercy-seat, the man who could not live without
his God, to whom God is his exceeding joy, the help and the
health of his countenance, the man who dwells in God,—this is
the godly man. This is the man who shall dwell for ever with
God, for he has a God-like-ness given to him ; and in the Lord's
good time he shall be called away to that blessed place where he
shall see God, and shall rejoice before him for ever and ever.

Judge ye, by these tests, whether ye are godly or not. Let
conscience make sure work about this matter. Possibly, while I
am preaching, you may be helped to perform this very needful
work of self-examination. The text itself is a test by which we
may tell whether we are among the godly : "For this shall every

one that is godly pray unto thee in a time when thou mayest be found."

The first is, THE UNIVERSAL MARK OF GODLINESS: "For this shall every one that is godly pray unto thee."

When a man is beginning to be godly, this is the first sign of the change that is being wrought in him, "Behold, he prayeth." *Prayer is the mark of godliness in its infancy.* Until he has come to pleading and petitioning, we cannot be sure that the divine life is in him at all. There may be desires, but if they never turn to prayers, we may fear that they are as the morning cloud, and as the early dew, which soon pass away. There may be some signs of holy thought about the man, but if that thought never deepens into prayer, we may be afraid that the thought will be like the seed sown upon the hard highway, which the birds of the air will soon devour. But when the man comes to real pleading terms with God, when he cannot rest without pouring out his heart at the mercy-seat, you begin to hope that now he is indeed a godly man. Prayer is the breath of life in the new-born believer. Prayer is the first cry by which it is known that the new-born child truly lives. If he does not pray, you may suspect that he has only a name to live, and that he lacks true spiritual life.

And as prayer is the mark of godliness in its infancy, it is equally *the mark of godliness in all stages of its growth.* The man who has most grace will pray most. Take my word for it as certain, that when you and I have most grace, we may judge of it by the fact that there is more of prayer and praise in us than there was before. If thou prayest less than thou once didst, then judge thyself to be less devout, to be less in fellowship with God, to be, in fact, less godly. I know of no better thermometer to your spiritual temperature than this, the measure of the intensity of your prayer. I am not speaking about the quantity of it, for there are some who, for a pretence, make long prayers; but I am speaking about the reality of it, the intensity of it. Prayer is best measured by weight rather than by length and breadth; and in proportion as thou growest in grace, thou wilt grow in prayerfulness, depend upon it.

When the child of God reaches the measure of the fulness of the stature of a man in Christ Jesus, then he becomes like Elias, a man mighty in prayer. One such man in a church may save it from ruin. I go further, and say that one such man in a nation may bring down upon it untold blessings. He is the godliest man who has most power with God in his secret pleadings; and he who has most power with God in his secret pleadings has it because he abounds in godliness. Every one that is godly shall pray unto the Lord, whether he be but the babe in grace who lisps his few broken sentences, or the strong man in Christ who lays hold upon the covenant angel with Jacob's mighty resolve, "I will not let thee go, except thou bless me." The prayers may vary as the degree of godliness differs, but every godly man has, from the beginning to the end of his spiritual life, this distinguishing mark, "Behold, he prayeth."

Further, *true prayer is an infallible mark of godliness.* If thou dost not pray, remember that old true saying, "A prayerless soul is a Christless soul." You know how often it has been the case that the highest professions of holiness have been sometimes accompanied by the practice of the deadliest vices. For instance, wherever the doctrine of human perfection has been much held, it has almost always engendered some horrible licentiousness, some desperate filthiness of the flesh which is unknown to anything but that doctrine. In like manner, I have known persons to become, as they say, so conformed to the mind of God, so perfectly in accord with the divine will, that they have not felt it necessary to pray. This is the devil in white,—nothing else; and the devil in white is more of a devil than when he is dressed in black.

If anything leads you to decline in prayerfulness, or to abstain altogether from prayer, it is an evil thing, disguise it as you may. But wherever there is real prayer in the soul, take it as certain that the lingering of holy desire in the spirit proves that there is life in the spirit still. If the Lord enables thee to pray, I beseech thee, do not despair. If thou hast to pray with many a groan, and sigh, and tear, think none the less of thy prayers for that reason; or if thou thinkest less of them, the day may come when thou wilt think better of thy broken prayers than of any others. I have known what it is to come away from the throne of grace, feeling that I have not prayed at all; I have despised my prayer, and wept over it; yet, some time after, in looking back, I have thought, "I wish I could pray

as I did in the time when I thought that I did not pray at all."
We are usually poor judges of our own prayers; but this judgment we may make,—if the heart sighs, and cries, and longs, and
pleads with God, such signs and tokens were never in an un-
regenerate heart. These flowers are exotics; the seed from which
they grow must have come from heaven. If thou dost pray a
truly spiritual prayer, this shall be indeed a sure mark that the
spirit of God is striving within thee, and that thou art already
a child of God.

Once more, *prayer is natural to the godly man.* I do think
that it is a good thing to have set times for prayer; but I am
sure that it would be a dreadful thing to confine prayer to any
time or season, for to the godly man prayer comes to be like
breathing, like sighing, like crying. You have, perhaps, heard
of the preacher who used to put in the margin of his manuscript
sermon, "Cry here." That is a very poor sort of crying that can
be done to order; so, you cannot make the intensity of prayer to
order, it must be a natural emanation from the renewed heart.
Jacob could not always go and spend a night in prayer;
possibly he never spent another whole night in prayer in all his
life after that memorable one. But when he spent that one by
the brook Jabbok, he could "do no other," as Luther said.
Pumped-up prayer is little better than the bilge water that
flows away from a ship. What you want is the prayer that
rises from you freely, like the fountain that leaped from the
smitten rock. Prayer should be the natural outflow of the soul;
you should pray because you must pray, not because the set
time for praying has arrived, but because your heart must cry
unto your Lord.

"But," says one, "sometimes I do not feel that I can pray."
Ah! then indeed you need most to pray; that is the time when
you must insist upon it that there is something sadly wrong
with you. If, when the time has come for you to draw near to
God, you have the opportunity and the leisure for it, you feel
no inclination for the holy exercise, depend upon it that there
is something radically wrong with you. There is a deadly
disease in your system, and you should at once call in the
heavenly Physician. You have need to cry, "Lord, I cannot
pray. There is some strange mischief and mystery about
me, there is something that ails me; come, O Lord, and

set me right, for I cannot continue to abide in a prayerless condition!"

A prayerless condition should be a miserable and unhappy condition to a child of God, and he should have no rest until he finds that once more his spirit can truly pour itself out before the living God. When you are in a right state of heart, praying is as simple as breathing. I remember being in Mr. Rowland Hill's chapel at Wotton-under-Edge, and stopping at the house where he used to live; and I said to a friend who knew the good man, "Where did Mr. Rowland Hill use to pray?" He replied, "Well, my dear sir, I do not know that I can tell you that; and if you were to ask, 'Where did he not pray?' or, 'When did he not pray?' I should be unable to tell you. The dear old gentleman used to walk up and down by that laurel hedge, and if anybody was outside the hedge, he would hear him praying as he went along. Then he would go up the street, and keep on praying all the time. After he had done that, he would come back again, praying all the while; and if he went indoors, and sat down in his study, he was not much of a man to read, but you would find that he was repeating some verse of a hymn, or he was praying for Sarah Jones who was ill, or he would plead for Tom Brown who had been backsliding." When the old man was in London, he would go up and down the Blackfriars Road, and stand and look in a shop window; and if anybody went to his side, it would be found that he was still praying, for he could not live without prayer. That is how godly men come to be at last; it gets to be as natural to them to pray as to breathe. You do not notice all the day long how many times you breathe; when you come home at night, you do not say, "I have breathed so many times today." No, of course you do not notice your breathing unless you happen to be asthmatical; and when a man gets asthmatical in prayer, he begins to notice his praying, but he who is in good sound spiritual health breathes freely, like a living soul before the living God, and his life becomes one continual season of prayer.

To such a man, *prayer is a very happy and consoling exercise.* It is no task, no effort; his prayer, when he is truly godly, and living near to God, is an intense delight. When he can get away from business for a few quiet minutes of communion with God, when he can steal away from the noise of the world, and get a little time alone, these are the joys of his life. These are the delights that help us to wait with patience through the long days of our exile till the King shall come, and take us home to dwell with himself for ever.

Those prayers of the godly, however, may be *presented in a great many forms*. Some praying takes the good form of action; and an act may be a prayer. To love our fellow-men, and to desire their good, is a kind of consolidated practical prayer. There is some truth in that oft-quoted couplet by Coleridge,—

> "*He prayeth best, who loveth best*
> *All things, both great and small.*"

There comes to be a prayer to God in giving alms, or in preaching the Gospel, or in trying to win a wanderer, or in taking a child upon your knee, and talking to it about the Saviour. Such acts are often most acceptable prayers; but when you cannot act thus, it is well to pour out your heart before the Lord in words; and when you cannot do that, it is sweet to sit quite still, and look up to him, and even as the lilies pour out their fragrance before him who made them, so do you, even without speaking, worship God in that deep adoration which is too eloquent for language, that holy nearness which, because it is so near, dares not utter a sound, lest it should break the spell of the divine silence which engirds it. Frost of the mouth, but flow of the soul, is often a good combination in prayer. It is blessed prayer to lie on your face before God in silence, or to sigh and cry, or moan and wail, as the Holy Spirit moves you. All this is prayer, whatever shape it assumes, and it is the sign and token of a true believer's life.

Secondly, there is, in the text, A POTENT MOTIVE FOR PRAYING: "For this shall every one that is godly pray unto thee in a time when thou mayest be found."

The motive seems to be, first, *because God heard such a great sinner as David was.* Possibly you know that this passage is very difficult to interpret. It appears to be simple enough, yet there are a great many interpretations of it. In the Revised Version you will find the marginal reading, "In the time of finding out sin." Let me read the context: "I acknowledged my sin unto thee, and mine iniquity have I not hid: I said, I will confess my transgressions unto the Lord; and thou forgavest the iniquity of my sin. For this let every one that is godly pray unto thee in the time of finding out sin." It runs all right, and the connection seems to warrant it. I am not sure that it is the correct translation, but the sense harmonizes with it; so let us learn from it this lesson, that God has heard the prayer of a great sinner. There may be, in this house of prayer, someone who has gone into gross and grievous sin, and this reading of the passage may be a message from the Lord to that person. David had sinned very foully, and he had added deceit to his sin. His evil deeds have made the ungodly to rail at godliness even until the present day, so that infidels ask in contempt, "Is this the man after God's own heart?" It was an awful sin which he committed; but there came to him a time of finding out his sin. His heart was broken in penitence, and then he went to God, and found mercy; and he said in effect, that it was so wonderful that such a wretch as he was should be forgiven, that every godly man, as long as the world stood, would believe in the confession of sin to the Lord, and in the power of prayer to obtain pardon for the guilty. I like that meaning of the text, for it is sometimes necessary to us, when we are under a sense of sin, to think of such sinners as Manasseh, and Magdalene, and the dying thief, and Saul of Tarsus. There are times, even with those whom God has greatly blessed, when nothing but the sinner's Saviour will do for them, and when they feel that, if there were not salvation for the vilest of the vile, there would be no salvation for them. So, God gives us a case like that of David, that every one that is godly may pray unto him in the time of finding out his sin. We might have been afraid to come if David had not led the way. "Come," says he of the broken heart, he who wrote the fifty-first Psalm, "God forgave me; and he did it that he might show forth in me all longsufferings, for a pattern to them who should hereafter repent and believe."

Another motive for prayer which I think the text brings before us is this, *we all need pardon daily*: "For this shall every one that is godly pray unto thee;" "for this covering of sin, for this blotting out of iniquity. I hope that all of you pray unto God daily for the forgiveness of sins; I am sure that all the godly amongst you do so. If you commit no sins, then the

Saviour made a great mistake when he left us the prayer, "Forgive us our trespasses." What is the need of that petition if we have no trespasses to be forgiven? But for this, that is, for the pardon of his sin, every one who is godly will pray unto the Lord.

And every one who is godly will pray unto God for this reason also, namely, *because he has received the pardon of sin.* You remember when you made your confession to the Judge of all, and received absolution from him. You recollect when, with broken heart and downcast eye, you acknowledged your sin unto him, and he put away your transgression. Well then, that is the reason why you should always be praying. He who heard you then will still hear you. He who put away your sin then, by that one great washing in the fountain filled with blood, will continue to put away your sin by that foot-washing which he gives to us continually, of which Jesus said, "He that is washed needeth not save to wash his feet, but is clean every whit." Blessed be God, we shall not cease to pray for pardon although we have received pardon; we will crave the daily renewal of the divine token of reconciliation. If we received it when we were sinners, much more shall we receive it now that we are reconciled to God by the death of his Son. If we received it when we were outcasts, much more shall we receive it now that we are his dear children.

Again, "For this shall every one that is godly pray unto thee," that is to say, *because troubles come,* for the connection teaches us this lesson. "Surely in the floods of great waters they shall not come nigh unto him. Thou art my hiding-place; thou shalt preserve me from trouble." Brethren, the Lord takes care to keep us praying, does he not, by giving us constant needs? Suppose that I had a friend upon whom I was dependent, and whose society I greatly loved, and that he said to me, "I will give you, in a lump sum, as much money as will last you till this time next year, and then you can come and see me, and receive another year's portion; or, as you like to come to my house, would you prefer to have the amount quarterly?" I should reply, "I will choose the latter plan, for then I should come to you four times in the year, and have four dinners with you." "Well, then, would you like it monthly?" "Oh, yes! I would like to come monthly, and spend a day with you every

month." "Perhaps," says he, "you would like to come daily."
"Oh, yes! I should prefer that; I should like to have a daily
portion at your table." "Perhaps you would like to stop with
me always, as Dr. Watts did when he went to Sir Thomas
Abney's, to stay for a week, and I think that 'week' lasted for
twenty-eight years, for he never went away till he died. Perhaps you would like to receive everything from my own hand,
and have nothing but what I give you." "Oh! yes, my friend,
this continual indebtedness, this constant dependence, would
give me so many opportunities of better knowing you whom I
love so much that I should like to have it so."

You have heard of "a hand-basket portion." There is a maid
to be married, and her father says to her, "There, my girl, I
will give you so many hundred pounds; do your best with it,
for it is all I shall have for you." Another girl is married, and
her father says, "I shall send you down a basketful of things on
such a day;" and so, every week, a present goes to her. It is a
hand-basket portion, and it is always coming; it never comes
to an end, and she gets a great deal more from the old man than
the other does, who has her fortune all at once. At any rate, it
comes, every time, "with father's love." If it is given only once,
and is done with, perhaps an ill-feeling springs up; but if it
comes, "with father's love," fifty or a hundred times a year, see
how affection is increased between father and daughter. Give
me a hand-basket portion. You who like may go and gather a
week's manna; it will stink before the end of the week. I like
to have mine fresh every day, just as it comes warm from the
ovens of heaven, and ready for the heavenly appetite of the
man who learns to live upon the daily gift of God. For this shall
every one that is godly pray unto God. He shall have trouble
to drive him, he shall have grace to draw him, he shall have
weights to lift him, and they shall be so adjusted that, though
they threaten to hold him down, they shall really raise him
up.

Once more, I think that, broadly speaking, the word "this"
here means, "*Because God does hear prayer*, for this reason shall
every one that is godly pray unto him." Now, it always will be
a dispute between the true believer and the mere professor
whether God does hear prayer. Of course, the outside world
will always sneer at the idea of God hearing prayer. A man said

to me, one day, "You say that God hears your prayers." "Yes,
I do say it." Said he, "I do not believe it." "No," I said, "I
never thought you did; and if you had believed it, I might have
thought that it had been a mistake. I did not expect a carnal
mind to receive the truth of God." "Oh!" said he, "there is
nothing in it." Then I asked him, "Did you ever pray, my
friend? Did you ever try God?" No, he never did. "Very
well, then," I said, "do not say anything about what you do not
know. If you know nothing about what it is, hold your tongue
till you do, and let those of us who have tried it speak of what
we know." If I were put in a witness-box to-morrow, any
lawyer in London would like to have me for a witness; so, when
I stand here, and declare solemnly that hundreds and even
thousands of times God has answered my prayers, I claim to be
as much accepted as an honest witness as I should be in the
High Court of Justice; and I can bring forward, not myself
only, but scores and hundreds of you. Brethren, tell me, does
not God hear prayer? [Voices: "Yes! Yes! Yes!"] I know
he does; and you godly folk can all bear witness that it is so.
Calmly and deliberately, you could tell of many instances in
which you called upon the Lord, and he answered you. I am
loth to argue this point, for it is not a point to be argued. If a
man said that I had not any eyes, he might say it, and my eyes
would twinkle as I heard him say it; and when anyone says,
"God does not hear prayer," I am sorry for the poor soul that
dares to make an assertion about a thing which he has never
tested and tried. God does hear prayer, and because he hears
it we will call upon him as long as we live. "For this shall every
one that is godly pray unto thee," because there is reality in it,
and there is a blessed result from it. Prayer does move the arm
that moves the world, though nothing is put out of gear by our
praying. The God who ordained the effects that are to follow
prayer ordained the prayer itself; it is a part of the grand
machinery by which the world swings upon its hinges.

The last point is one to which I want to call your earnest
attention; that is, THE SPECIAL OCCASION WHEN PRAYER IS
MOST USEFUL. "For this shall every one that is godly pray
unto thee in a time when thou mayest be found," or, "in a time
of finding," as the margin of our Bibles has it. Is there any set
time when God is to be found?

Well, in general, it is *the time of this mortal life*. So long as you live here, and pray to God, he has promised to answer. Though it be the eleventh hour, do not hesitate to pray. Christ's word is, "He that seeketh findeth." There is a special promise to those who seek the Lord early; but this does not exclude those who seek him late. If you truly seek him, he will be found of you.

I think, too, that the time of finding is *under this gospel dispensation*. God has always heard prayer, but there seems to be a larger liberty allowed us in prayer now. The Mercy Seat is unveiled, and the veil is rent away that we may come with boldness. But besides that, there are special times of finding God, namely, *in visitations of his Spirit*. Revival times are grand times for prayer. How many there are who put in their suit with God because they feel moved thereto by a heavenly impulse! There is "the sound of a going in the tops of the mulberry trees," as there was with David, and they begin to bestir themselves.

In closing, I will dwell only upon this one point: *there are special times of finding for individuals*, and one of these is the time of the finding out of sin. Come back to the translation which I gave you before. The time when you will find out sin, is the time when you will find God. "Why!" say you, "it is a horrible thing for me to find out my sin." It is, in itself; but it is the best time to find out God. When thine eyes are blinded with tears of penitence, thou canst best see the Saviour. Do not say, "I find myself to be so guilty, and therefore I have no hope." Nay, rather, because thou findest thyself to be guilty, therefore have hope, for the Saviour came to seek and to save such guilty ones as thou art. The time, I say, when sin finds us out, and we are humbled and ashamed, is the time when we may find our God through Jesus Christ.

So, too, a time of decision is a time for finding God. Some remain shilly-shallying; they have not decided whether they will live for the world and perish, or seek Christ and live eternally. But when the Spirit of God comes upon you, and you say to yourself, "I must find Jesus Christ, I must get for-giveness, and lay hold of eternal life; give me Christ, or else I die;" you shall have him. God has promised that, if we seek him with our whole heart, he will be found of us. When you are decided for God thoroughly and intensely, it will be with you a time of finding.

So will it be when you come to God in full submission. Some of you have not laid down your weapons of rebellion yet. You cannot be reconciled to God while your sword is in your hand; down with it, man! Some of you have fine feathers on your helmets, and you come before God as great captains; off with those feathers! He will accept you in rags, but not in ribbons. He will receive you if you come confessing your sin, but not boasting of your supposed merits. Down with you into the very dust. Yield to God. Oh, that his mercy might make us all pliant as the willow before his mighty power! Then shall we find peace through Christ.

I believe that it is a time of finding when you come to concentration. I have known men sometimes say, with a holy determination, "I am resolved that I will find Christ; I will find salvation, and everything else shall go till I do. I shall go upstairs to my room, and shut the door, and not come out again till I have found the Lord." When the whole soul is bent on seeking Christ, then will the Lord speedily appear, and it shall be a time of finding.

But especially is it a time of finding when the heart at last trusts wholly and implicitly to the Lamb of God that taketh away the sin of the world. You shall find that God has found you when you have done with yourself, and taken the blood and righteousness of Christ to be the sole hope of your soul. God lead you to this, this very hour!

I know that there are some here who are seeking the Lord. There are some who have lately begun to come under great anxiety. I hope that you will not be long in that anxious state, but that you will come right out of it by trusting yourselves with Christ. It is a wonderful end to anxiety when you have somebody to trust to, and when you do trust that somebody. Now, trust Jesus; he will save you. Ay, he does save you the moment that you trust him; and he will never let you go, but will bring you to his glory home above.

V

THE NEW SONG ON EARTH

"He hath put a new song in my mouth, even praise unto our God: many shall see it, and fear, and shall trust in the Lord."—Psalm 40: 3.

THIS man who talks about his song, and seems to be very much struck with the fact that he has become a singer, was formerly a man of prayer. I doubt not that he was still praying while he was praising; but he began to pray before he began to praise. It is ill to go in the choir first; we must begin our spiritual experience at the "penitent form." He who sings without having wept may have to weep, by-and-by, where he can never sing.

Listen to what this man's experience had been: "I waited patiently for the Lord; and he inclined unto me, and heard my cry." That is where God gets his singers, out of the place of praying and weeping. Where they learn to pray they begin to sing. Oh, yes, even in heaven itself, the sweetest voices that there praise God and the Lamb belong to those who came out of great tribulation, and washed their robes and made them white in the blood of the Lamb! Therefore are they before the throne of God, and serve him day and night in his temple. Do not try to get the joy of Christ without first having sorrow for sin.

*"The path of sorrow, and that path alone,
Leads to the land where sorrow is unknown."*

This man, who says that God has put a new song in his mouth, began with a new prayer in his heart: "I waited patiently for the Lord; and he inclined unto me, and heard my cry."

Further, this man, who sings so well that he cannot help talking about it, was once in a very deplorable state where there was no singing for him; but God brought him up out of it.

54

Hear what he says, "He brought me up also out of an horrible pit, out of the miry clay, and set my feet upon a rock, and established my goings." Nowadays, people do not seem to know much about that horrible pit; I wish they did. There are more gentle, quiet conversions,—and I little care how men are converted so long as they are really converted; but, after all, the old-fashioned sort of conversions wear best. Men who know from what they are saved, men who have felt the iron rod of the law, and have been crushed and broken beneath the millstones of conviction, these are they who appreciate "free grace and dying love" to the full, and speak of it, and sing of it. I do not find so much of this singing now, and the reason is because there has been so little of the deep experience of which our good old fathers used to speak. The Psalmist says, "He brought me up also out of an horrible pit, out of the miry clay, and set my feet upon a rock, and established my goings; and therefore it is that this new song is in my mouth."

First, notice that we have here A MAN WONDERING TO FIND HIMSELF SINGING, for the text is evidently a declaration that God had put a new song into his mouth, and that it was a marvel even to himself. Here is, then, a man wondering to find himself singing, and it would not be difficult to find one like him here.

What makes you wonder so, my friend? Other people sing: why is it at all a wonder that you should? He answers, "It is a wonder that I should sing *because I have been so used to sighing*. Had you seen me, sir, when the arrows of God stuck fast in me, you would have heard many sighs, but never a song. If you had tracked me home, you would have found my pillow wet with tears; but I was no nightingale, I could not sing in the dark. I woke in the morning, almost sorry to think that I had to face the world again, and that I had my burden still to bear; but I chanted no morning hymn, and I went about the world still burdened till night came on again. Those around me talked of vesper hymns, but I had no such hymns. I had my evening moans and groans, for sin was heavy upon me, and an angry God seemed to make the darkness about me a darkness that might be felt. Had you seen me then, you would not think it strange that I should wonder and be a wonder to myself that now I sing." Oh, yes, if you have ever known the depths of sorrow for sin, you will be amazed to think that you can be as happy as you are because Christ has loosed the burden from your shoulder, and made you free, saying, "Go, and sin no more. Thy sins, which are many, are all forgiven thee."

Well, my friend, I can see why you are astonished at your singing; is there any other reason? "Yes," he answers, "if you had known me a little farther back, before I came under the hand of God, and was awakened to a sense of sin, you would have known a fellow that could sing; but *the wonder now is that I can sing 'a new song.'* I am glad, sir, that you did not hear me sing in those days, for my songs would have done you no good. They were very light and trifling, sometimes lewd and sometimes profane. Oh, how I set my companions in a roar with my jests; and when I had a little drink in me, how I liked to thunder out some loose verses, and bid the others take up the chorus; and 'jolly good fellows' were all of us said to be when those hymns of the devil were upon our tongues." Oh, you are that man, are you? Yet I heard you sing just now, and I think you sang it from your heart,—

> "*My heart is resting, O my God;*
> *I will give thanks and sing;*
> *My heart is at the secret source*
> *Of every precious thing.*
>
> "*And a 'new song' is in my mouth,*
> *To long-loved music set;*
> *Glory to thee for all the grace*
> *I have not tasted yet.*

Ah, now I wonder, too, that such a man as you once were, should be singing such a song as that! O brethren and sisters, there are some of us here who must be wonders to ourselves when we think of what we used to be! Some of you forget the dunghills where you grew; but if you have any honesty in you, you cannot but feel the tears starting up between your eyelids at the recollection of how God has changed you. What a miracle of mercy you are! Surely, it took almighty power to make a saint of such a sinner as you were. The utmost bound of infinite love must have been reached in the case of some who are in this house of prayer praising redeeming love, and wishing that they had a thousand tongues with which to shout the Saviour's praise. Yes, friend, I can see why it is that you tell us as a wonder that a new song is put into your mouth. The time past well suffices us to have sung the songs of Belial; now let us sing unto the Lord with all our strength, and tell to all around what great things his grace has done for us.

Still, you who are so much wondering at yourself, you tell me that you marvel to find yourself singing because you so lately were sighing, and, farther back, were singing such a different tune. Is there any other wonder in it? "Well, yes, sir, my greatest wonder is because I am singing a new song. *It is a totally new song*; it is new to me, for I knew nothing of it once. I ridiculed what I did not understand; I cast scorn on what I had not the candour to wish to know. I said that religion was all cant, and that religious people were all hypocrites. I did not know this for a fact, but I said it all the same. I did not want to know anything about Christ crucified and the Gospel of his grace. I said that these were only terms that were used by fanatical people, and that had no meaning in them; and as to the songs of Zion, why, sir, I sometimes parodied them to give a little zest to my profane merriment; but, as to singing them myself, that I felt could never be the case." Yes, beloved, there are some who are now singing of free grace and dying love who, years ago, would not have believed it possible, even if a prophet of God had told them it would be so. They would have spat at any man who should have said, "And you, too, will take up the cross, and follow the Nazarene." Yet now they are singing a song altogether new to them. These low notes of penitence, the deep bass of confession, are all new to them, and these highest notes, the *jubilates* that rise even to the skies, are all new to them. None of this score did they ever read in their days of sin, they never tuned their harps to such psalms as this in the time of their unregeneracy. It is all new to you. Do I not remember when it was all new to me? Yet I heard it when I was a child, I was never away from the hearing of it; but when I came to know it, it was just as new to me, nursed on the lap of piety, as it was to you who lived in the midst of a wicked world, for I was blind in the light as you were blind in the dark; I was deaf in the midst of music, and you were only deaf in the midst of discord. There was but a slight difference between us after all; and truly, we do wonder to think that we should be singing a new song.

It is not only called a new song because it is new to us, but because it is so uncommon. Rich and rare things are often called in the Bible new. There is a new covenant, there is a new commandment; I will not quote the many things in Scripture that are called new because they are so rare. And, oh, the praises of God are indeed rich and rare! If an angel, fresh from heaven, were asked his judgment of the various kinds of music played or sung below, I know what he would say. Your finest operas and your noblest lyrics concerning things of time and sense would be but doggerel in his ear, and discord to his heart; but the hymns in which we praise our dying yet risen Lord, the psalms in which we exalt the God of heaven and earth, these would be music indeed to him, and he would write these down as truly sweet. Yes, and so it is to us. Dull is the song that does not praise our Lord; but the burst of united psalmody, from a vast congregation that exalts him, brings tears into our eyes, as Augustine says it did to his when he heard the singing at Milan. When first he entered the church there, to hear the many simple folk praise God touched his soul. But if it be not so, if the music be not to the praise of the Lord, there is nothing rich and rare in it for us. Oh, believe us, we have learnt a rare song now that we have learnt to praise the Lord our God!

And, truth to tell, there is a wonder about our new song because it is always new. Do you ever tire—you who love your Lord,—do you ever tire of him? You who praise him, do you ever weary of singing his praises? You may very well weary of me, poor creature that I am, I who have addressed you so many hundreds of times; but you never weary of my subject when I talk of Jesus. You may very well weary of the monotony of any human voice, but you can never be tired of the many-stringed harp which is to be found in that one name, the name of Jesus. His name fresh? Oh, I think it is newer to me now than when I first heard it! It may seem a paradox, but the Gospel is to me fresher the longer I know it. Did not my heart leap at the sound of Christ's name nearly forty years ago? Yes; but not as it does now. The music of his name will refresh our soul in death with a new depth of sweetness. It is all new as you go on in Jesus. You seem sometimes to fancy that you are coming to an end, but there is no end to this music. Did you ever sail up or down the Rhine? If so, standing in the steamboat, you thought you were in a lake rather than in a river, and you wondered how you could proceed any farther. You turned a corner, and the river opened up before you with a fresh stretch of beauty; and where it seemed to end again, the end was all a delusion, for it still went on and on. So is it with the song which the Lord has taught us, it is always fresh and always new.

Yet again, if you wonder that we call it new, let me remind you that it is new because it seems to have woke us up into a newness of life. I have seen men excited; look at them whenever there is an election, but there is a far better kind of excitement than that which is produced by politics. When a man comes to know Christ, and to love him, it wakes him up from the crown of his head to the sole of his foot. We steady-going people, you know, try to be very serene and quiet, and our worship is apt to get terribly stiff and dull, but if we could let our souls have their liberty, if we could speak and sing as we feel, what a noise we should make sometimes! There would be hallelujahs and hosannas indeed; and it is wonderful that we can restrain them, for the Gospel of Christ somehow brings out of a man new faculties which he does not know of himself till a glorious breeze of everlasting life has blown through him. Then odours, which else had lain asleep, odours such as God delights in, are poured forth on every side. This is indeed a new song, for it makes us new. God grant that many of you may so continually sing it that you may know what I mean, and a great deal more than I can say! There is a wonderful thing, then, a new man singing a new song.

There is a further wonder yet. My friend, you have been telling us that you marvel that you have a new song, what is it that makes you so surprised? You have told us much; tell us a little more. And he answers, "Well, sir, I wonder at my new song because *it is raised unto our God:* 'even praise unto our God'." It should not be, but still it is, a marvel when a man praises his God. We are by nature so averse to this sweet exercise that, when we come to do it, and to do it heartily, it is a marvellous thing. Look. We praise God's grace; we sing,—

"Grace! 'tis a charming sound!
Harmonious to the ear!"

and each saved man among us feels it to be so in his case. We
praise God's power. What power he has put forth in bringing
us up out of our graves of sin, and turning us from darkness to
light, and from the power of Satan unto God, by that same
mighty power which he wrought in Christ when he raised him
from the dead, and set him at his own right hand. Yes, every
man whom God has saved praises his grace and his power.

The pith of the song is this: "praise unto *our* God." You
cannot praise another man's God; at least, there is no sweetness
in such a song; but there is a blessed melody when it is "praise
unto *our* God"—our covenant God, the God who belongs to us,
the God who by a perpetual covenant has given himself up to
us to be our possession for ever: "praise unto our God." I like
to have it put in the plural. My soul can praise my God; but
the highest note is reached when many of us together can
praise "our God"—yours and mine. We who are brethren in
Christ, we who know each other, and love each other, find a
peculiar sweetness in our new song when it is "praise unto our
God." If you all knew the sweetness of bringing others to
Christ, more of you would live for it, and be prepared even to
die for it.

I have had some very happy days in my life; but my happiest
times have been such as I had one day last week, when I shook
hands with somewhere about a hundred persons who called
me their spiritual father. It seemed to them to be quite a grand
day to touch my hand, while to me—the tears standing in my
eyes as I saw each one of them,—it was as the days of heaven
upon earth, for I had never seen all those people before. Perhaps some of them had been in this house now and then, but I
did not know them. They had read the sermons, and as I
went from village to village, and found them standing at their
doors, begging me to stop just to hear how such a sermon was
"blessed to me," and "my old father read your sermons, and
died in peace after reading them,"—there, I could have died of
joy, for this is the truest happiness we can have on earth. Seek
sinners, my brethren, seek their conversion with all your heart
and soul. If you would be happy men and women, and would

sing the sweetest song that could be sung on earth, let it be "praise unto our God"; not yours alone, but the God also of those whom infinite mercy shall permit you to bring to the same dear Saviour's feet.

There is one more wonder about this song, and then I shall have finished what I have to say about this friend of ours. You tell us that you sing, and that you sing a new song; what is the greatest wonder about that song? "Why, sir, to tell you the truth, I do not know which is the greatest marvel; there is a world of wonders in my singing this new song, but there is one point I have not told you, and that is this: '*He hath put a new song in my mouth.*'" Oh, I see, then; you did not learn it of anybody? You did not make it up yourself? "No, no, no; a thousand times, no; it was God that put it into my mouth." Well now, when God puts a song into a man's mouth, that is a grand thing, for the devil himself cannot get it out. If God puts a new song into a man's mouth, he has a right to sing it, and he ought to sing it, and he must sing it; therefore, let him sing it. Magnify the Lord if he has done this great thing to you, if he has put this new song into your mouth. All that we ever do for ourselves never has the sweetness in it of that which God does for us. You may labour and toil and tug, and all the wage you get you may hold in the hollow of your hand, and it shall melt in the morning sun; but if God shall give it to you of his free, rich, sovereign grace, it shall be within you a well of water springing up into everlasting life, and neither life, nor death, nor things present, nor things to come, shall ever take it away from you. If God hath put this new song in your mouth, that is the best thing you can tell us about it. So, my good friend, I will ask you no more questions. Sing away, sing away, as long as ever you like, sing praise unto our God.

> "*Sing, though sense and carnal reason*
> *Fain would stop the joyful song:*
> *Sing, and count it highest treason*
> *For a saint to hold his tongue.*"

Now, secondly, we have here A MAN WHO IS RESOLVED TO KEEP ON SINGING, for, you notice, he says, "He hath put a new song in my mouth, even praise unto our God: many shall see, and fear, and shall trust in the Lord;" so that this man means to keep on singing. I must have you back again, old friend, and ask you why it is that you mean to keep on singing.

He answers, first, "*Because I cannot help it.*" When God sets a man singing, he must sing. Good Rowland Hill once had sitting on the pulpit-stairs a person who sang with such a cracked, squeaking voice that it put the dear man out of heart; and this person with the cracked voice of course sang more loudly than anybody else. So Mr. Hill said to him, while the hymn was being sung, "Be quiet, my good man, you make such a dreadful noise that you put us all out." "Oh!" said the man, "I am singing from my heart, Mr. Hill." "I beg your pardon, my friend," said the preacher, "go on, go on, go on with your singing if it comes from your heart." So we would not stop any man, whatever his voice is, if he sings from his heart. But, what is more, we not only say that we would not stop him, but we could not stop him if we wanted to do so. If, as men say, "murder will out," I am sure that grace will. You cannot put salvation into a bottle, and put the cork in. It will burst the bottle, for it must come out. If God has put a song into thy mouth, thou must sing it. Therefore, again I say, sing away.

But, my friend over yonder, do not sing before everybody; perhaps it would be casting pearls before swine. "Oh!" says he, "but I must; *I mean to sing before many.*" Why? "Well, I used to sing before many in my evil days. I was not ashamed to sing for the devil. When I ought to have been ashamed, I was not; and now that I ought not to be ashamed, I will not be ashamed, and I will sing. Besides, why should I be so tender and considerate of their nerves? They are not thoughtful about mine." The ungodly sometimes complain of us for preaching outdoors, they say that it disturbs them. Bless their dear delicacy! What a noise they make at night, sometimes, when they keep us from sleeping while they noisily declare that they "won't go home till morning"! Surely, we may sing as loudly as they do; and when we sing songs of Zion, we can well reply to them that, when they are quiet, and will suspend their music, we may consider when we will suspend ours.

Still, my friend, do you think that it is worth while to sing at this rate? "Yes," says he, "I do, for *I believe that it is good for them to hear it.*" Do you? What good can it do them? And he answers me thus. "Look at your text, sir, and you will not need to ask me that question; what does your text say?" "Many shall see, and fear, and shall trust in the Lord." It is good to preach the Gospel, but it is better to preach and sing the Gospel. I mean that if you and I, in our daily lives, were to sing the Gospel more, especially by a holy cheerfulness of character, we should bring the truth home to a great many who now turn aside from it, and do not feel its power. Sing you of Christ your Lord, tell out his love to you, tell out how you were converted, tell how he brought you up out of the horrible pit, out of the miry clay, and as you do it, others will long to experience the same deliverance, and so will be drawn to the Saviour by your sweet testimony to his grace. There are many more flies caught with honey than with vinegar; and there are many more sinners brought to Christ by the gracious tidings of his love than ever will be driven to him by all the threatenings of his law. I do not know a better soul-trap than a happy Christian experience. This will catch them; therefore be sure to use it. Sing, sing, sing unto the Lord a new song. Sing his praise unto the ends of the earth; for many will see, and fear, and put their trust in the Lord.

If I had come here knowing that there were persons here that were ailing, and were to say, "Now, listen; I will tell you how I suffered from your complaint," you would be sure to attend to me; and if I then mentioned a certain remedy, and said, "I took it, and I have experienced a very remarkable cure," you would listen with both your ears, and you would ask, "Where is that remedy to be purchased?" You would begin thinking whether you could get some of it to-morrow morning, especially if you were very ill yourselves as I had been; and you would go away thankful to think that you had met with someone who, through his own experience, could guide you to a perfect cure. Well now, that is exactly what I want you to do with regard to yourselves, you who are sick of sin, and care, and fear, and grief. I, too, as a youth, was sick of sin, and I was made to feel it, and to endure great grief on account of it. I sought to be delivered from it; I gave up many things in which I had indulged, and I hoped by self-denial that I should come to peace; but I did not, I was as far off as before I began. I said that I would very diligently attend the means of grace, and I did so. Thrice on the Sabbath I was found somewhere or other hearing the Word. But mere sermon-hearing brings no peace. Then I said that I would read good books. How I remember reading *Alleine's Alarm*, and *Doddridge's Rise and Progress*, and *Baxter's Call to the Unconverted*; and how they ploughed me, and brought tears into my eyes; but I found no rest to my soul by all the godly books I read,—the best that could be read. Whatever was proposed to me that looked likely to bring me rest, I was eager to try. I was willing, I am sure, to become a monk, or aught else beneath the sun that would promise peace to my spirit, for I wanted to be right, and longed to be at peace with God. At last, I found rest. The preacher pictured Christ upon the tree, bleeding for sinners; and he said, in his Lord's own words, "Look unto me, and be ye saved, all ye ends of the earth;" and I looked. It was all I could do, it was all I was asked to do, I looked. It was but a look; yet in that moment all my fears were ended, my doubts were solved, my burden was removed, and I, too, could say, "He hath put a new song in my mouth. He brought me up also out of an horrible pit, out of the miry clay, and set my feet upon a rock, and established my goings."

Now, after trying and testing this salvation for a good many years,—well nigh on to forty,—I have only this to say of it, it is a simple salvation, but it is as sound as it is simple. It is fitted for the poorest of us, but it is as enriching as it is suitable to our poverty. The weakest may look to Jesus, but by looking he shall soon be ranked among the strongest. He who is at death's door may look to Jesus crucified, but the life that look brings is life everlasting, which shall never die. There is the remedy, and I have tried it. That is all I can say to you, except that I beg you to try it yourselves. Try it yourselves. Look to Christ. Look to Christ. Trust Jesus, that is all; trust, simply trust. It does seem as if this could not be all, but it is. Thou with the broken heart, trust. Thou with the heart that will not break, trust to have it broken. Thou that art deeply penitent, trust; not in thy repentance, however, but in Christ. And thou that canst not repent, but wishest to repent, look to Christ for repentance. Trust; trust; trust, as the drowning man trusts to the life-buoy, as the shipwrecked mariners trust to the life-boat. Trust; trust in God almighty, incarnate in the bleeding Man of sorrows, for it is God that hangs on the cross in the body of the Nazarene. Trust thou in Jesus Christ, the Son of God, and the Son of Mary, and as surely as he lives, as surely as God lives, thou shalt live, and live for ever. Heaven and earth may pass away; but that Word shall never pass away, "He that believeth on the Son hath everlasting life."

VI

"OUT OF THE DEPTHS"

"For innumerable evils have compassed me about: mine
iniquities have taken hold upon me, so that I am not able to
look up; they are more than the hairs of mine head: therefore
my heart faileth me. Be pleased, O Lord, to deliver me: O
Lord, make haste to help me:"—Psalm 40: 12, 13.

YOU remember that these were the words of a man of God,
a man after God's own heart, a man undoubtedly the
possessor of the grace of God. They were the words, also, of a
preacher, one who could say, "I have preached righteousness
in the great congregation. . . . I have declared thy faithfulness
and thy salvation: I have not concealed thy lovingkindness
and thy truth from the great congregation."

This teaches us that, however eminent for grace a man of
God may be, it may happen to him, sometimes, that the thought
of his sin may be paramount over his faith. There are times when
the Lord seems to give his servants a new start; it is not a
second conversion, but it is something very like it. They are
made to see once more the deformity of their character, the
defilement of their nature, the inward sinfulness of their hearts,
that they may prize more than ever they have done the cleansing fountain of atoning blood, and the wonderful power of the
sanctification of the Holy Spirit.

I mention this fact so that, if any of you are in sore trouble
like that described in the text, you may be comforted by
knowing that there are the footprints of a fellow-believer in this
dark part of the way you have to travel. Others have been
here before you, others who were undoubtedly the people of
God, others who were saved in the Lord with an everlasting
salvation. You have had to write bitter things against yourself;
so have other people. Have you ever felt as though you were
surrounded by sin, so that you could not look up? You are not
the first man who has been in such a plight, and you are not
likely to be the last. This part of the road has been frequented

by full many of the pilgrims to Zion's city bound. All the people of God have not taken this route; there are different ways of travelling along the road to heaven; but some of the true saints of God have gone by this rough path, and I mention this fact in order that no troubled heart may fall into despair because of the painful experience through which it is at the present time passing.

In trying to describe a soul in the condition mentioned in our text, let me say, first, that we have evidently before us A SOUL BESET: "For innumerable evils have compassed me about: mine iniquities have taken hold upon me, so that I am not able to look up; they are more than the hairs of mine head."

The text describes a man, who is, first, made to see *the countless number of his sins*. He did not know so much about them before; he said that he was a sinner, and he meant it, but then he wrote the word in very small letters. Now, a further enlightenment has been granted to him; the Spirit of judgment and of burning has come to deal with him, and now he writes the sentence, "I AM A SINNER," in capitals so large that he wants the whole sky and all the sea as well to make the page on which to emblazon the terrible words. With an emphasis, of which he used to know nothing, he now calls himself a sinner, for sins that he had forgotten come up before his memory. Now he sees that there is a great number of sins in any one sin, like so many Chinese boxes shut up one inside another. Moreover, things which he formerly did not recognize as sins he now perceives to be among the deadliest of transgressions. He realizes that the imagination of evil is sin, that sin is any want of conformity to the perfection of God. Now he seems as if he swarms with sins; and yet, a little while ago, he thought himself clean and pure in the sight of God. It is wonderful what a ray of light will do; the sun suddenly shines into a room, and the whole air seems full of innumerable specks of dust, dancing up and down in the sunbeam. The light does not make the room full of dust; it only shows you what was always there, but which you did not see until the sun shone in; and if a beam of God's true light were to shine into some of your hearts, you would think very differently of yourselves from what you have ever done.

I question whether any one among us could bear to see himself as God sees him. I think it is highly probable that, if any man were to see his own heart as it really is, he would go mad; it would be a sight too dreadful for an awakened conscience and a sensitive reason to endure. And when the Lord does come to any of his servants, and reveals sin in its true character, unless there is a corresponding revelation of the cleansing blood, it puts a man into a very dreadful condition of mind. He says that his sins are more than the hairs of his head; he feels that that is a very poor comparison, so he says they are innumerable, they cannot be counted. In the process of trying to count them, we should have sinned again I know not how many times, sinned in our very judgments about our sins; our thoughts about our sins would only increase the number of them. Now, this is no morbid feeling of a perverted brain; it is a true and strictly accurate statement of a sad fact. It is not possible for any of us to think too badly of ourselves as we really are in the sight of God. Comfort does not come by trying to lessen our sense of sin, it comes in a much better and more effectual way, as I will presently try to show you.

This man, then, is troubled by the number of his sins. He also seems to be greatly perplexed by *a sort of omnipresence of sin*, for he says, "Innumerable evils have compassed me about." He looks that way, and says, "Surely there is a gap there; I have not sinned in that direction." But no; there are sins in that quarter. He turns sharply round, and he looks this way, and says, "Perhaps I shall find a lane there, through which I may escape; I hope I have not sinned in that way;" but when he steadily looks, he finds that he has sinned there, too. These innumerable evils have compassed him about. David said of his enemies, "They compassed me about like bees;" they were all around him. When a swarm of bees gets about a man, they are above, beneath, around, everywhere stinging, every one stinging, until he seems to be stung in every part of his body. So, when conscience wakes up the whole hive of our sins, we find ourselves compassed about with innumerable evils; sins at the board and sins on the bed, sins at the task and sins in the pew, sins in the street and sins in the shop, sins on land and sins at sea, sins of body, soul, and spirit, sins of eye, of lip, of hand, of foot, sins everywhere, every way sins. It is a horrible discovery when it seems to a man as if sin had become well-nigh as omnipresent with him as God is. It cannot be actually so, for sin cannot be everywhere, as God is; but it is hard to say where sin is not when once conscience is awake to see it. Our whole life, from our first responsible moment even until now, appears defiled. There are sins even in our holy things; only half the heart is laid upon God's altar, and the sacramental bread itself is defiled as it passes into our mouth. Oh, it is dreadful when the heart is awakened to see that it is even so!

But that is not all; this man is so beset with sin that *it seems to hold him in a terrible grip.* Read this: "Mine iniquities have taken hold upon me," as though they were so many griffins, or other monsters of the old fables. They come and fix their claws into him; they have taken hold upon him. Did any of you ever feel the grip of a single sin? I hope that you have, for you have never been rightly delivered from it if you have never felt its grasp. I once knew a young man who had not a true sense of sin; he believed himself to be a sinner, but he never had a real conviction of sin. He was a working-man, steady and upright, and he prided himself upon his sobriety and industry. One day, in some little frolic, he upset an oil-can, and when his employer came in, and asked, "Who did that?" he said that he did not. No one ever found out who did upset that oil-can, but he knew that he did it. Knocking over that can was not, in itself, an act of criminality; but he felt mean and despicable because he had told a lie, and that lie just fixed itself upon his heart, and clawed at it, and tore away at it so that he could not get away from its cruel clutches. He came to the house of prayer on the Sabbath-day, to try to get rid of this iniquity that had taken hold upon him, but it kept its hold month after month, hissing in his ear, "You have been a liar." Nobody knew of it but himself; yet that one sin was quite enough to take hold upon him, and to fix him with an awful grip. It was in this house that he was delivered from that sin through the precious blood of Christ; and I said within myself, when I heard the whole story, "Well, I am glad that sin took hold of that young man, for there were many sins beside which he afterwards thought of, and acknowledged with tears before his God; but they had all passed by unnoticed, they had never laid hold on him as that one lie had.

"Let me tell you, friend, if you have a number of sins which have once taken hold on you, you will be something like a stag when the whole pack of hounds has seized him, and his neck and his flanks and every bone in him seem to feel the hounds' teeth gnawing at them. I speak what I do know; I have felt these dogs upon me, and I have had to cry to God for deliverance; and peradventure I am speaking to some soul that is in that condition to-night. It is no child's play when this is the case. Here we have to deal with stern facts; and it is only God, by some great act of grace, who can set free a poor soul that is once beset in this way.

Here is, secondly, A SOUL BEWILDERED: "Mine iniquities have taken hold upon me, so that I am not able to look up." Do you hear that, "not able to look up"? That is the only hope that a man has when he is under a sense of sin; his one way of escape is by looking up; but the psalmist says, "I am not able to look up."

Does it not mean, first, that *he did not dare to look his sins in the face?* He felt so guilty, so self-condemned, that, as the judge, when he pronounces the death-sentence, covers his head by putting on the black cap, so this culprit felt that he must hide his own face. He wants to have a handkerchief tied over his eyes, for he is shocked at the sight that meets his gaze. He dares not look up, that is, he cannot face his sin.

It means, also, that *he is unable to excuse himself.* He used to be as big a braggart as anybody; at one time, he could talk as glibly as anyone about there being no God, and no hell, but that kind of speech is all gone out of him now. The Lord can soon knock such folly as that out of a man. Just one prick of the conscience, and the boaster is brought to his knees, and he does not try to look up for a single moment, to justify or excuse himself. All he can do is to hang his head, and murmur, "Guilty, guilty, guilty."

A man in this state of bewilderment *dares not look up to read God's promises.* I come to him, and I say, "Friend, do you not know that there is a Bible full of promises for such as you are? 'This is a faithful saying, and worthy of all acceptation, that Christ Jesus came into the world to save sinners, of whom I am chief.'" I put my hand on his shoulder, and I say, "Now, look at that promise." He cannot look up. We read, in the 107th

Psalm, of some who were so ill that, when the most dainty food was brought to them, they shook their heads, for they could not touch it: "Their soul abhorreth all manner of meat; and they draw near unto the gates of death." Well, that is the condition of this man. "But," you say, "my dear fellow, do look at this passage, 'All manner of sin and blasphemy shall be forgiven unto men.' 'Whoso confesseth and forsaketh his sins shall have mercy.'" "Ah!" says he, "it is too late for me, it does not apply to me."

Now, this is all a mistake, you know; the Lord is willing to receive you, however horrible your offences may have been. If you are up to your neck in blasphemy and iniquity, Christ can make you clean in a moment. He has such sovereign power that, with a word, he can forgive you; aye, and with a word, he can change your nature, and make a saint out of a sinner, an angel out of a very human devil; such power does Christ possess to save the vilest of the vile.

Perhaps, we try what effect *the testimony of others* will have upon him. We stand in front of him, and we say, "Do look at us for a moment." There was a dear brother, who prayed at the prayer-meeting before the service, "Lord, save the big sinners, for, since thou hast saved me, I believe that thou canst save anybody." Now, that was good pleading; and I can say the same. There are many here who would say to you, "We looked unto Christ, and were lightened. We came with all our sin heavy upon us; and we did but look to Jesus, and we found peace, and rest, and new hearts, and changed lives. What he has done for us, he can do for you, for he has shown forth in some of us, as he did in Paul, all longsuffering for a pattern to all others who will believe in him unto life everlasting." Still, the man cannot look up; his sins have so bewildered him, his sense of guilt has so muddled his poor thoughts, that he dares not look up; and yet he ought to do so.

If I were suffering from a certain disease, and a number of persons came to me, and said, "We were afflicted exactly as you now are, but we went to Dr. So-and-so, and he cured us almost at once," I think that I would go to that doctor, and I would try the medicine that had healed others. Oh, I wish that some of you would try my Saviour! You young people, would God that you would try him in your youth! You older ones, I pray that you may be led to Jesus now, though your sin rises like a mountain, for he is able to forgive and to save unto the uttermost all that come unto God by him.

But this poor soul cannot yet look up; so we put our hand upon him again, and we say, "But, dear heart, if you will not look to the promises in the Bible, and you will not look to us who are specimens of what divine grace can do, yet do *look to Jesus on the cross.* Have you never heard the story of how he lived, and how he died? Do you not know the meaning of those blessed wounds of his? He was the Son of God, and he suffered all this for sinful men. He was pure, and holy, and innocent, yet he died, 'the Just for the unjust, to bring us to God.' Must there not be great merit in the sacrifice of Jesus Christ? Look up. Look to him. Look up to Jesus on the cross."

> *"There is life for a look at the Crucified One:*
> *There is life at this moment for thee:*
> *Then look, sinner—look unto him, and be saved—*
> *Unto him who was nail'd to the tree."*

We try again, and we bid him *look up to Jesus on the throne.* We say, "Do you not know that Jesus has risen from the dead? He has gone up into heaven, and he is at the right hand of God, making intercession for the transgressors. The business of Christ in heaven is to plead for sinners. Oh, how I wish that you would look up to him! Do!" Thus we plead, but our pleading is not sufficient. Spirit of God, break these poor creatures away from their infatuation, and help them now just to look up to the living Saviour who is seated at the right hand of God, pleading for the guilty, for such as they are! Look to Jesus; only trust him. In the name of Jesus Christ of Nazareth, I do not merely advise, but speaking by his authority, I bid you look and live! May he set his seal to that command, as he did when Ezekiel bade the dry bones live, and they did live!

Follow me while I notice, in the third place, that here is A SOUL FAINTING; "Mine iniquities have taken hold upon me, so that I am not able to look up: they are more than the hairs of mine head: therefore my heart faileth me."

Why, that is the man who used to come in here as big as

anybody, and now he cries, "My heart faileth me." You used to sing above all the rest, did you not? And you despised those poor weeping ones; but now your lament is, "My heart faileth me." When a man's heart faileth him, it is as when the standard bearer of an army fainteth, everything gets in disarray.

"My heart faileth me." You have come to a fainting condition; and when the heart fails, *death is approaching.* You feel as if you must die, you are so utterly faint. You dare not hope; energy, you have none; what can you do? "To will," say you, "is present with me; but how to perform that which is good I find out."

"My heart faileth me." This is the language of one in whom *fear is working.* Why, there is poor Mercy! Poor Mercy! You, as a young girl said, "I will not come to Jesus yet, I can come to him whenever I like;" and now you are fainting outside the gate because the big dog barks at you; and your heart faileth you. Oh, lie not there to die, dear swooning one! Jesus Christ will come to you in all your faintness. Is it not written, "When we were yet without strength, in due time Christ died for the ungodly"? "When we were yet without strength." Now, you see what there is in yourself, do you not? Nothing at all. Your very heart fails you; and if sovereign grace does not interpose, you are lost, you know you are.

"Yes," you say, "that is quite true, *I am lost.*" I am so glad that you confess this, for your confession proves that you are the one whom God has chosen unto eternal life from before the foundation of the world. You are the sort for whom Jesus died when he poured out his heart's blood. You are already called by his grace to come to him, for he said, "Come unto me, all ye that labour and are heavy laden, and I will give you rest." You are the very characters whom he describes as being the objects of his love. Come to him, just as you are, and cast yourselves upon him. Fainting heart, do not wait till thou art revived, but faint on the bosom of Jesus! Failing heart, do not wait till thou growest strong again, but come and confess thy failure, thy spiritual bankruptcy at Christ's feet!

"But I have no good feelings," says one. I am glad of it; come to Christ for them. "But I cannot repent as I would, or believe as I would." Then listen to Joseph Hart

"True belief, and true repentance,
Every grace that brings you nigh,
Without money,
Come to Jesus Christ and buy."

He wants nothing of you but that you will agree to let him be everything to you. "Free grace and dying love"—I delight to ring those charming bells; oh, that every ear would welcome their blessed music!

Here is A SOUL PLEADING: "Mine iniquities have taken hold upon me, so that I am not able to look up. . . . My heart faileth me. Be pleased, O Lord, to deliver me: O Lord, make haste to help me."

"Oh!" says one, "I would plead with God, but I do not know how to go to him." Do you not? Did you ever teach your girl how to come to you when she wanted anything? She comes, and she says, "Father, I want so-and-so." You do not send her to school, do you, and pay so much a week to teach her that art? No, she knows it naturally. If there is anything to be got out of a father, trust a boy or a girl for knowing how to do it. You smile; let that smile go a little deeper. Smile again, if you like, that it may go right down deep. It is in this way that you should deal with God; just as your children, being evil, know how to ask good gifts of their father, so you should know how to ask good gifts of your Father who is in heaven; and the more childlike you can be in your praying, the better. Come to God in the simplest way possible, and tell him all that is in your heart, pour out your desires before him, expecting that he will hear you, and answer you; and go your way rejoicing that you have such a God to go to. The easiest thing in the world to a child of God should be to talk to his Father. He should not feel as if he had to put his best coat on in order to approach the Lord. Let him stand out in the yard, in his shirt-sleeves, and pray. Why not? Wherever you are, if you should wake up in the middle of the night, begin to pray. You would not think of going to see a person in your shirt-sleeves; but your boy may come to you like that whenever he pleases.

A person said to me, some time ago, "Would you mind telling me what to say when I pray?" I answered, "Say what you feel, ask God for what you desire." "But," she said, "I am such a poor ignorant woman that I would like you to tell me the words to say." Then I thought of the passage in Hosea, "Take with you words, and turn to the Lord: say unto him, Take away all iniquity, and receive us graciously." Thus, the very words were put into the suppliants' mouths; and in our text, David does, as it were, make a prayer that is suitable for many of you. May the Lord put it into your mouths and hearts!

I will only briefly call attention to the drift of the prayer; and, first, it is *a prayer distinctly to God.* This poor bewildered heart does not look to itself, or to a priest, or to a sacrament, but it turns to God, and to God alone, and says, "Be pleased, O Jehovah, to deliver me: O Jehovah, make haste to help me." Your only hope is in your God; salvation must come from God alone. You know how I pictured this matter some little time ago, about the baby picked up in the street. There is somebody who is going to tell us what that baby wants. He wants some milk, and he wants to be washed, and he wants some clothes, he wants nursing, he wants soothing to sleep; he wants,—well, we can go on for a week, and hardly tell all that he wants; but I will put in one word what the baby wants, and that is, his *mother.* And you, poor soul, you want—you want—you want so many, many things that I will not stay to mention them; I will put them into one word, you want your *God.* Nobody but he who made you can ever new-make you; therefore, as you need remaking, re-creating, you need your God. Oh, poor prodigal, I know you want a new pair of boots, and a new pair of trousers, and a good dinner, and a great many other things; but most of all you want to go home to your Father, and if you go home to your Father, then you will get all the other things that you need. Cry unto God, then, thou who hast never prayed before.

And then, do you notice the style of the prayer in our text? "Be pleased, O Jehovah, to deliver me." It is *an appeal to the good pleasure of God.* There is no arguing of merit, there is no plea but that of God's good pleasure. No man has any right to God's grace; if it be given to anyone, it is given by the free favour of God, as he pleases, and to whom he pleases. Shall he not do as he wills with his own? But do thou, as a suppliant, take this lowly ground: "Be pleased, O Jehovah, to deliver me, for thy mercy's sake, for thy goodness' sake! Universal Ruler as thou art, and able to save whom thou wilt, for the rights of life and death are in the hands of the King of kings, be pleased, O Lord, to deliver me!" That is the way to plead with God.

And then you may, if you like, use that last sentence: "Make haste, O Jehovah, to deliver me!" You may *plead urgency*: you may say, "Lord, if thou dost not help me soon, I shall die. I am driven to such distress by my sin that, if thou dost not hear me soon, it will be too late. Innumerable evils have compassed me about, so that I am not able to look up. I am driven to such dire distress that my case is urgent; O Lord, help me now!" Oh, how I wish that such a prayer as that might go up from many and many a heart in this audience! You are not truly awakened to a sense of your lost condition if you want to be saved to-morrow. If you are really convinced of sin, your prayer will be, "Make haste, O Lord, to deliver me." I pray that you may be brought to that point so that you may not dare to go to bed till you have found your God, and put your trust in him.

VII

THE STORY OF GOD'S MIGHTY ACTS

"We have heard with our ears, O God, our fathers have told us, what work thou didst in their days, in the times of old."—Psalm 44 : 1.

PERHAPS there are no stories that stick by us so long as those which we hear in our childhood, those tales which are told us by our fathers, and in our nurseries. Now, among the early Christians and the old believers in the far-off times, nursery tales were far different from what they are now, and the stories with which their children were amused were of a far different class from those which fascinated us in the days of our babyhood. No doubt, Abraham would talk to young children about the Flood, and tell them how the waters overspread the earth, and how Noah alone was saved in the ark. The ancient Israelites, when they dwelt in their own land, would all of them tell their children about the Red Sea, and the plagues which God wrought in Egypt when he brought his people out of the house of bondage. Among the early Christians we know that it was the custom of parents to recount to their children everything concerning the life of Christ, the acts of the Apostles, and the like interesting narratives. Nay, among our Puritan ancestors such were the stories that regaled their childhood. Sitting down by the fireside, before those old Dutch tiles with the quaint eccentric drawings upon them of the history of Christ, mothers would teach their children about Jesus walking on the water, or of his multiplying the loaves of bread, or of his marvellous transfiguration, or of the crucifixion of Jesus. Oh how I would that the like were the tales of the present age, that the stories of our childhood would be again the stories of Christ, and that we would each of us believe that, after all, there can be nothing so interesting as that which is true, and nothing more striking than those stories which are written in sacred writ ; nothing that can more truly move the heart of a child than the marvellous works of God which he did in the olden times.

Now, it seems that the Psalmist who wrote this most musical ode had heard from his father, handed to him by tradition, the stories of the wondrous things which God had done in his day; and afterwards, this sweet singer in Israel taught it to his children, and so was one generation after another led to call God blessed, remembering his mighty acts.

I intend to recall to your minds some of the wondrous things which God has done in the olden time. My aim and object will be to excite your minds to seek after the like, that looking back upon what God has done, you may be induced to look forward with the eye of expectation, hoping that he will again stretch forth his potent hand and his holy arm, and repeat those mighty acts he performed in ancient days.

To begin then, with THE WONDERFUL STORIES WE HAVE HEARD OF THE LORD'S ANCIENT DOINGS.

We have heard that God has at times done very mighty acts. The plain every-day course of the world hath been disturbed with wonders at which men have been exceedingly amazed. God·hath not always permitted his Church to go on climbing by slow degrees to victory, but he hath been pleased at times to smite one terrible blow, and lay his enemies down upon the earth, and bid his children march over their prostrate bodies. Turn ye back then, to ancient records, and remember what God hath done. Will ye not remember what he did at the Red Sea, how he smote Egypt and all its chivalry, and covered Pharaoh's chariot and horse in the Red Sea? Have ye not heard tell how God smote Og, king of Bashan, and Sihon, king of the Amorites, because they withstood the progress of his people? Have ye not learned how he proved that his mercy endureth for ever, when he slew those great kings and cast the mighty ones down from their thrones? Have you not read, too, how God smote the children of Canaan, and drove out the inhabitants thereof, and gave the land to his people, to be a possession by lot for ever? Have you not heard how when the hosts of Jabin came against them, the stars in their courses fought against Sisera? The river of Kishon swept them away, "that ancient river, the river Kishon," and there was none of them left. Hath it not been told you, too, how by the hand of David, God smote the Philistines, and how by his right hand he smote the children of Ammon? Have you not heard how Midian was put to confusion, and the myriads of Arabia were scattered by Asa in the day of his faith? And have ye not heard, too, how the Lord sent a blast upon the hosts of Sennacherib, so that in the morning they were all dead men? Tell—tell ye these, his wonders! Speak of them in your streets. Teach them to your children. Let them not be forgotten, for the right hand of the Lord hath done marvellous things, his name is known in all the earth.

The wonders, however, which most concern us, are those of the Christian era. Have you never read how God won to himself great renown on the day of Pentecost? Peter the fisherman stood up and preached in the name of the Lord his God. A multitude assembled and the Spirit of God fell upon them; and it came to pass that three thousand in one day were pricked in their heart by the hand of God, and believed on the Lord Jesus Christ. And know you not how the twelve Apostles with the disciples went everywhere preaching the Word, and the idols fell from their thrones. The cities opened wide their gates, and the messenger of Christ walked through the street and preached. It is true that at first they were driven hither and thither, and hunted like partridges upon the mountains : but do ye not remember how the Lord did get unto himself a victory, so that in a hundred years after the nailing of Christ to the cross, the Gospel had been preached in every nation, and the isles of the sea had heard the sound thereof? And have ye yet forgotten how the heathen were baptised, thousands at a time, in every river? What stream is there in Europe that cannot testify to the majesty of the Gospel? What city is there in the land that cannot tell how God's truth has triumphed, and how the heathen has forsaken his false god, and bowed his knee to Jesus the crucified? The first spread of the Gospel is a miracle never to be eclipsed.

And have ye never heard of the mighty things which God did by preachers some hundreds of years from that date? Hath it not been told you concerning Chrysostom, the golden-mouthed, how, whenever he preached, the church was thronged with attentive hearers; and there, standing and lifting up holy hands, he spake with a majesty unparalleled, the word of God in truth and righteousness; the people listening, hanging forward to catch every word, and anon breaking the silence with the clapping of their hands and the stamping of their feet ; then silent again for awhile, spell-bound by the mighty orator; and anon carried away with enthusiasm, springing to their feet, clapping their hands, and shouting for joy again? Numberless were the conversions in his day, God was exceedingly magnified, for sinners were abundantly saved.

And have your fathers never told you of the wondrous things that were done afterwards when the black darkness of super-stition covered the earth, when Popery sat upon her ebon throne and stretched her iron rod across the nations and shut the windows of heaven, and quenched the very stars of God and made thick darkness cover the people? Have ye never heard how Martin Luther arose and preached the Gospel of the grace of God, and how the nations trembled, and the world heard the voice of God and lived? Have ye not heard of Zwingly among the Swiss, and of Calvin in the holy city of Geneva, and of the mighty works that God did by them? Nay, as Britons have ye forgotten the mighty preacher of the truth—have your ears ceased to tingle with the wondrous tale of the preachers that Wickliffe sent forth into every market town and every hamlet of England, preaching the Gospel of God? Oh, doth not history tell us that these men were like fire-brands in the midst of the dry stubble; that their voice was as the roaring of a lion, and their going forth like the springing of a young lion. Their glory was as the firstling of a bullock; they did push the nation before them, and as for the enemies, they said, "Destroy them." None could stand before them, for the Lord their God had girded them with might.

To come down a little nearer to our own times, truly our fathers have told us the wondrous things which God did in the days of Wesley and of Whitefield. The churches were all asleep. Irreligion was the rule of the day. The very streets seemed to run with iniquity, and the gutters were filled full with the iniquity of sin. Up rose Whitefield and Wesley, men whose hearts the Lord had touched, and they dared to preach the Gospel of the grace of God. Suddenly, as in a moment, there was heard the rush as of wings, and the Church said, "Who are these that fly as a cloud, and as the doves to their windows?" They come! they come! numberless as the birds of heaven, with a rushing, like mighty winds that are not to be withstood. Within a few years, from the preaching of these two men,

England was permeated with Evangelical truth. The Word of God was known in every town, and there was scarcely a hamlet into which the Methodists had not penetrated. In those days of the slow coach, when Christianity seemed to have bought up the old waggons in which our fathers once travelled,—where business runs with steam, there oftentimes religion creeps along with its belly on the earth,—we are astonished at these tales, and we think them wonders. Yet let us believe them; they come to us as substantial matters of history. And the wondrous things which God did in the olden times, by his grace he will yet do again. He that is mighty hath done great things and holy is his name.

There is a special feature to which I would call your attention with regard to the works of God in the olden time; they derive increasing interest and wonder from the fact that they were all sudden things. The old stagers in our churches believe that things must grow, gently, by degrees; we must go step by step onward. Concentrated action and continued labour, they say, will ultimately bring success. But the marvel is, all God's works have been sudden. When Peter stood up to preach, it did not take six weeks to convert the three thousand. They were converted at once and baptised that very day; they were that hour turned to God, and became as truly disciples of Christ as they could have been if their conversion had taken seventy years. So was it in the day of Martin Luther: it did not take Luther centuries to break through the thick darkness of Rome. God lit the candle and the candle burned, and there was the light in an instant—God works suddenly. If any one could have stood in Wurtemburg, and have said, "Can Popery be made to quail, can the Vatican be made to shake?" The answer would have been :—"No; it will take at least a thousand years to do it. Popery, the great serpent, hath so twisted itself about the nations, and bound them so fast in its coil, that they cannot be delivered except by a long process." "Not so," however, did God say. He smote the dragon sorely, and the nations went free; he cut the gates of brass, and broke in sunder the bars of iron, and the people were delivered in an hour. Freedom came not in the course of years, but in an instant. The people that walked in darkness saw a great light, and upon them that dwelt in the land of the shadow of death, did the light shine.

So was it in Whitefield's day. The rebuking of a slumbering Church was not the work of ages; it was done at once. Have ye never heard of the great revival under Whitefield? Take Cambuslang as an instance. He was preaching in the church-yard to a great congregation, that could not get into any edifice; and while preaching, the power of God came upon the people, and one after another fell down as if they were smitten; and at least it was estimated that not less than three thousand persons were crying out at one time under the conviction of sin. He preached on, now thundering like Boanerges, and then com-forting like Barnabas, and the work spread, and no tongue can tell the great things that God did under that one sermon of Whitefield. Not even the sermon of Peter on the day of Pente-cost was equal to it.

So has it been in all Revivals; God's work has been done suddenly. As with a clap of thunder has God descended from on high, not slowly, but on cherubim right royally doth he ride; on the wings of the mighty wind does he fly. Sudden has been the work; men could scarce believe it true, it was done in so short a space of time. Witness the great revival which is going on in and around Belfast now, in 1859. After carefully looking at the matter, and after seeing some trusty and well-beloved brother who lived in that neighbourhood, I am convinced, not-withstanding what enemies may say, that it is a genuine work of grace, and that God is doing wonders there. A friend who called to see me tells me that the lowest and vilest men, the most depraved females in Belfast have been visited with this extraordinary "epilepsy," as the world calls it; but with this strange rushing of the Spirit, as we have it. Men who have been drunkards have suddenly felt an impulse compelling them to pray. They have resisted; they have sought to their cups in order to put it out; but when they have been swearing, seeking to quench the Spirit by their blasphemy, God has at last brought them on their knees, and they have been compelled to cry for mercy with piercing shrieks, and to agonize in prayer; and then after a time, the Evil one seems to have been cast out of them, and in a quiet, holy, happy frame of mind, they have made a profession of their faith in Christ, and have walked in his fear and love.

Roman Catholics have been converted. I thought that an

extraordinary thing; but they have been converted very frequently indeed in Balymena and in Belfast. In fact, I am told the priests are now selling small bottles of holy water for people to take, in order that they may be preserved from this desperate contagion of the Holy Spirit! This holy water is said to have such efficacy, that those who do not attend any of the meetings are not likely to be meddled with by the Holy Spirit—so the priests tell them. But if they go to the meetings, even this holy water cannot preserve them—they are as liable to fall a prey to the Divine influence. I think they are just as likely to do so without as with it.

All this has been brought about suddenly, and although we may expect to find some portion of *natural* excitement, yet, I am persuaded it is in the main a real, *spiritual*, and an abiding work. There is a little froth on the surface, but there is a deep running current that is not to be resisted, sweeping underneath, and carrying everything before it. At least, there is something to awaken our interest, when we understand that in the small town of Ballymena on market day, the publicans have always taken one hundred pounds for whiskey, and now they cannot take a sovereign all day long in all the public houses. Men who were once drunkards now meet for prayer, and people after hearing one sermon will not go until the minister has preached another, and sometimes a third; and at last he is obliged to say, "You must go, I am exhausted." Then they will break up into groups in their streets and in their houses, crying out to God to let this mighty work spread, that sinners may be converted unto him. "Well," says one, "we cannot believe it." Very likely you cannot, but some of us can, for we have heard it with our ears, and our fathers have told us the mighty works that God did in their days, and we are prepared to believe that God can do the like works now.

I must here remark again, in all these old stories there is one very plain feature. Whenever God has done a mighty work it has been by some very insignificant instrument. When he slew Goliath it was by little David, who was but a ruddy youth. Lay not up the sword of Goliath—I always thought that a mistake of David—lay up, not Goliath's sword, but lay up the stone and treasure up the sling in God's armoury for ever. When God would slay Sisera, it was a woman that must do it with a hammer and a

nail. God has done his mightiest works by the meanest instru-
ments: that is a fact most true of all God's works. Peter the
fisherman at Pentecost, Luther the humble monk at the Reformation, Whitefield the potboy of the Old Bell Inn at Gloucester
in the time of the last century's Revival; and so it must be to the
end. God works not by Pharaoh's horses or chariot, but he works
by Moses' rod; he doth not his wonders with the whirlwind and
the storm; he doth them by the still small voice that the glory
may be his and the honour all his own.

Doth not this open a field of encouragement to you and to
me? Why may not we be employed in doing some mighty work
for God here? Moreover, we have noticed in all these stories of
God's mighty works in the olden time, that wherever he has
done any great thing it has been by some one who has had very
great faith. I do verily believe at this moment that, if God
willed it, every soul in this hall would be converted now. If
God chose to put out the operations of his own mighty Spirit,
not the most obdurate heart would be able to stand against it.
"He will have mercy upon whom he will have mercy." He will
do as he pleases; none can stay his hand. "Well," says one,
"but I do not expect to see any great things." Then, my dear
friend, you will not be disappointed, for you will not see them;
but those that expect them *shall* see them. Men of great faith
do great things. It was Elijah's faith that slew the priests of
Baal. If he had had the little heart that some of you have,
Baal's priests had still ruled over the people, and would
never have been smitten with the sword. It was Elijah's faith
that bade him say, "If the Lord be God, follow him, but if
Baal, then follow him." The reason why God's name was so
magnified, was because Elijah's faith in God was so mighty and
heroic.

When the Pope sent his bull to Luther, Luther burned it.
Standing up in the midst of the crowd with the blazing paper
in his hand he said, "See here, this is the Pope's bull." And
when he went to Worms to meet the grand Diet, his followers
said, "You are in danger, stand back." "No," said Luther,
"if there were as many devils in Worms as there are tiles on
the roofs of the houses, I would not fear; I will go;"—and into
Worms he went, confident in the Lord his God. It was the same
with Whitefield; he believed and he expected that God would do

great things. When he went into his pulpit he believed that God would bless the people, and God did do so. Little faith may do little things, but great faith shall be greatly honoured.

All the mighty works of God, have been attended with great prayer, as well as with great faith. Have ye ever heard of the commencement of the great American Revival? A man unknown and obscure, laid it up in his heart to pray that God would bless his country. After praying and wrestling and making the soul-stirring enquiry, "Lord, what wilt thou have *me* to do? Lord, what wilt thou have me *to do?*" he hired a room, and put up an announcement that there would be a prayer-meeting held there at such-and-such an hour of the day. He went at the proper hour, and there was not a single person there; he began to pray, and prayed for half-an-hour alone. One came in at the end of the half-hour, and then two more, and I think he closed with six. The next week came round, and there might have been fifty dropped in at different times; at last the prayer-meeting grew to a hundred, then others began to start prayer-meetings; at last there was scarcely a street in New York that was without a prayer-meeting. Merchants found time to run in, in the middle of the day, to pray. The prayer-meetings became daily ones, lasting for about an hour; petitions and requests were sent up, these were simply asked and offered before God, and the answers came; and many were the happy hearts that stood up and testified that the prayer offered last week had been already fulfilled. Then it was when they were all earnest in prayer, suddenly the Spirit of God fell upon the people, and it was rumoured that in a certain village a preacher had been preaching in thorough earnest, and there had been hundreds converted in a week. The matter spread into and through the Northern States—these revivals of religion became universal, and it has been sometimes said, that a quarter of a million of people were converted to God through the short space of two or three months.

Now the same effect was produced in Ballymena and Belfast by the same means. The brother thought that it lay at his heart to pray, and he did pray, then he held a regular prayer-meeting, day after day they met together to entreat the blessing, and the fire descended and the work was done. Sinners were converted, not by ones or twos, but by hundreds and thousands, and the Lord's name was greatly magnified by the progress of his gospel. Beloved, I am only telling you *facts*.

I have now to make a few observations upon THE DISADVAN-TAGES UNDER WHICH THESE OLD STORIES FREQUENTLY LABOUR. When people hear about what God used to do, one of the things they say is, "Oh, that was a very long while ago." They imagine that times have altered since then. Says one, "I can believe anything about the Reformation—the largest accounts that can possibly be given, I can take in." "And so could I concerning Whitefield and Wesley," says another, "all that is quite true, they did labour vigorously and successfully, but that was many years ago. Things were in a different state then from what they are now." Granted; but I want to know what the things have to do with it. I thought it was God that did it. Has God changed? Is he not an immutable God, the same yesterday, to-day, and for ever? Does not that furnish an argument to prove that what God has done at one time he can do at another? Nay, I think I may push it a little further, and say what he has done once, is a prophecy of what he intends to do again—that the mighty works which have been accomplished in the olden time shall all be repeated, and the Lord's song shall be sung again in Zion, and he shall again be greatly glorified.

Others among you say, "Oh, well, I look upon these things as great prodigies—miracles. We are not to expect them every day." That is the very reason why we do not get them. If we had learnt to expect them, we should no doubt obtain them, but we put them up on the shelf, as being out of the common order of our moderate religion, as being mere curiosities of Scripture history. We imagine such things, however true, to be prodigies of providence; we cannot imagine them to be according to the ordinary working of his mighty power. I beseech you, my friends, abjure that idea, put it out of your mind. Whatever God has done in the way of converting sinners is to be looked upon as a precedent, for "his arm is not shortened that he cannot save, nor is his ear heavy that he cannot hear." If we are straitened at all, we are not straitened in him, we are straitened in ourselves. Let us take the blame of it ourselves, and with earnestness seek that God would restore to us the faith of the men of old, that we may richly enjoy his grace as in the days of old.

Yet there is another disadvantage under which these old stories labour. The fact is, we have not seen them. Why I may talk to you ever so long about Revivals, but you will not believe them half so much, nor half so truly, as if one were to occur in your very midst. If you saw it with your own eyes, then you would see the power of it. If you had lived in Whitefield's day, or had heard Grimshaw preach, you would believe anything. Grimshaw would preach twenty-four times a week; he would preach many times in the course of a sultry day, going from place to place on horseback. That man *did* preach. It seemed as if heaven would come down to earth to listen to him. He spoke with a real earnestness, with all the fire of zeal that ever burned in mortal breast, and the people trembled while they listened to him, and said, "Certainly this is the voice of God." It was the same with Whitefield. The people would seem to move to and fro while he spoke, even as the harvest field is moved with the wind. So mighty was the energy of God that after hearing such a sermon the hardest-hearted men would go away and say, "There must be something in it, I never heard the like." Can you not realise these as literal facts? Do they stand up in all their brightness before your eyes? Then I think the stories you have heard with your ears should have a true and proper effect upon your own lives.

This brings me in the third place to the PROPER INFERENCES THAT ARE TO BE DRAWN FROM THE OLD STORIES OF GOD'S MIGHTY DEEDS.

I would that I could speak with the fire of those men whose names I have mentioned. Pray for me, that the Spirit of God may rest upon me, that I may plead with you for a little time with all my might, seeking to exhort and stir you up, that you may get a like Revival in your midst. The first effect which the reading of the history of God's mighty works should have upon us, is that of gratitude and praise. Have we nothing to sing about to-day?—then let us sing concerning days of yore. If we cannot sing to our Well-beloved a song concerning what he is doing in our midst, let us, nevertheless, take down our harps from the willows, and sing an old song, and bless and praise his holy name for the things which he did to his ancient Church, for the wonders which he wrought in Egypt, and in all the lands wherein he led his people, and brought them out with a high hand and with an outstretched arm. When we have thus begun to praise God for what he has done, I think I may venture to impress upon you one other great duty. Let what God has done suggest to you the prayer that he would repeat the like signs and wonders among us.

Oh! men and brethren, what would this heart feel if I could but believe that there were some among you who would go home and pray for a Revival of religion—men whose faith is large enough, and their love fiery enough to lead them from this moment to exercise unceasing intercessions that God would appear among us and do wondrous things here, as in the times of former generations. Why, look you here in this present assembly what objects there are for our compassion. Glancing round, I observe one and another whose history I may happen to know, but how many are there still unconverted—men who have trembled and who know they have, but have shaken off their fears, and once more are daring their destiny, determined to be suicides to their own souls and put away from them that grace which once seemed as if it were striving in their hearts. They are turning away from the gates of heaven, and running post-haste to the doors of hell; and will not you stretch out your hands to God to stop them in this desperate resolve? If out of this congregation there were but one unconverted man and I could point him out and say, "There he sits, one soul that has never felt the love of God, and never has been moved to re-pentance," with what anxious curiosity would every eye regard him. I think out of the thousands of Christians here, there is not one who would refuse to go home and pray for that solitary unconverted individual. But, oh! my brethren, it is not one that is in danger of hell fire; here are hundreds and thousands of our fellow-creatures.

Shall I give you yet another reason why you should pray? Hitherto all other means have been used without effect. God is my witness how often I have striven in this pulpit to be the means of the conversion of men. I have preached my very heart out. I could say no more than I have said, and I hope the secrecy of my chamber is a witness to the fact that I do not cease to feel when I cease to speak; but I have a heart to pray for those of you who are never affected, or who if affected still quench the Spirit of God. I have done my utmost. Will not you come to the help of the Lord against the mighty? Will not your prayers accomplish that which my preaching fails to do? Here they are; I commend them to you. Men and women whose hearts refuse to melt, whose stubborn knees will not bend; I give them up to you and ask you to pray for them. Carry their cases on your knees before God. Wife! never cease to pray for your unconverted husband. Husband! never stay your supplication till you see your wife converted. And, O fathers and mothers! have you no unconverted children? have you not brought them here many and many a Sunday, and they remain just as they have been? You have sent them first to one chapel and then to another, and they are just what they were. And do you refuse to pray for them?

We do not know what God may do for us if we do but pray for a blessing. Look at the movement we have already seen; we have witnessed Exeter Hall, St. Paul's Cathedral, and Westminster Abbey, crammed to the doors, but we have seen no effect as yet of all these mighty gatherings. Have we not tried to preach without trying to pray? Is it not likely that the Church has been putting forth its preaching hand but not its praying hand? O dear friends! let us agonise in prayer, and it shall come to pass that this Music Hall shall witness the sighs and groans of the penitent and the songs of the converted. It shall yet happen that this vast host shall not come and go as now it does, but little the better; but men shall go out of this hall, praising God and saying:—"It was good to be there; it was none other than the house of God, and the very gate of heaven."

Another inference we should draw is that all the stories we have heard should correct any self-dependence which may have crept into our treacherous hearts. Perhaps we as a congregation have begun to depend upon our numbers and so forth. We may have thought, "Surely God must bless us through the ministry." Now let the stories which our fathers have told us remind you, and remind me, that God saved not by many nor by few; that it is not in us to do this but God must do it all; it may be that some hidden preacher, whose name has never been known; some obscure denizen of St. Giles will yet start up in this City of London and preach the Word with greater power than bishops or ministers have ever known before. I will welcome him ; God be with him ; let him come from where he may ; only let God speed him, and let the work be done. Mayhap, however, God intends to bless the agency used in this place for your good and for your conversion. If so, I am thrice happy to think such should be the case. But place no dependence upon the instrument. No, when men laughed at us and mocked us most, God blessed us most ; and now it is not a disreputable thing to attend the Music Hall. We are not so much despised as we once were, but I question whether we have so great a blessing as once we had. We would be willing to endure another pelting in the pillory, to go through another ordeal with every newspaper against us, and with every man hissing and abusing us, if God so pleases, if he will but give us a blessing. Only let him cast out of us any idea that our own bow and our own sword will get us the victory. We shall never get a Revival here, unless we believe that it is the Lord, and the Lord alone, that can do it.

Why should not every one of my hearers be converted? Is there any limitation in the Spirit of God? Why should not the feeblest minister become the means of salvation to thousands? Is God's arm shortened? When I bid you pray that God would make the ministry quick and powerful, like a two-edged sword, for the salvation of sinners, I am not setting you a hard, much less an impossible task. We have but to ask and to get. Before we call, God will answer ; and while we are yet speaking he will hear. God alone can know what may come of this sermon, if he chooses to bless it. From this moment you may pray more ; from this moment God may bless the ministry more. From this hour other pulpits may become more full of life and vigour than before. From this same moment the Word of God may flow, and run, and rush, and get to itself an amazing and boundless victory. Only wrestle in prayer, meet together in your houses, go to your closets, be instant, be earnest in season and out of season, agonize for souls, and all that you have heard shall be forgotten in what ye shall see ; and all that others have told you shall be as nothing compared with what ye shall hear with your ears, and behold with your eyes in your own midst.

Oh ye, to whom all this is as an idle tale, who love not God, neither serve him, I beseech you stop and think for a moment. Oh, Spirit of God, rest on thy servant while a few sentences are uttered, and make them mighty. God has striven with some of you. You have had your times of conviction. You are trying now, perhaps, to be infidels. You are trying to say now—"There is no hell—there is no hereafter." It will not do. You know there is a hell and all the laughter of those who seek to ruin your souls cannot make you believe that there is not. You sometimes try to think so, but you know that God is true. I do not argue with you now. Conscience tells you that God will punish you for sin. Depend upon it you will find no happiness in trying to stifle God's Spirit. This is not the path to bliss, to quench those thoughts which would lead you to Christ. I beseech you, take off your hands from God's arm; resist not still his Spirit. Bow the knee and lay hold of Christ and believe on him. It will come to this yet. God the Holy Spirit will have you. I do trust that in answer to many prayers he intends to save you yet.

Give way now, but oh, remember if you are successful in quenching the Spirit, your success will be the most awful disaster than can ever occur to you, for if the Spirit forsake you, you are lost. It may be that this is the last warning you will ever have. The conviction you are now trying to put down and stifle may be the last you will ever have, and the angel standing with the black seal and the wax may be now about to drop it upon your destiny, and say, "Let him alone. He chooses drunkenness—he chooses lust—let him have them; and let him reap the wages in the everlasting fires of hell." Sinners, believe on the Lord Jesus: repent and be converted every one of you. I am bold to say what Peter did. Breaking through every bond of every kind that could bind my lip, I exhort you in God's name repent and escape from damnation. Oh! fly to Christ while yet the lamp holds out and burns, and mercy is still preached to you. Grace is still presented; accept Christ, resist him no longer; come to him now. The gates of mercy are wide open to-day; come now, poor sinner, and have thy sins forgiven. To-day if ye will hear his voice, harden not your hearts as in the provocation. Oh, to-day lay hold on Christ, "Kiss the Son, lest he be angry, and ye perish from the way, when his wrath is kindled but a little. Blessed are all they that put their trust in him."

VIII

REPENTANCE AFTER CONVERSION

"The sacrifices of God are a broken spirit: a broken and a contrite heart, O God, thou wilt not despise."—Psalm 51 : 17.

THE French have a phrase which signifies in English assisting at a service. A person who has been present at some grand function of the church speaks of himself as having "assisted" at the service. I want that many of us should literally carry out that expression just now. I do not want so much to preach as to lead you in the offering of sacrifices. Somebody says, perhaps, "But I have no bullock, no lamb." No, but you have a heart; and it is a broken and a contrite heart that I propose that we should present to God.

I would have you specially notice that, in this Psalm, David puts the sacrifice in its right position, and I would put it in the same position. You observe that he has first of all sought pardon for his sin, and he has found it. He has prayed, "Purge me with hyssop, and I shall be clean: wash me, and I shall be whiter than snow." His sin, then, is forgiven. He has next asked for a restoration of purity: "Create in me a clean heart, O God, and renew a right spirit within me." That also has been done. I will suppose it, to have been done in your case also, that you have been renewed in the spirit of your mind by the grace of God. Then, next, joy has also been restored to David, for he says, "Restore unto me the joy of thy salvation;" so that it is not a question with him as to whether he is saved or not, he is a man who is saved, and living in the assurance of salvation. Sin is pardoned, and the impurity engendered by grievous transgression has been put away, and he has peace with God; that is the man who brings the sacrifice, that is the man who presents to God a broken heart and a contrite spirit.

More than that, he has become a preacher; his gratitude to God has led him to be useful to others, as he says in the thirteenth verse, "Then will I teach transgressors thy ways; and sinners shall be converted unto thee." And even more than that, he has gone from the pulpit to the choir; he has become a singer, and he sings a sweet song of thankfulness to the great God who has saved him. Now, this is the man whose lips the Lord has opened, and whose mouth is showing forth God's praise; this is the man who says, "The sacrifices of God are a broken spirit: a broken and a contrite heart, O God, thou wilt not despise."

Perhaps you have the notion that repentance is a thing that happens at the commencement of the spiritual life, and has to be got through as one undergoes a certain operation, and there is an end of it. If so, you are greatly mistaken; repentance lives as long as faith. Towards faith I might almost call it a Siamese twin. We shall need to believe and to repent as long as ever we live. Perhaps also you have the idea that repentance is a better thing. It is sometimes bitter: "They shall be in bitterness for him, as one that is in bitterness for his first-born;" but that is not the kind of repentance that I am talking of now. Surely that bitterness is past, it was all over long ago; but this is a sweet bitterness which attends faith as long as ever we live, and becomes a source of tender joy. I do not know whether I shall quite convey my meaning to you; but I can assure you that the greatest joy I have ever known has not been when I have laughed, but when I have cried. The most intense happiness I have ever felt has not been when I have been exhilarated and full of spirits, but when I have leaned very low on the bosom of God, and felt it so sweet to be so low that one could scarcely be lower, and yet did not wish to be any higher. I want you to indulge yourselves in this most rare and *recherché* delight of sorrow at the feet of Jesus,—not sorrow for unpardoned sin, but sorrow for pardoned sin, sorrow for that which is done with, sorrow for that which is forgiven, sorrow for that which will never condemn you, for it was laid on Christ long ago, and is put away for ever.

First, LET US CONSIDER WHAT THIS SACRIFICE IS. It is a broken spirit, a broken and a contrite heart.

If you and I have a broken spirit, *all idea of our own importance is gone.* What is the use of a broken heart? Why, much the same as the use of a broken pot, or a broken jug, or a broken bottle! Men throw it on the dunghill. Hence David says, "A

broken and a contrite heart, O God, thou wilt not despise," as if
he felt that everybody else would despise it. Now, do you feel
that you are of no importance? Though you know that you are
a child of God, do you feel that you would not give a penny for
yourself? You would not wish to claim the first place; the rear
rank suits you best, and you wonder that you are in the Lord's
army in any rank at all. Oh, brothers, I believe that the more
God uses us, the less we shall think of ourselves; and the more
he fills us with his Spirit, the more will our own spirit sink
within us in utter amazement that he should ever make use of
such broken vessels as we are! Well now, indulge that feeling
of nothingness and unimportance; not only indulge it as a
feeling, but go and act upon it, and be you in the midst of
your brethren less than the least, humble yourselves in wonder
that God should permit your name to stand on the roll of his
elect of all. Admire the grace of God to you, and marvel at it
in deep humiliation of spirit. That is part of the sacrifice that
God will not despise.

Next, if you and I have a broken and a contrite heart, it
means that *frivolity and trifling have gone from us*. There are
some who are always trifling with spiritual things, but he who
gets a broken heart has done with that sort of spirit. A broken
heart is serious, and solemn, and in earnest. A broken heart
never tries to play any tricks with God, and never shuffles texts
as though even Scripture itself were meant only to be an
opportunity for testing our wit. A broken spirit is tender,
serious, weighed down with solemn considerations. Indulge
that spirit now, be solemn before God, grasp eternal things; let
slip these shadows; what are they worth? But set you your
soul on things divine and everlasting. Pursue that vein of
thought, and so bring before God a broken and a contrite
spirit.

Further, a broken spirit is one out of which *hypocrisy has
gone*. That vessel, whole and sealed up, may contain the most
precious otto of roses, or it may contain the foulest filth; I know
not what is in it. But break it, and you will soon see. There is
no hypocrisy about a broken heart. Oh, brethren and sisters,
be before men what you are before God! Seem to be what you
really are. Make no pretences. I am afraid that we are all
hyprocites in a measure; we both pray and preach above our

own actual experience full often, and we perhaps think that we have more faith than we actually have, and more love than we have ever known. The Lord make us to have a broken heart that is revealed by being broken!

Once more, a broken spirit signifies that now *all the secrets and essences of the spirit have flowed out.* You remember what happened when that holy woman broke the alabaster box; we read that "the house was filled with the odour of the ointment." A broken heart cannot keep secrets. Now is all revealed, now its essence goes forth. Far too much of our praying, and of our worship, is like closed-up boxes; you cannot tell what is in them. But it is not so with broken hearts; when broken hearts sing, they do sing. When broken hearts groan, they do groan. Broken hearts never play at repenting, nor play at believing. There is much of religion, nowadays, that is very superficial, it is all on the surface; a very small quantity of gospel paint, with just a little varnish of profession, will go a very long way, and look very bright. But broken hearts are not like that; with broken hearts, the hymn is a real hymn, the prayer is a real prayer, the hearing of sermons is earnest work, and the preaching of them is the hardest work of all. Oh, what a mercy it would be if some of you were broken all to pieces! There are many flowers that will never yield their perfume till they are bruised. When God has put sweetness into our hearts, it is then that breaking develops the sweetness. Oh, to worship God in spirit and in truth! One has well said, "No one ever worshipped God with his whole heart unless he worshipped him with a broken heart; and there never was a heart that was truly broken that did not thereby become a whole heart."

Now, in the second place, LET US OFFER THE SACRIFICE.

I have told you a little of what the sacrifice means, now we will try, as God shall help us, to bear our brokenness of heart before the Lord. Come, my brothers and sisters, let us mourn a while on account of our past sin; we will do so from several points of view.

First, let us deeply regret that *we have sinned against so good a God.* While I regarded God as a tyrant, I thought sin a trifle; but when I knew him to be my Father, then I mourned that I could ever have kicked against him. When I thought that God was hard, I found it easy to sin; but when I found God so kind, so good, so overflowing with compassion, I smote upon my breast to think that I could have rebelled against one who loved me so, and sought my good. Will you not now think of the goodness of God, brothers and sisters, and shall it not lead you to repentance? Shall we not feel within our hearts a burning indignation against sin, because it is committed against so holy, so good, so glorious a being as the infinitely-blessed God?

Let me help you again, and may the arrow pierce your very hearts this time! Let us mourn to think that *we have offended against so excellent and admirable a law.* If the law of God were like the laws of men, it might sometimes be a virtue to break it; but where a law is so balanced, so perfect, oh, how could we have run contrary to it? Brethren, the law of God, when it says to us, "Thou shalt not," only sets up a danger signal to tell us where it is injurious to go. And when the law says, "Thou shalt," it does but lift up a kindly hand to point out to us the best and safest path. There is nothing in the law of God that will rob you of happiness; it only denies you that which would cost you sorrow. We know that it is so, and therefore we stand here, and bow our head, and mourn that we should have been so foolish as to transgress, so wilfully and suicidally wicked as to do that evil thing which God hates and which so grievously injures us.

You remember that I am talking to those of you who are saved, to those of you whose sins are forgiven. In my heart, I think that I can hear some others say, "Will you not let us join with you in repenting though we are not pardoned?" Bless your hearts, yes, yes! God help you to join with us; and if you do, you will find pardon, too, for pardon comes in this way! A broken heart can never long be divided from the broken Saviour. You shall have peace with him when you are at war with sin.

More than that,—and this is a very tender point,—let us grieve that *we have sinned against a Saviour's love.* I like that verse we sang just now,—

> "'Tis I have thus ungrateful been,
>   Yet, Jesus, pity take!
> Oh, spare and pardon me, my Lord,
>   For thy sweet mercy's sake!"

The greatest crime that was ever committed against high heaven was that crime of deicide, when men nailed the Son of God to the tree, and put him to death as a criminal. Where are the wretches that did this awful deed? They are *here*; I will not say that they are before us, for each of us harbours one of them within his bosom. "'Tis I,"—"'Tis *I* have thus ungrateful been." How can I speak to you thus? Well, perhaps, all the better, because from my very heart I ask that we may stand together at the foot of the cross, and count the purple drops, and say, "These have washed away my sins, yet I helped to spill them. Those hands, those feet, have saved me, yet I nailed them there. That opened side is the refuge of my guilty spirit, yet I made that fearful gash by my sin. It was my sin that slew my Saviour." O sin, thou thrice-accursed thing, away with thee! Away with thee! Come, let us be filled with mournful joy, with pleasurable sorrow, while we sit beneath the bloody tree, and see what sin has done, and yet see how sin itself has been undone by him who died upon the cross of Calvary.

Beloved, the more you love your Lord, the more you will hate sin. If you often sit at the table with him, and dip your hand into his dish, if you lean your head upon his bosom with the blessed John, if you are favoured and indulged with the choicest brotherliness towards the Well-beloved, I know that you will often find occasion to seek a quiet place where you may shed tears of bitter regret that you should ever have sinned against such a Saviour as Jesus is.

Let me help you again, however, while I remind you of *our sins against the Holy Ghost*. Oh, what do we not owe to the Holy Spirit? I speak to you who know him. It is the Holy Ghost who quickened you, the Holy Ghost who convinced you of sin, the Holy Ghost who comforted you; and oh, how sweetly does that Divine Comforter still comfort! Yet we resisted him, and grieved him. Do you not remember, in your youthful days, how you strangled your convictions, how you held down conscience, and would not let it reprove you? That blessed Spirit, whom we vexed and spurned, might have left us, and gone his way, never to strive with us again; but he loved us so that he came and took up his abode with us, and now he dwelleth in us. Within the narrow cell of our poor heart he has condescended to find a temple for his perpetual indwelling. O my soul, how couldst thou ever grieve him? How couldst thou ever have resisted that best and tenderest Friend?

Let us go a step further, and *set our sin in the light of God's countenance.* I speak to you, beloved, who are God's elect. He loved you from before the foundation of the world, and yet you have sinned against him. He chose you from among men, of his own sovereign grace, and ordained you to belong to Christ, and gave you to Jesus to be his for ever. Alas, you knew it not, and you continued to sin against this distinguishing and discriminating grace! Oh, that even the elect of God should have done this! See that you crucify the sin that suffered you to act so shamefully. Then in due time you were redeemed. For you, beloved, Jesus shed his precious blood; he shed it not for all men, but with a special view to the redemption of his elect. Christ loved the Church, and gave himself for *it.* He hath redeemed us from among men. We have been the object of that special and peculiar redemption, and yet against that dear Christ, who loved us, and gave himself for us, we rebelled and transgressed. Ordained to be of the blood-royal of heaven, and yet a rebel! Ordained on earth to have the love of God within your spirit, and in heaven to behold his face for ever, ordained by divine decree to this high destiny, and yet for many a year a rebel, a wilful rebel against such wondrous love as this! I do not know what to say to myself; I despise myself, I loathe myself, that I should thus have acted against such extraordinary love.

Then remember also that you are God's child, adopted into his family, his twice-born, divinely regenerated. You are an heir of God, a joint heir with Jesus Christ; and yet—and yet, you have acted so sinfully! O God, thou hast forgiven thy servants; but we have never forgiven ourselves, and we never mean to, we shall always mourn, even amid our joy for pardoned guilt, that we, the favourites of heaven, should have so grieved the Lord!

Go a little further. I want you to *set sin in the light of your marvellous experiences.* Oh, there are some of us who, without boasting, can tell of answered prayer when we have come back from the top of Carmel, and we have cried, "I have won the day;" and yet to us who have been privileged thus to have power with God it was not always so. Perhaps the very lips that now prevail in prayer were once habituated to blasphemy. Oh, mourn, my brother, if it was so! Can you ever help mourning? When John Newton wrote the *Cardiphonia*, or voice of the hear., when he left us that choice treasure, I am sure that he must often and often have smitten upon his breast, and grieved over the thought that he was once in Africa, a blasphemer, and everything that was foul and bad. Oh yes, wonders of grace have been ours! Wonders of grace! Wonders of grace! We have tasted the wines on the lees well refined; yet once we drank of the wine of the clusters of Sodom and Gomorrah. What has grace not done for us, brothers and sisters? You and I have been in the King's banqueting house, and his banner of love has waved over us, and our Beloved has caught us away "from the top of Amana, from the lions' dens, from the mountains of the leopards," and manifested his love to us in the secret places where no eye saw except our own and his. There did he reveal to us his great love. Yet we were the very ones who once despised him, broke his Sabbaths, refused to read his Word, neglected prayer, perhaps ridiculed holy things. We were proud, covetous, unholy; but we are washed, but we are sanctified. Oh, let us sit here, and sweetly repent, and present to our God the sacrifices of a broken and contrite spirit!

Besides, think of *the injury you have done to others by your example.* What a powerful preacher a mother is to her boy! What an influential preacher is a father to his son! What a mighty preacher one workman may be to another, especially if he is a man of stronger mind than his fellows! Whatever any of us do, we are sure to have some who will copy us; it cannot be avoided. You are all writing copies every day, even though you are not schoolmasters; and there are some who will learn either bad or good writing from you, for they will copy your handwriting; I mean, that they will imitate what they see in you. In years to come, when you have forgotten what you did, some may be following your former example. I would urge young men,—and I am glad to see a great many of them present,—to pray that they may begin life in such a way that they may not have much back reckoning. Suppose a man to be converted after his children are born, if those children have seen the father do wrong, they will perhaps remember the evil

better than the good example of their converted father. When
your children have once left your roof, what opportunities of
influencing them aright you have lost! Though you may
yourselves be saved by faith in Christ, yet you cannot call back
the boys and the girls from those sinful ways into which you
yourself led them in the days of your ungodliness. This thought
has a sharp sting in it for any who, by word or by example,
have taught others to do that which is evil in the sight of the
Lord.

If that is not enough, I want to lead you a little further, and
bid you think of all *the opportunities that we lose whenever we fall
into sin.* I do repent of sin unfeignedly because it has hindered
my progress. I am now speaking only to the people of God,
mark you. If any of you sinners want to creep in among them,
you may; still, I am specially addressing them. There is one
here who, not long ago, was a pilgrim on the road to the
Celestial City, and he went part of the way up the Hill Difficulty,
climbing splendidly on his hands and knees. He made the best
of his way up, but it came to pass that, when he had gone
about half-way up the hill, he found a little arbour by the road-
side. It was built there by the Lord of the way that he might
rest himself a little in it, and then go on his way; but this
brother sat down in the arbour, and he sat on till he went to
sleep; and he slept there I do not know how long. Just lately,
he has been awaked, and he has gone on his way again, climbing
up, but he has discovered that he has lost the roll that he used
to carry in his bosom. It was a roll that he had when first he
started at the head of the way, and he meant to present it to
the Lord of the Celestial City when he came to his journey's
end. But he has lost his roll. You know what Mr. Bunyan
says of this matter. It was getting late, but Christian had
lost his roll, so he had to go back; and he wisely went back to
the place where he had fallen asleep, all the way moaning and
sighing and crying to himself, "I have lost my evidences, I
have lost my roll. Where shall I find it?" He was so glad,
when he looked under the settle, to see the roll there. I warrant
you that he quickly picked it up, and put it in his bosom again;
but then, you see, he had to go over that part of the road three
times. If he had not lost his roll, and had to go back, he might
by that time have been much further on the road. There were

lions in that region, and that was ugly for him. If he had got into the House Beautiful earlier in the day, he would not have suffered the fears he now had; so he went along in a very sad state of mind, and all through that careless sleeping in the arbour. Oh, what some of you might have been if it had not been for your sins since conversion! What a preacher I might have been! What workers in the Sunday-school you might have been! Oh, what winners of souls you might have become by this time! But you have been asleep, and had to go back, perhaps, and so you have missed many opportunities of serving Christ.

Let us sit and think this matter over, and begin to say, "Lord, we do present to thee a broken and contrite heart, mourning and lamenting, for if we are straitened, we are straitened in ourselves, and not in thee. If we are mourning in darkness, we ourselves made the darkness. If we are desponding, we have in a large measure created the despondency. Lord, we grieve and sorrow for all this." Do not talk about years; they go so quickly, and our friends pass away quickly, too. The other day a man of God sat at his table writing; he had dipped his pen in the ink, but he never laid it on the paper, for he fell asleep there and then, and he was gone home. We, too, shall soon pass away. "Perhaps in a few days I shall be among the angels,"—say that to yourself, my brother. "Perhaps in a few weeks I shall behold the face of him I love,"—say that, my sister. It will come true. Perhaps in a few years; nay, drop the "perhaps" now, and say, "Certainly, within a few years, I shall behold the beatific vision."

> "Father, I long, I faint to see
> The place of thine abode."

I see myself walking over that street of gold that shines like glass. Earthly gold is dull, you cannot see into it. If you could, you would see the tears of the oppressed and sometimes the blood of crushed-down men in it; but the gold of heaven is good, and you can see into it, as you could into a sea of glass. I think I am walking there. I hardly know myself, and there I meet one and another of you whom I knew here, and we go together down that golden street, and look in at the many

mansions, whence come out many to welcome us; and we thread
our way into the centre. There is no temple there, no taber-
nacle of worship there; but we get into the centre, and we stand
upon the glassy sea, into which all the streets seem to run; and
as we look around, we see angels and elders bowing there before
the throne of the infinite majesty, and we are there ourselves,
and we bow with them; and when we lift up our eyes to that
light we sing, "Unto him that loved us, and washed us from
our sins in his own blood, and hath made us kings and priests
unto God and his Father; to him be glory and dominion for
ever and ever."

Now I want you to *think of your sins in the light of that glory*.
Oh, how could those who are predestinated to these heavenly
seats ever have wandered into sin? What! Was it so—that
we, who were born to behold the face of God, ever loved the
theatre, and all its abominations? What! Did we, who were
ordained to be peers with cherubim and seraphim, ever love
the race-course and all its gambling? What! Were we, whom
God has made to be conformed to the image of his firstborn
Son, ever seen to be drunken, and staggering through the streets,
defiled with unchastity, or polluted with gluttony, or guilty of
covetousness, or cursed with pride? What! We whom the Lord
has loved with an everlasting love, and without whom Christ
himself will not be content to reign in heaven, grovelling in
iniquity? Oh, I think these questions must have helped to
make sin seem contemptible and loathsome! I point at it the
finger of scorn. O dear children of God, scorn your sins, lament
your sins, weep over your sins! Indulge that feeling, and God
will accept it when it is mixed with faith in his dear Son; for
"the sacrifices of God"—that is, all sorts of sacrifices put
together, sin-offerings, burnt-offerings, peace-offerings, scape-
goats, and all together—"the sacrifices of God are a broken
spirit." One broken spirit is worth them all. "A broken and a
contrite heart,"—though there be but one such,—"O God,
thou wilt not despise."

IX

FEARING AND TRUSTING—TRUSTING AND NOT FEARING

"What time I am afraid, I will trust in thee."—Ps. 56: 3.
"I will trust, and not be afraid."—Isa. 12: 2.

I INTEND to have two texts, though I shall not therefore have two sermons. Our first text, which will suffice to begin with, is in the 56th Psalm, at the 3rd verse:—"*What time I am afraid, I will trust in thee.*"

David was one of the boldest of men. From his youth up, he was noted for his courage. As a youth he went, in simple confidence in God, and attacked the giant Goliath. Throughout life there was no man who seemed to be more at home in wars and battles, and less likely to be afraid. But yet this hero, this courageous man, says that he was sometimes afraid, and I suppose that there are none of us but must plead guilty to the impeachment that sometimes the brave spirit gives way, and that we tremble and are afraid. It is a disease for which the cure is here mentioned, "What time I am afraid, I will trust in thee; when my soul suffers from the palsy of fear, I will lay hold upon the strong one, and get strength from him, and so my fears shall all be cast out."

To be afraid is, in some cases, *a very childish thing.* We expect to see our little children sometimes frightened, and that they will not bear to be alone in the dark, but we are surely not afraid to be there. The more we are afraid, the more childish we become. Courage is manly, but to be afraid, is to be like a child. It is not always so, however, for there are some great and sore dangers which may well make the very boldest man tremble.

To be afraid is always *a distressing thing.* The heart beats quickly, and the whole system seems to be thrown out of order. There have been known cases of men who have had to endure severe terror for several hours, and their hair has all turned grey in a single night. No doubt, too, there have been diseases which have brought men to their graves, and which have been caused by fright. Fear is always distressing, and whether it be the fear of outward danger, or fear of inward sin, it is always a terrible thing to have to go mourning because of being afraid.

And to be afraid, too, is always *a weakening thing*. The man who can keep calm in the midst of difficulty is better able to meet it. If he be at sea in a storm, if his mind be quiet, he is likely to steer his vessel safely through the danger, but if he be perturbed and cast down with agitated alarm, we can have but little confidence in him, for we know not where he may steer the bark. A man who is afraid often runs into worse dangers than those from which he seeks to escape. He plunges himself into the sea to escape from the river, and it is as though he fled from a lion, and a bear met him.

To be afraid, then, is generally a very mischievous thing, and though sometimes exceedingly excusable, yet full often is exceedingly dangerous also. David, however, here gives us the cure for fear, "What time I am afraid, I will trust in thee."

SOMETIMES WE ARE AFRAID OF TEMPORAL TROUBLES. If some of you have such a smooth path in life that you are untried in this respect, yet the great proportion of mankind have a hard fight to find bread to eat, and raiment wherewith they shall be clothed, and in the lives of the poor, especially, there must often be sad times when they are afraid lest they should not be able to provide things necessary, and should be brought to absolute starvation. Such a fear must very often afflict those who are in extreme poverty. And you, too, who are in business, in this age of competition, you are, no doubt, frequently afraid lest, by a failure in this direction or in that, you should not be able to meet your engagements, and the good ship of your business should drive upon the rocks.

Such fears, I suppose, fall to the lot of all young tradesmen when they are starting in business life, and, peradventure, there are few older ones who have done longer and rougher work, are quite free from such times of anxious fear. And even if we have none of these troubles about what we shall eat and what we shall drink, yet we have our domestic troubles, that make us to be much alarmed. It is no small thing to see the child sick, or, worse still, to see your life's partner gradually fading away, and to know, as some do, that the case is beyond all medical skill, and that she, who is so dear, must be taken away.

And you wives, perhaps, are some of you dreading the hour when you may become widows, and your little children may be fatherless. You have often been afraid as you have looked forward to the calamity which seemed to overshadow you. God has not made this world to be a nest for us, and if we try to make it such for ourselves, he plants thorns in it, so that we may be compelled to mount and find our soul's true home somewhere else, in a higher and nobler sphere than this poor world can give.

Now, whenever we are tried with these temporal affairs, David tells us we are to trust in God. "What time I am afraid, I will trust in thee." I will just do this; after having done my best to earn my daily bread and to fight the battle of life, if I find I cannot do all I would, I will throw myself upon the promise of God, wherein he has said, "Thy bread shall be given thee, and thy water shall be sure." I will believe that my Heavenly Father, who feeds the ravens, will feed me, and that if he does not suffer even the gnats that dance in the sunbeam to perish for lack of sustenance, he will not suffer a soul that rests upon him to perish for lack of daily bread. Oh! it is a sweet thing, though, mayhap, you may some of you think it a hard thing—it is a sweet thing when God enables you to leave the morrow with him, and to depend upon your Father who is in heaven.

To the tradesman I speak, and all who have often to do business in great waters, who seem to go from water-spout to water-spout, and over whom all God's waves and billows seem to go— I believe you will find yourselves much stronger to do battle against these difficulties if it be your constant habit to commit all your cares to him who careth for you. It will all go wrong with us, even in smooth waters, if we do not have God to be the Pilot; and as to rough weather, we shall soon be a wreck if we forget him. I know of nothing more delightful to the believer than every morning to commit the day's troubles to God, and then go down into the world feeling, "Well, my Father knows it all," and then at night to commit the troubles of the day again into the great Father's hands, and to feel that he has said, "I will never leave thee, nor forsake thee." It is sweet sleeping when you can have a promise for the pillow at your head.

You know, perhaps, the good old story which is told of the woman on ship-board who was greatly afraid in a storm, but she saw her husband perfectly at peace, and she could not understand it. Her husband said he would tell her the reason, so snatching up a sword, he pointed it at her heart. She looked at it, but did not tremble. "Well," said he, "are you not afraid? The sword is sharp and I could kill you in a moment." "No," said she, "because it is in your hands!" "Ah!" he replied, "and that is why I am not afraid, because the storm is in my Father's hands, and he loves me better than I love you."

A second great fear, through which some of you have never passed, but through which all must pass who enter into heaven, is a FEAR CONCERNING THE GUILT OF PAST SIN.

Do not tell me with regard to temporal troubles that they are sharp and bitter! Believe me, that trouble for sin is far more bitter and keen. Do you remember when God was pleased to awaken you from your long sleep, when you looked within, and saw that you were all defiled, and full of pollution, and all manner of evil? Do you recollect how the thoughts pierced you like poisoned arrows—"God requireth that which is pure"; "For every idle word that men shall speak, they shall give an account thereof at the day of judgment"? Do you recollect how it seemed as though hell flared up right before you where you stood, and it seemed as though there were a step only betwixt you and death? The terrors of the Lord got hold upon you, and the very marrow of your bones seemed to freeze as you thought upon an angry God, and of how you, in your sins, without any preparation, could meet him! Oh! it is not so long ago with some of us but what we recollect being startled in our sleep under a sense of sin ; and all day long the common joys of men were no joys to us, and though before we had been sprightly and cheerful like others, yet our mirth was now turned into mourning, and all our laughter into lamentation!

Perhaps some of you are passing through this state of mind now. You are conscious now of your old sins : the sins of your youth are coming up before your remembrance. Now, if so, listen to what David says, "What time I am afraid, I will trust in thee." Beloved! if you would ever get rid of the fear of your past sins, remember that the Lord Jesus Christ came into the world to suffer for the sins of all who will trust him. All the sins of all his people were reckoned as upon him, and all that they should have suffered on account of those sins Jesus Christ suffered in their stead. The mighty debt, too huge for us to calculate, was all laid upon him, and he paid it to the last farthing. The whole tremendous debt that was due to God, the debt caused by the sins of all his people were paid by him.

Now, it is a blessed thing when sin burdens us to fly away to Christ, and stand in spirit beneath the cross, and feel that under that crimson canopy no flash of divine penalty shall ever fall upon us. "Smite me! Great God? Thou canst not, for hast thou not smitten the redeeming Christ on my account? Is it not recorded that for those who trust him, thy Son is both surety and substitute?" Faith thus clings to the cross, and feels, nay! knows, that all is safe. Only look on Jesus, and though you had committed all the sins that are committable by mortal man, yet Jesus Christ can put them all away. If every form of iniquity were heaped upon you, till you were dyed through and through with it, like the scarlet that has been lying long a-soak in the dye, yet let the crimson blood of Jesus come into contact with your crimson sins, and they "Shall vanish all away, Though foul as hell before."

Now, I know it is very easy when we do not feel our sins to trust in Christ, but the business of faith is to trust in Christ when you *do* feel your sins. Brethren, it would be cheap faith to take Christ as the saints' Saviour, but it is the faith of God's elect to take him as the sinner's Saviour. When I can see marks of grace in myself, to trust Christ is easy; but when I see no marks of anything good, but every mark of everything that is evil, and then come and cast myself upon him, and believe that he can save me, even me, and rest myself upon him—this is the faith which honours Christ and which will save us.

A third fear that is remarkably common is FEAR LEST WE SHOULD BE DECEIVED.

Amongst the best and most careful of believers this fear intrudes itself, "Lest, after having preached to others, I myself should be a castaway." Lest, after having been united to the church, I should prove to be a dead member, and so be cut out of the living vine. All these fears have I met with. One has said, "I fear I was never chosen of God." Another has said, "I fear I never was effectually called." And yet a third has said, "I fear I never possessed the repentance that needeth not to be repented of." Still others have confessed, "I am afraid my faith is not the faith of God's elect." Very frequently have I heard this, "I am afraid I am a hypocrite," which is one of the oddest fears in all the world, for nobody that was a hypocrite was ever afraid of it. It is the hypocrite who goes on peacefully, without fear, confident where there is no ground for confidence. But these fears abound, and, in some respects, they are healthy. Better go to heaven doubting, than to hell presuming. Better to enter into life halt and maimed, than, having two eyes and hands, and feet, to be cast into the destroying fire. We cannot say too much in praise of assurance, and we cannot speak too much against presumption. Dread that! shun it with all your might.

But when you and I are besieged by these doubts and fears— and I very often am—as to whether we are the children of God or not, what is the best thing for us to do? "What time I am afraid, I will trust in thee." This is the short cut with the devil. Go straight away to Christ. Do not stop to argue with Satan. He is a crafty old liar, and he will be sure to defeat you if it comes to argument between you. Say to him, "Satan, if I be deceived, if all I have ever known up till now has been only head-knowledge, if I am nothing but a mere hypocrite, yet now:—

> "Black, I to the fountain fly;
> Wash me, Saviour, or I die."

It is a blessed thing to begin again; to be always beginning, and yet always going on, for no man ever goes on to perfection who forgets his first love, his first faith, and forgets to walk in Christ Jesus as he walked in him at the first.

Beloved, whatever may be the doubt that comes to you, I beseech you recollect it is still, "Him that cometh unto me I will in no wise cast out." If you have been a backslider, weep over it; if you have been a great sinner, be sorry for it, but still remember, "All manner of sin and of blasphemy shall be forgiven unto men," and "Where sin abounded, grace doth much more abound." The Gospel's voice still is, "Return, ye backsliding children, for I am married unto you, saith the Lord." "Come, now, let us reason together; though your sins be as scarlet, they shall be as wool; though they be red like crimson, they shall be whiter than snow." Come, come, come, thou doubting one; trembling and broken to pieces; come again, a guilty, weak, and helpless worm, and cast thyself into Jesus' arms.

A fourth fear, which is frequent enough to cause Christians much distress, is A FEAR THAT WE SHALL NOT HOLD ON, AND HOLD OUT, TO THE END.

Many thousands of God's saints are quite unnecessarily troubled with this. Remember, that where God begins to work, he does not ask us to finish it. He always completes his own work. If you have begun the work of salvation, you will have to carry it on, but if God has begun the good work in you, he will carry it on, and bring to its perfection of completeness in "the day of Christ." Yet there are thousands who say "Should I be tempted, I might fall: working as I do with so many others, none of whom fear God, but who sneer and ridicule at divine things, I might, perhaps, turn aside and prove like one of them." It is very proper that you should have that fear, very proper that you should be distressed at it. But, dearly beloved, what time you are afraid, do not say, "I shall be able to hold out"; do not trust in yourselves, or you will trust to a broken reed, but what time you are afraid, renew your trust in Christ. Go with the temptation which you now experience, and which you expect to recur to-morrow, to the Lord, and he will, with the temptation, show the way of escape out of it. I remember a miner who had been a sad, drunken man, and a great blasphemer, but he was converted among the Methodists, and a right earnest man he was, but he seemed to have been a man of strong passions, and on one occasion he was praying, and he prayed that sooner than that he might ever go back to his old sins, if God foresaw that he would not be able to bear up under temptation, he would take him to heaven at once, and while he was praying the prayer in the prayer-meeting he fell dead. God had answered him. Now, if you are to be tried in the order of Providence in a way that you cannot bear, and there is no other way of escape for you, God will take you clear away to where no temptation shall ever come near you. What time you are afraid, put your trust in him, and all will be well.

The last fear I have to mention, is this : THE FEAR OF DEATH.

There are some "who, through fear of death, are all their life-time subject to bondage"; but Christ came to deliver such, and where Christ works he delivers us from that fear. Beloved, do you ever get afraid of death? You do, perhaps, when you feel very sick, when you are very ill and low-spirited. You begin to look forward, and you say, "I have run with the footmen and they have wearied me ; what shall I do when I have to contend with the rider on the pale horse? My trials have been so great that I have scarcely found faith enough to bear them ; what shall I do in the last great trial of the swellings of Jordan?" Now, what ought you to do at what time you are afraid of dying, but to say, with David, "What time I am afraid, I will trust in thee"? Oh! fear not to die! If you are in Christ, death is nothing. "But the pain, the dying struggle," you say. Oh! there is no pain in death. It is the life that is full of pain. Death! What is it? Well, it is but a pin's prick, and then it is over. "Many lie a-dying for weeks or months together," say some. Nay! say they live, for 'tis living that makes them full of pain and anguish, but death ends all that. Death is just the passing through the narrow stream that is the entrance in the fields where "Everlasting spring abides, and never-withering flowers."

To be afraid to die must be because we do not understand it, for believers know that to die is but to enter into the arms of Jesus Christ. What time you are afraid of dying, trust in the living Saviour, for in him are life and immortality. Recollect :—

> *"Jesus can make our dying bed*
> *Feel soft as downy pillows are,*
> *Whilst on his breast we lean our head,*
> *And breathe our life out softly there."*

He will keep you where you shall sing :—

> *"Oh! if my Lord would come and meet,*
> *My soul would stretch her wings in haste;*
> *Fly fearless through death's iron gate,*
> *Nor fear the terror as she passed."*

Now, brethren, I have taken you far, like a guide conducting a number of travellers up the first road on a mountain, and I think we have gathered something even there, but now I want you to go up higher still. I feel as if, in handling this text, we have been travelling third class to heaven, but now I want you to get into the first class. My second text will let you know what I mean. It is in the 12th chapter of Isaiah and the 2nd verse :—"*I will trust and not be afraid.*"

This is several stages beyond the first text. David says, "What time I am afraid, I will trust in thee." Isaiah says, "I will trust and not be afraid," which is far better. When David is afraid he trusts in God, but Isaiah trusts in God first, and then he is not afraid at all. I told you in the first case that there was a disease, and that faith was the remedy, but you know prevention is always better than cure. I have heard of a man who had the ague, and he was thankful to have a medicine which helped him through it ; but his neighbour said he should not be very thankful for that, for he had a remedy which prevented him from ever having the malady. So with you who are doubting and fearing : it is a good thing that faith can bear you through it, but how much better it will be if you get a faith that does not have these doubts, that lives above these fears and troubles.

Let us take the fears which we have already mentioned over again. Faith saves from THE FEAR OF TEMPORAL TROUBLE.

The man who fully trusts in God is not afraid of temporal trouble. You have read, perhaps, the life of Bernard Palissy, the famous potter. He was confined for many years on account of his religion, and he was only permitted to live at all because he was such a skilful workman that they did not like to put him to death. King Henry the Third of France said to him one day, "Bernard, I shall be obliged to give you up to your enemies to be burned, unless you change your religion." Bernard replied, "Your Majesty, I have often heard you say you pity me, but believe me I greatly pity you, though I am no king but only a poor humble potter, but there is no man living that could compel me to do what I believe to be wrong ; and yet you say you will be compelled ; those are kingly words for you to utter !" And he could say this to the king, in whose hands his life was ! Bernard was a very poor man. As I have told you, he used to earn his bread by making pottery, and he used to

say in his poverty that he was a very rich man, for he had two
things, he had heaven and earth, and then he would take up a
handful of the clay by which he earned his living. Happy man!
Though often brought to the depths of poverty, he could say,
"I will trust and not be afraid."

Take as another example, Martin Luther. They came to
Martin one day, and they said, "Martin, it is all over with the
Reformation cause now, for the Emperor of Germany has sworn
a solemn oath to help the Pope." "I do not care a snap of my
finger for both of them," said he, "nor for all the devils in hell!
This is God's work, and God's work can stand against both
emperors and popes." There was a man who trusted, really,
intensely, and because of this he was not afraid. Is not that
much better than being afraid, and then having to trust to
banish the fear? Now, God is with me, and come what may :—

> "Should earth against my soul engage,
> And hellish darts be hurled;
> Now I can smile at Satan's rage,
> And face a frowning world.
>
> "Let cares like a wild deluge come,
> And storms of sorrow fall:
> I shall in safety reach my home,
> My God, my heaven, my all."

Oh! if we can all get to this brave assurance of faith, happy shall
we be in the midst of the worst trouble.

Faith also saves from the FEAR CONCERNING PAST SIN.

He is in a blessed state who is delivered from such fear. One
of you knows a man, perhaps, who has got into debt, and who
owed a great deal. But some little time ago a friend paid all his
debts for him, and he has got the receipt. Now, when he walks
the streets, is this man afraid of the sheriff's officer? Does he
fear that he shall be arrested? Why, no; he knows he shall not,
because he has got the receipt about him. Every man who
trusts Christ perceives his own sin, but he also perceives that
Christ paid for all his sin. He that believeth hath the witness
of his pardon in himself, which he carries about him as a receipt,
and which eases his conscience and prevents his fears. Oh! if

you can but know that Christ died for you; if you can but rest alone in him so as to know that he is yours, then all the sins that you have ever committed, though you lament them, shall never cause you a moment's uneasiness, for they are drowned beneath the Red Sea of the Saviour's blood, and therefore may you say, "I will trust and not be afraid."

As to that third fear which I mentioned—the fear lest we should be hypocrites, or LEST THE WORK OF GRACE SHOULD NOT BE RIPENED IN OUR HEARTS, there is one way of getting rid of that fear entirely. If you take a sovereign across the counter, you may not know whether it is a good one; you may have some doubts about it. But if you get it straight from the Mint, I do not suppose you will have any suspicion of it at all. So when a man asks, "Is my faith right? Is my religion right?" If he can say, "I got it straight from the throne of God by trusting in the blood of Jesus Christ"—then he will know that he received it from headquarters, and there can be no mistake about it. A Christian has no right to be always saying:—

"Do I love the Lord or no?
Am I his, or am I not?"

He may be compelled to say it sometimes, but it is far better for him to come just as he is, and throw himself at the foot of the cross, and say, "Saviour, thou hast promised to save those that believe! I do believe, therefore thou hast saved me." I know some think this is presumption, but surely it is worse than presumption not to believe God, and it is true humility to take God at his word, and to believe him.

I think I once illustrated this truth in this place in this way. A good mother has two children. Christmas is drawing near, and she says to one of them, "Now, John, I shall take you out on Christmas Day to such a place, and give you a great treat." She promises the same to William. Now, Master John says to himself, "Well, I do not know: I do not know whether my mother can afford it: or perhaps I do not deserve it: I hardly think she will take me: it will be presumption in me to believe that she will." But as for little Master William, he is no sooner told that he is to go out on Christmas Day than he claps his hands, and begins to skip, and tells all his playmates

to-morrow that his mother is going to take him out on Christmas Day: he is quite sure of it. They begin to ask him, "How
do you know?" "Why," he says, "mother said so." Perhaps
they mention some things that make it look rather unlikely.
"Oh! but," he says, "my mother never tells lies, and she told
me she would take me, and I know she will." Now, which of
those children, do you think, is most to be commended—the
bigger boy, who raised difficulties and suspected his mother's
word? Why, he is a proud little fellow, who deserves to go
without the pleasure; but as for his little brother William, who
takes his mother at her word—I do not call him proud. I
consider him truly humble, and he is the child who really
deserves the mother's fondest love.

Now, deal with God as you would have your children deal
with you. If he says he will save you if you trust him, then if
you do trust him, why, he will save you. If he is a true God,
he cannot destroy the soul that trusts in Christ. Unless this
Bible is one great lie from beginning to end, the soul that trusts
in Christ must be saved. If God be true, every soul that trusts
in Jesus must be safe at the last. Whatever he may be, and
whoever he may be, if he trusts his soul with Christ, and with
Christ alone, cast away he cannot be, unless the promise of God
can be of no effect. "I will trust and not be afraid."

So, brethren, it will be with other fears—time fails us to
mention them—whatever they may be. May you get into such
a blessed state of confidence in the love of God, in the love of
Christ's heart, in the power of Christ's arm, in the prevalence
of Christ's plea, that at all times you may trust in him, and in
nothing whatever be afraid.

X

GOD IN HEAVEN, AND MEN ON THE SEA:
A SERMON FOR SAILORS

"By terrible things in righteousness wilt thou answer us, O
God of our salvation; who art the confidence of all the ends of
the earth, and of them that are afar off upon the sea."—
Psalm 65: 5.

PLEASE read the sixty-fifth Psalm through. May it do you
good, whether as landsmen you read of the Lord's settling
the furrows, or as sailors you hear of his stilling the noise of the
seas. Notice the first two verses: "Praise waiteth for thee,"
"O thou that hearest prayer." *Holy men of old were accustomed
to mix praise and prayer together:* this is a happy mixture. We
are not tied to one thing. We spread the sails of prayer, and
fly the flag of praise. To praise God without praying to him
would be impossible. To pray to God without praising him
would be ungrateful. Praise takes in a cargo of gold for the
King of kings; and prayer stokes the fires to make the good
ship steam towards the royal city. Brothers, keep to this
throughout all the watches: *pray and praise,* and when you
want a change, *praise and pray.* Keep the boat of the soul
going with these two oars, praise and prayer.

Notice, also, in this psalm, that when the saints of the olden
time offered prayer and praise, *they addressed themselves at once
to God, and not to saints and angels.* David is not satisfied with
talking about God, but he talks *to* him, as in our text: "Thou
wilt answer us, O God of our salvation." There's nothing like
straight sailing: let us go to God direct. We ought not to think
of what our fellow-men will say of our praises; if they are not
musical in the ears of men it matters little, so long as they are
sweet to the Lord our God. When we engage in public prayer,
it is a pity to be thinking about how our words will sound in the
opinion of our brethren; let us only think of the Lord to whom
we are speaking. We can't steer two ways at once: if we make
for the mercy-seat we need not consider the pews. Let us fix

our eye on the lighthouse at the mouth of the harbour, and
leave the church on the hill, and the windmill over yonder, for
other people to look at. Brothers, look to your captain, and
let your mates think what they like. Let us know our port, and
steer for it; and let the twin-ship of prayer and praise never
take any course but that which carries our whole heart straight
to heaven.

First, then, let us consider WHAT THE LORD IS TO US. He is
the "God of our salvation." It is clear from this that *we all need
salvation.* If it were not clear in this text, we could not doubt it,
for the evidence surrounds us on every side. We have sadly
sufficient proof of our lost estate. Human nature is water-
logged, and ready to sink, and in God alone is our hope.

The text tells us where salvation is, namely, in God. God is the
God of our salvation. You have neither right ideas of yourself,
nor right ideas of God, unless you see that by nature you have
need of being saved from sin—saved by nothing less than a
divine hand. The greatest saint on earth is still a sinner. Let
him have safely sailed on the sea of life for sixty years, he will
be on the rocks before the morning watch, unless the Lord save
him. The most intelligent man, and the man of longest experience, still needs saving. The oldness of a ship does not
increase its seaworthiness. Ask at Lloyd's if a ship is any safer
because it has been afloat more than sixty years. No man that
lives is safe from rocks, and quicksands, and tempests, or even
from foundering at sea, unless the Lord God shall be always the
God of his salvation. We have all need to ask for salvation
from the guilt of sin, the power of sin, and the curse of sin;
and it should be our great joy that the Lord graciously con-
descends to provide all this for us in the person of the Lord
Jesus Christ, our Saviour.

It is this salvation which brings God to us, and us to God. I do
not think that very many find out God by what they see in
nature. Men see the works of God, but they do not see God in
his works. There is such a thing, I suppose, as going "from
nature up to nature's God," but it is a hard climb for cripples,
like the most of us. To lift your foot even from the top of the
highest mountain to the lowest step of the throne of God is a
tremendous effort. Human nature does not care for such an
upward climb. The ready way to God, by which tens of

thousands have come to him, is by Jesus Christ our Saviour. No man ever does come to God except by Jesus, who is the way of salvation. There may be other channels, but this is the only navigable one. Our boats draw too much water to get to God along the shallow straits of human learning. We shall be wise to keep to the deep waters of redeeming love, for by this channel God came to us. The glorious God came here to earth in the person of his Son, that he might reconcile us to himself, and so save us. Where there is depth enough for God to come to man, there is a fair sea-way for man to come to God. Remember that the Lord Jesus came for our salvation. "God sent not his Son into the world to condemn the world; but that the world through him might be saved." Salvation brought God to us, and salvation must bring us to God, or else we shall be cast-aways. Blessed for ever be our gracious and glorious God; for in every man that is saved, he is the God of his salvation in Christ Jesus.

The salvation that we get is entirely from God. If you ever hear of salvation that does not come from God, depend upon it, it is not seaworthy, but will turn out to be one of those worm-eaten coffin ships. I would not trust a dog on board of it. If I were to preach a merely human salvation to you, it would not be worth your while to listen to me. "Salvation is of the Lord" is the saying of Jonah, from the depths of the sea. This salvation began in God's everlasting purpose, in his sacred covenant, in his divine choice of his people. It is carried out by the life and death of our Saviour. It is wrought in us by the Holy Ghost, by whom we are quickened, illuminated, converted, and brought to faith in Jesus. Salvation is of the Lord, from stem to stern, from truck to keel. There is not a bit of rope on board, nor even a spar up aloft, which is of man's merit or working. Christ is not only the helper of our salvation, but the God of it, the Maker of it, the All-in-all of it. Have any of you a salvation which you have manufactured for yourselves? Then drop it overboard and row away from it as fast as you can, lest it should be a torpedo to work your ruin.

It is a remarkable thing that *in this salvation there is a strange mixture of the terrible and the gracious.* "By terrible things in righteousness wilt thou answer us, O God of our salvation." In the death of our Lord Jesus we see the salvation of God; in this the Lord is terrible against sin, but most tender to the sinner. God did not put up the sword of his justice, for he was bound to use it. "Shall not the Judge of all the earth do right?" To do right he must punish sin. And, oh, how terrible it is to view our Lord Jesus, the Son of God, bowing his head to death in the sinner's place, and bearing in his own innocent person the wrath of God on account of sin. Our children's hymn puts the truth exactly:—

> "He saw how wicked men had been,
>   And knew that God must punish sin;
>   So, out of pity, Jesus said
>   He'd bear the punishment instead."

It was indeed a display of terrible things in righteousness when the perfect Son of God was made to sweat great drops of blood, and to be in an agony in Gethsemane. Terrible things in righteousness were manifest when he was scourged, and spit upon, and nailed to a tree and made to die without the comfort of his father's presence, crying in anguish, "My God, my God, why hast thou forsaken me?" Ah, friends, when the Father's Best Beloved bore those unknown sufferings by which the honour of the divine government was maintained, it was a very terrible day. Not even the pains of the lost are more terrible for a tender and devout mind to think upon, than our Lord's being made a curse for us when he was hanged upon the tree. We seek salvation: the Lord Jehovah answers us, and bids us behold it in the blood of his Only-begotten Son—"By terrible things in righteousness wilt thou answer us, O God."

So, also, when God came to deal with us by his Spirit he mixed the terror with the grace. If you have been praying to God to save you, then, if he has answered you, you have had a vision of terrible things. To see your guilt, your present ruin, and your future doom, is to be made to tremble terribly. When the Lord Jesus Christ comes to our vessel, walking on the sea, he finds us in an awful storm. The sails are gone to ribbons, and every timber groans. We see ourselves wrecked by nature before we see ourselves saved by grace. Conviction of sin does not come to every sinner with the same degree of force; but to some of us when we were under the bondage of the law neither sun nor moon appeared, the sea wrought and was tempestuous, and all hope that we should be saved was taken away from us. We reeled to and fro, and staggered like drunken men, and were at our wits' ends: we did not then know that the God of our salvation has his way in the whirlwind. He designs to make us give up self-righteousness and self-confidence, and come and lay hold on Christ, to be our all in all. Men won't take to the life-boat of salvation while they think their own craft can be kept afloat; but when their vessel is settling down at the head they are glad to see the life-boat near.

The difficulty with most men is that they will not have God to be their Saviour; they want to save themselves. Every man thinks he can be his own pilot to the port of glory. But what can we do? What merit? what wisdom? what strength have we? We are proud fools, and deceive ourselves. I have heard a story of a man on board a vessel which was coming home from the other side of the world. He was very conceited, and interfered with everything. Every now and then a captain does get such a man on board. He was always grumbling and making trouble. The ship met with rough weather, and this meddlesome gentleman picked up the notion that things were in a very bad way, and the ship might go down. He was getting into everybody's way, and so the captain, calling him on one side, told him that it was highly important that he should keep very quiet for the next hour or two; especially, that he should hold fast a certain rope to which he pointed him. Nobody could tell what might depend on his holding on to that rope, and saying nothing to anybody. Our noisy friend felt himself to be a person of consequence, put his feet down and set his teeth together, and in a very determined manner stuck to his rope. If anybody came along, instead of talking, as he was used to do, he held his tongue. Just as you must not speak to the man at the wheel, so he felt that no one was allowed to speak to him. Did not the safety of the ship depend upon his being quiet and holding tightly to that rope? He kept his post with due gravity till the wind dropped, and then he did not say much; for his sense of merit made him modest, of course. He waited patiently for the passengers to present him with a piece of plate for having saved the ship. He felt, at any rate, that deep gratitude was due to him for his wonderful exertions. It was about the most difficult thing he had ever done in his life; for he had held his tongue for hours, and thus made a martyr of himself to save them all. As nobody thanked him, he began to hint at the importance of the service he had rendered. But they did not seem to see it; for, you know, people will not always see a thing that is very plain. At last he stated his case more fully, and became so exacting that the captain had to tell him that he had only given him that bit of rope to hold just to keep him quiet, and that, really, he had not contributed, in the least degree, to the safety of the vessel. That is just what I feel inclined to do with certain vastly important persons who think they can do wonders in the things of God. If you will keep from boasting, and stand out of the Lord's way, that is as much as I hope for from you. And if the Lord leads you to trust yourself in Jesus' hands, then all will be safe enough. With God to save us, what is there for us to do but to trust, and not to be afraid?

I have set forth what God is to us. Now, let us see WHAT GOD WILL DO FOR US. Don't doubt it, the Lord has an open ear to hear his people's prayers.

He will answer us. This shows that *we must all pray*. Every believing man in the world must pray; and we shall never get into such a state of grace that we have no need to pray. *But what do we pray for?* Well, according to the text, one of the most important things is to *pray against sin*. "Iniquities prevail against me: as for our transgressions, thou shalt purge them away." Do we not need to pray daily for cleansing? This must be the prayer of the man who is seeking the Lord for the first time. Does the leak of sin gain upon you? Are the pirates of temptation all around you so that you cannot get away from them? Are you compelled to say, "Iniquities prevail against me"? Cry to the Lord Jesus to come to the rescue. A word from him will stop the leak, and drive the demons back when they are boarding you. Pray to him at once.

Do I address a backslider? Did you once own the name of Christ? Have you taken down the old flag? Are you now trading under other colours? Are you sorry it is so? Do iniquities prevail against you? Ah, then, come to the Lord again! Ask him to come and take possession of you. The pirates are on board now, and you cannot get rid of them; but as for your iniquities, he can "purge them away." He can sweep the deck of them.

If you have been long a Christian, and have not backslidden, you will have, as you grow in grace, more and more a sense of the sin that dwelleth in you. You will be crying out every day, "Lord, keep me; for I shall perish utterly, even now, after all my experience, unless thou preserve me from my inbred sin, and the temptations of the world, the flesh, and the devil." Cry to God in that fashion. Ask to be steered clear of all evil, and to be presented faultless. When we are close in shore we need a pilot more than ever. We shall be wrecked in the river's mouth unless the Lord preserve us. Iniquities will prevail unless omnipotent grace prevails. In this direction we shall always need to cry mightily unto the Preserver of men.

We also pray *for nearer fellowship with God.* Just let me read you the next words. "Blessed is the man whom thou choosest, and causest to approach unto thee." Lord, help me to approach unto thee, so as to know thy love and love thee in return. Let us go on reading the record: "That he may dwell in thy courts." Lord, help me to be one of thy court, and always to live in thy presence.

"We shall be satisfied with the goodness of thy house, even of thy holy temple." Do you not long for that satisfaction? Is there not in your hearts, my beloved brethren, a great desire to get nearer to God, and to abide in his house?

Oh, to have a continual enjoyment of the favour of God! May the love of God be shed abroad in our hearts by the Holy Ghost! Blessed be the name of the Lord our God, he will hear and answer that prayer. As he will help you to conquer sin, so will he also help you to grow in grace. There is no reason why we should not be far happier and far holier than we are. If we are straitened at all, we are not straitened in God, but in ourselves. It is not that there is no wind, but we do not spread enough sail. If you do not enter into the deep things of God with understanding, and if you do not enjoy them with delight, you must blame yourselves. You have not, because you ask not, or because you ask amiss.

But, remember, if we pray to be delivered from sin, and to be brought nearer to the Lord, *he may answer us by terrible things in righteousness.* I will like to whisper these words in the ears of all praying men. Often you know not what you ask; and perhaps if you really knew how God would answer you, you would not pray as you now do. You were praying the other day that God would sanctify you, and now you see more of the workings of evil in your nature than ever before. Crosses and losses have come upon you thick and threefold; temptations and evil thoughts have beset you more fiercely than ever; and you are saying, "Lord, is this the answer to my prayer?" Yes, by terrible things in righteousness he is answering you. A trial has been love's reply to earnest desire. God's wisdom often chooses to give us a head wind to prevent our rushing upon sunken rocks.

God will answer you surely, though he answer you strangely. He answers roughly, but rightly. The help of no other can suffice you; but if you cry to God you shall find his strength to be all-sufficient, both for crushing sin and for growth in grace.

The third point is this: WHAT THE LORD IS TO "THE ENDS OF THE EARTH." He is "the confidence of the ends of the earth." All men have a confidence, and they are wise who place all their confidence in God.

Who are "the ends of the earth"? They may be those who live in the extremes of climate—the dwellers at the poles and at the equator. These are so tried by cold and by heat, that one would think they would hardly live in such regions if they did not confide in God. Those who live at the ends of the earth *are farthest off.* God is worthy to be the confidence of those who are farthest off from his Church, from his Gospel, from hope, from anything that is good, and from God himself. This sermon may, one of these days, reach somebody who will say to himself, "I think that I am the farthest off from God of anybody that ever lived. I have been guilty of cursing and swearing, and I have committed all manner of vice, and so I have gone as far away from God and the very name of religion as it is possible for a man to go." Friend, our God is worthy to be *your* confidence, even yours. You are permitted to put your trust in him and find salvation in him, even in his Son Jesus Christ, who cries "Look unto me, and be ye saved, all the ends of the earth."

The ends of the earth may mean, also, *those that are least known.* Are there not men scattered abroad of whom nobody knows anything? They do not themselves know who their father and mother were, and nobody cares to own them. Nobody calls them brother, or knows where they came from. They wish to be forgotten: they would not like to have their stories told. Their character is such that they can get on better without it than with it. Well, but Jesus Christ is worthy to be the confidence of those who are least known. They are known to him: he knows their past and their present. Oh, that sinners who are far off in that way, and least known, would come and put their trust in him!

The ends of the earth may also mean *the most tried*. Where the cold is most severe, or where the dog-star burns most furiously, there we have the ends of the earth. And you who are most poor or most sick, or who have least of ability and talent, you are those who should make God your confidence, for he delights to be the strength of the weak, the fulness of the empty. God's grace is the hospital for sick souls; come ye and enter it. He lifts the poor from the dunghill to set him among princes. Driven to your wits' end, brought down to life's dregs, take the Lord for your confidence, and it shall be well with you.

"The ends of the earth." Well, they are *the hardest to reach*. We have around us men and women who are as hard to get at as the North Pole. We do not know how to speak to them so that they will understand us, for they are so ignorant. We would, if we could, do them good, but they are so depraved that we are half afraid that they will do *us* harm. It may be, they are so proud and conceited that we can hardly get a good word in edgeways with them. Sailors, you must have met with fellows to whom you give a wide berth. You never felt inclined to take them on board. These ships are too far gone to be towed into harbour; and you clear out, lest when they sink you should be sucked down with them. Yet the Lord is ready to help even these. Those whom no man can pity, and no man can help, God can love and save. A mortal arm is too short to reach these shipwrecked souls. Ho, my comrades, when you are at your worst, God is still at his best. When you are all misery, he is all mercy. When you are at "the ends of the earth," you may be at the beginnings of heaven.

I have come to the last point, which is this: WHAT IS GOD

TO SEA-FARING MEN? What should he be to sailors? He is the confidence of all them that are "afar off upon the sea."

In the life of a sea-faring man we have a picture of *the voyage of faith*. Hundreds of years ago, when men went to sea at all, their boats kept always within sight of shore. Your Greek or Roman mariner might be quite master of his galley; but he could not bear to lose sight of a headland which he knew; for he had no compass, and knew little or nothing of astronomical observations. Here and there a lighthouse might be placed, but it would be regarded as a wonder. But at this day a ship may not sight land for a month, and yet its position on the chart will be as certain as your position in the pew. The vessel will be steered entirely by observations of the heavenly bodies, and by chart and compass; and yet at the end of thirty days it will reach a point which was never within sight, and reach it as accurately as if it had been running on a tram-line instead of sailing over the pathless ocean. Its way is as certain as if it had traversed a railway from port to port. Such is the life of a Christian—the life of faith. We see not spiritual things, but yet we steer for them with absolute certainty. We ought not to wish to see; for "We walk by faith, not by sight." We take our bearings by the things in the heavens. We are guided by the Word of God, which is our chart, and by the witness of the blessed Spirit within, which is our compass. We see him who is invisible, and we seek a heaven full of "things not seen as yet." Glory be to God, we shall reach the harbour as sure as a bullet goes to the mark. Don't shift a point, brothers. As the Captain of your salvation has set the helm, so let it remain. Trusting in God, we shall come to our desired haven in due time, and shall not miss our way. We need not fear shipwreck; for he that taught us to sail the spiritual sea will guide us safely till we come to the Glory Land.

Those that are "afar off upon the sea" are *on an unstable element*, but God is their confidence. They are never quiet, the boat is always rocking or rolling from side to side. On the sea they have no continuing city. Is it not so with us? We also dwell upon an unstable element. We talk of the solid earth, but it is only so in contrast with the waves. All things beneath the moon are changing. The elements which make up our life are no more to be depended upon than the waters of the sea.

What is our life but a vapour? What does it depend upon but air?—the breath of our nostrils. Remember, you may die at any moment. Death may board you before the next watch. Oh, to live like a man at sea! He has loosed his hold from all things, and feels himself committed to an unstable element, upon whose calm condition he cannot depend; for at any moment a storm may bear him away. The godly sailor's confidence is in God. In God he has a foundation that cannot be moved. God is the mariner's *terra firma*, and he is ours. All else is fickle, but God is immutable.

Next, they that are upon the sea are *liable to great dangers*. They cannot tell at any time that there may not come up from the North a howling blast, or from the South a tremendous cyclone. When above them all is clear blue, save "a cloud the size of a man's hand," they know that within an hour the heavens may gather blackness, and the sea, which now sleeps in calm, may rage in fury. A sailor's life makes him see the dangers which surround him; but you and I know that we also live in a world where tempests of trial may be upon us in a moment. When I go home after a time of spiritual enjoyment, and feel supremely happy, I say to myself, "I may expect trying news. I cannot be long at ease." In fact, one gets in this world to be afraid of too profound a calm, lest at the back of it should lurk a terrible tempest. At sea we may reckon upon all sorts of weathers: we must therefore keep the boat trim, and never neglect to set the helm, and keep the watch wide awake. The sailor must keep his eyes open; for rocks and quicksands lie below, and hurricanes and cyclones lurk above. If he is a Christian man, his confidence is in his God, and his watchfulness is towards the world. O true believer, let your confidence be in God, whether on sea or shore. Say, "O God, my heart is fixed; my heart is fixed. I will sing and give praise."

But the men on the sea also *are familiar with trouble*. It is not only liability to storm, but the storm does break over them. I speak to many who have weathered no end of tempests. In your voyages across the mighty deep, you have found it no child's play to be tossed up and down like a ball in the hand of the storm. You have even been floating on the angry waves, clinging to a hen-coop, or lashed to the rigging. I do not envy you your trying experience; but, spiritually, we drink from the same cup; for we, too, have had our rough passages, and have been well-nigh cast away.

You do not want to see any more of such nights as you can remember, when sea and sky were blended in dread confusion; neither do I wish to see those months in which to me also the winds were contrary. What a mercy in such seasons to have confidence in God! What is to be done if this fails us? But while God is with us it does not matter whether we live or die. We shall be with the Lord if we die, and if we live the Lord will be with us.

Beloved friends, those that go down to the sea in ships *soon find out their own weakness.* A man looks like a man when he is on shore, or in command of a fine barque sailing along merrily before the wind; but in a great storm what a poor creature a man is. There he goes: yonder wave has swept him from the deck as if he were a spar. You hear one plaintive cry, and it is all over with him. The hungry deep thinks nothing of so small a mouthful. The wind howls still, and the waves dance with a horrid glee. If not thus drowned, the strong man is often rendered useless as to helping others. He cannot stir, for he could not keep his footing. He needs to be lashed to the rigging, or he will be washed away. The bravest, the wisest, the strongest man is just nothing at all in the day of storm. Then the man almost envies the sea-bird that is tossed "up and down, up and down, from the base of the wave to the billow's crown;" because it is always safe, and comes up from the spray as fresh as ever. You and I are often brought into conditions in which we feel that we are not worth half so much as the sea-swallows. We have no strength left at all; we are less than nothing and vanity. Oh, then, let God be our confidence!

I exhort all believers here to have more confidence in God than in all beside. Believe in the Lord a thousand fathoms deep. You will never believe too much nor too well of God. If friends forsake, if all means of comfort fail, let your confidence be so thoroughly in God that such things make no difference to you. It is a grand thing to get off the stocks, and really float on the main sea. It is glorious to have an anchor in the skies, and to hold to that alone, when everything else is dragging, and the earth itself is dissolved. A sailor is often brought to where, if God does not help him, he will be swallowed up; and you and I are always in the like condition. God is our all and we rest in him, but apart from him we are wrecked eternally.

God bless you, my shipmates! We are not yet come to the Pacific Seas; we still are rounding the Cape of Storms, but another name for it is the Cape of Good Hope. With God for our confidence we are not afraid. We shall all meet around the flag-ship of our Great Captain in the Fair Havens above.

XI

THE CHURCH'S PROBATION

"Thou, O God, hast proved us."—Psalm 66: 10.

THE psalmist, who spake these words in his song, told forth the experience of the godly in all generations. In the patriarchal age, when Abraham was called to leave his kindred, and go forth from Ur of the Chaldees; constrained to sojourn as a stranger among a people that he knew not; bidden to wait with patience for a son whom God would give him in his old age; and, at length, commanded to take that son to the top of a mountain, and offer him as a sacrifice,—he might well say, "Thou, O God, hast proved us." Isaac could say the same when he tabernacled in the Land of Promise, having not so much as a foot of it that he could call his own, except his father's sepulchre. Jacob learned the same stanza when he was tried in Laban's household, when he wrestled with God in Peniel, and triumphed over the angel at Jabbok; this he knew when he went down into Egypt, and, dying, blessed the sons of Joseph. All the patriarchs, as they fell asleep, could say, "Thou, O God, hast proved us."

And this was the song of the Church during her sojourn in Egypt, when she was lying among the pots, and during her wanderings in the wilderness, when she passed through a desert land by a way which she had not traversed aforetime. And this, too, was the voice of the Church under the conduct of Joshua, when Israel came through Jordan, and began to defy the hosts of the Canaanites,—when they drew the sword against mighty adversaries who dwelt in cities fenced with high walls, gates, and bars, and came forth to battle in chariots that had scythes of iron,—"Thou, O God, hast proved us." With such a word as this in their mouths, the judges fell asleep after they had avenged Israel, and done mighty deeds for the Lord of hosts. This David could well say, for he had seen affliction. This the kings, who walked in his steps, and this the prophets, who spoke in God's name, might all have said, "Thou, O God, hast proved us."

And God's dear Son, the Captain of our salvation, himself was tried and proved in all things too. He was thrust into the hottest part of the glowing coals, and tried as you and I have never been tried,—proved to such an extent as our heart hath not conceived. And, amongst the professed followers of Jesus, all the sons of God are witnesses to this truth, "Thou, O God, hast proved us;" whether they were proved in dungeons where they lay victims of damp and mildew, or on racks where every bone was dislocated and every muscle snapped, or at the stake where they mounted in chariots of fire to heaven, or on the rocks where they wandered about in sheepskins and goatskins, destitute, afflicted, tormented,—in all these temptations and trials God proved them. And even to this day, though by less severe methods, yet by other tests, as I shall have to show, the Church has still the same song to sing; and each dying saint must still subscribe his name to the long list; yea, and every bright spirit around the throne, in looking back upon his experience on earth, will have to swell the great chorus, "Thou, O God, hast proved us."

It is universal to every child of God. If you are a servant of the Lord, you must be proved; you shall never enter heaven unproved; you must be tried in the fire; the proof, the assaying must take place upon every one of us. Nor do I think we ought to shun it; perhaps it may happen that, in the feeble words I speak some reason may be given which shall reconcile your hearts to the sternness of the proof, and even make you kiss the hand of the Refiner when he puts you into the fire.

WHAT IS IT THAT THOU, O GOD, HAST PROVED IN THY PEOPLE? I think we may answer, *he has proved everything.* If we have anything that has not been proved, it either is to be proved, or else it is so bad that it is not worth proving. Everything we have, that God has given us, will have to be proved. There is not a grain of grace that will escape the probation; he is sure, in some way or other, to test and exercise it.

I think we can say, looking back upon our lives, those of us who are in Christ Jesus, that *the Lord has proved our sincerity.* Ah, how many put on the harness when we first put it on; and where are they now? In our little Gospel experience, how many have we seen who have turned their backs in the day of battle! Yes, the young knights went out gaily enough to the field; but say nothing about their return; "tell it not in Gath, publish it not in the streets of Askelon," how their shields were broken, their lances shivered, and their plumes trailed in the mire. When any turn from Zion's way, our best method of using their apostasy is as Cowper used it, for self-examination,—

> "*When any turn from Zion's way,*
> *(Alas, what numbers do!)*
> *Methinks I hear my Saviour say,*
> *'Wilt thou forsake me too?'*"

But, up to this time, one way in which God has tested our sincerity has been to keep our leaf green; and, through divine grace, that sincerity has kept its hold, while some who, in the first flush of religious excitement, promised well for heaven, afterwards withered and faded. While many, who were like the fair blossoms of the spring upon the tree, were blown down by the East wind, or fell with a shower on the ground, we have been left, by divine grace, to bring forth some little fruit, though not as much as we could desire. O brethren, it is a great mercy, when God proves our sincerity, if, notwithstanding the defection of man, and the fickleness and instability of our own hearts, we are able to say, "Lord, thou knowest all things; thou knowest that I love thee."

It is a privilege to have our sincerity tried, but it is one which must be purchased at a sharp cost; for we cannot know our sincerity for God without being put where we are much tempted and troubled. I believe many young people think they have the grace of God in their hearts, who, if they were really put in temptation's way, would soon discover that it is only a sort of hereditary profession, and not the true grace of God they possess. Some of you, I know, have had to suffer this trial. You have been shut up among blasphemers, you have been made to live among the ungodly and profane, or you have had temptations from the polite and the godless, yet, thanks be to God, you have been enabled to retain your hold on Christ. You can say, with the psalmist, "Thou, O God, hast proved us." And if you are sincere, mark you, as surely as ever you have true godliness, it must and will be put to the test.

And God has also tried *our vows of fidelity.* Perhaps, the fewer vows we make, the better; but when we do make them, how jealous should we be to keep them! What a mass of vows we once made when our blood was hot with the novelty of our new discovery of the beauty of religion! We think we will do, we know not what; our love laughs at impossibilities; we could leap like Curtius into the chasm, and sacrifice ourselves for Jesus. Would to God that we were always in that frame of mind! But then we get promising what we will do if we are put in certain positions, and our promissory notes are not written on stamped paper, they are only written on some common stuff of our own; and we put our signature, but still we dishonour the note when it comes due; we never pay our vows. God did not prompt us to the vow, but our own self-confidence; and, therefore, it gets broken. When I look back upon what you and I promised we would do when we first began the heavenly warfare, and how little we have really done, I think we can mournfully say, "O Lord, thou hast proved us."

Some people talk about the older Christians as being so dull and so lifeless; but, let me put it to yourselves, how much better are you? And I, sometimes, in the early days of my preaching, was wont to speak of the cool, freezing lips of some ministers, and of the dilatory way in which they discharged their duties; but I have had, in looking at my text, to say of myself, "Lord, thou hast proved me." And some of those vows that I made,—to wit, how I would be the pillar of fire in his cause, and lead the souls of men, and win them to the foot of the cross,—how signally have they been broken, for "Thou, O Lord, hast proved us." All those fine visions, like potters' vessels when smitten with a rod of iron, have been broken into vile potsherds.

But how the Lord has been pleased to prove *our professions and pretensions to eminence!* Do you recollect—with some of you, it will not be very difficult to look back, certainly not with me,—do you remember how you thought, when first you knew the Lord, how different you would be from that nervous Mrs. Muchafraid? You went to see her, when you were first converted, and sat down and talked with her; and as you came away, you said, "That woman is a bag of nerves; if ever I live to her age, you will not find me so desponding." You have been proved since then, and how has it been with you? Do you remember how when you came, one evening, from a prayer-meeting, when some friend had prayed so long and so drearily, you said, "Please God, if ever I have the privilege of praying aloud at a prayer-meeting, there shall always be life and earnestness in my prayer"? How has it been with you, brother? I question whether any man ever attained to the eminence in piety that he once marked out for himself, and whether we have not all had occasion to eat our words.

Whenever I have seen a Christian talking large things about his loftiness in grace and his attainments, I have always seen him, sooner or later, brought as low as the dust. I have known some brethren, who have said that they never had a doubt of their acceptance; and I have thanked God for them, and have hoped they never might; but I have seen some of them in such a condition as I pray I never may be in. Such professors as those will find that the Lord will bring them down ere long. Those big saints will one day be glad enough to creep into a mousehole, and feel themselves thrice happy if they are permitted to be numbered amongst the meanest of the Lord's people. As surely as we ever make these high pretensions to great things, we shall be brought down, and we shall have to cry, "O Lord, we did exalt ourselves, we did promise high and great things, but thou, O Lord, hast proved us; and when it came to the proof, what insignificant, what worthless, what despicable worms we turned out to be after all!"

But, beloved, we have not only been tried in our sincerity, and in our vows, and in our lofty pretensions, but *have we not also been tried in our strength*? How strong we are sometimes! As my friend Will Richardson, who, though he is a poor labouring man, is a divine I like to quote, just as some people would quote St. Augustine, said to me one day, "Brother Spurgeon, if you and I ever get one inch above the ground, we get that one inch too high, and the Lord will bring us down again." How true that is! And the old man said, "O sir, you know, in winter-time, I feel as if I could do such a deal of mowing, and as if I could reap the fields at such a rate!" but when the hot summer comes on, poor old Will wipes the sweat from his brow, and he thinks it is hard work reaping after all, and he will be very glad when he can get home and lie down, for he is getting an old man. "O sir," said he, "if I could reap in the summer as I think I can in the winter, then I should do." And is not that the way with us? When there is no trial to bear, we can do all things, or can bear all sufferings; when there are no duties to be performed, then our strength runs over, we have too much; we have enough, and some to give to our neighbours; but when we get into the work, and the struggle, and begin to reap and to mow, the sweat of weariness is such that we long to be away from it; our strength, when tried, is found to be less than nothing and vanity.

Moreover, *the Lord has proved our faith as well as our strength.* Our faith is indeed our real strength, because our faith is that by which we lay hold upon God's arm. Has not your faith been proved, brother? An untried faith is no faith; at least, I mean, if a man has had faith for some considerable length of time, and that faith has not been tried, I question whether it ever came from God. I may say truly of faith what the old naturalists used to say falsely of the salamander,—that it lives in the fire. The natural element of faith is fire, it never gets on well unless it has some fire to try it. What dost thou think faith is given us for unless it is to be tried? Didst thou ever know a man build a house, and then shut it up, and let no one live in it? Houses are built to be inhabited, so God does not give anything without a design. Dost thou know a man who keeps his wheat year after year, and never puts it through the mill? Let me tell thee that my God puts all his wheat through the mill, and you must all go between the big stones, and you must have your crushing. You will never come out fit to be offered unto the Lord unless you have been between the stones, there must be "the trial of your faith."

Your faith is much more precious than gold, so it also must be tried in the fire. You, Mr. Greatheart, must prepare for a great many battles. And you, "Valiant-for-Truth," depend upon it you will have to fight until your arm bleeds, and your sword grows to your hand, cemented with your own blood. "Father Honest," there is warfare for you before you enter heaven. You "Little-faiths" and "Despondencies" and "Much-afraids" may go on with but few trials, comparatively. Your faith must be tried.

Your religious principles will be tried. Why should they not be? There is a certain sort of Christians,—I do not know whether I shall think them Christians soon,—who profess to be better than anybody else. Never fear any attacks from nominal Christians, or proud, conceited persons, who think themselves too good to join with other churches, who, forsooth, are Babylon; they are the men of wisdom, and say, "Stand by, for we are holier than thou." But what of the Pharisees of modern times, what shall we say of them? Let them do their best, and their worst, and fight as they will. If our course be right, we can bear to have it proved. I like to see breezes spring up,— these fresh blasts that, every now and then, beat upon the good old ship. If she is all right, she will outlast them; and whether it be from disorders within or quarrels without, she will come out of the trouble.

If we have an ordinance, it ought to be tried: may baptism be tried! Let the Lord's supper be tried. The Church can never be reformed except by these trials. I always court the trials if they are sent by a brother in friendliness of spirit; it is only the bitterness with which they come that sometimes makes my blood boil about it; but I must look to the God that sends it, and not to the man who may happen to be the second cause. Whether as individuals, or as a church, or as a denomination, we shall have to say at last, "O Lord, thou hast proved us; blessed be thy name that thou hast."

And now let us turn to the second question, How has God proved us? The Lord has proved us in a thousand ways. Many men think that the only proof that God gives to his servants is that of trial. He often proves them by trials, by bereavements, by temporal losses, by sickness in body, by personal infirmity, by slander, by persecution, all these are, therefore, proofs to a Christian; and a man who can go through all these, and find his faith still keeping its hold, and that he is able to say, "The Lord gave, and the Lord hath taken away, blessed be the name of the Lord," such a man may thank God for the proof. And, after all, the only grace that is worth having is that which shall be with us when we go through fire, and through water, and when men ride over our heads. Do not tell me of your sunshiny religion; do not tell me of your summer-day godliness. You may sometimes see, on the Mediterranean, when the waters are calm and still, a little fleet with fair and beautiful sails floating gaily there; it is the nautilus coming up in the sunshine to float; but there is a black cloud yonder, and at the first breath of wind that comes whistling across the waveless sea, where is that fleet? Where is the nautilus? Every little creature has drawn itself into its shell, and fallen to the bottom of the sea. Oh, there are too many of this kind, too many Christians who are with us when everything goes well; but where are they when the times have changed? To use John Bunyan's expressive metaphor, they walk with Religion when she goes in her silver slippers; but when she is bare-foot, and men laugh at her through the streets, then where are they? Affliction does try men.

But mark you, believers, there are many others trials; let me mention some of them, that I often think severe. *There is a very sharp trial, which some Christians have to bear when they have fresh light given them*, and they shut their eyes against it. There are plenty of things that we never dreamt of in our philosophy, that are true after all. Am I like a man who, whereunto he hath attained, walks by the same rule, but is still ready to advance further if the rule is more fully revealed? Hold on to the old and tried truth of the grace of God which bringeth salvation, as with a death-grip; but, still, you are not perfect yet; there is a height beyond. Sometimes, when you are reading a passage of Scripture, you say, "Ah, yes, yes; it must mean that!" You pray over it. "Yes, it must mean that; but if it means that, what about that text our minister preached from last Sunday week, what about that?" And you are apt to say, "Well, now, I won't believe that, for it does not fit in with my system of theology." Is there not many a good "Hyper" brother, who has a full knowledge of the doctrines of grace; but when he is reading the Bible, one day, and he finds a text that looks rather wide and general, he says, "This cannot mean what it says; I must trim it down, and make it fit into Dr. Gill's Commentary"? That is the way many a brother does. Is not this the right thing to say? "Now, this does mean what it says; the Lord knows better how to write than I do; there may be faults in my reading, but there cannot be any faults in his writing; then, if such-and-such a thing be true, I will not doubt it; and if that other thing is true, I will not doubt it; and if they seem to contradict one another, I will believe them both; but

I can never entertain a thought that they really do contradict one another; I believe that there is some fault in me, not in the truth."

When we get to heaven, we shall see that conflicting truths, such as free-agency and divine sovereignty, were only different views, after all, of the same truth taken from a little different angle; and we shall see how God gave us both the truths, and how foolish we were to go against them. Now, that man, I take it, is proved to be right who, when he is thus tried with superior light, says, "Well, yes, I have been wrong in many of my thoughts and reasonings; the more I learn of God's revelation, the more I will open my heart to receive it." I like a brother who is ready to advance. I think, as a church, we ought always to be advancing.

Don't you think it is a very sharp trial to be tried by other loves? You have an only child; how fond you are of that girl; how your heart is knit to that boy! You have a dear husband, properly enough you love him; but, ah! improperly enough you idolize him. Or, alas! it is a brother, or sister, or some other Christian man, and your heart is set on that object. Do you know what Jesus says to you? He has said, "There is a disciple who loves me; he says he does; I will see if he does; I will give him that child, and I will see which he loves the better; I will give him that wife, I will give her that husband; I will see now whether I really am King in that heart or no." And in how many cases have we mournfully to suspect that Jesus Christ was not King! Oh, it is sad to think of how it would be if some of us were tried by that test: "If any man love father or mother, son or daughter, more than me, he is not worthy of me." If some are tried in that way, what a trial it must be to them! And there are many who fail here, and many more Christians would fail, perhaps, only that God, on a sudden, comes like a great iconoclast, and breaks their images in pieces, and utterly spoils their false gods; and then they are compelled to go to Christ, and say, "Yes, we do love thee." But perhaps that was hardly true while the idol was in the way. It is a hard trial to have these fair things put in competition with Jesus, happy are ye if ye have been tried, and yet have stood the trial!

I believe that *God often proves his servants by opening up to them fresh fields of labour.* It has been my lot, when I have been

busy about my Master's service, here and there to come to a
certain corner, and see before me what I had never seen before,
a great field ripe for the harvest; and perhaps flesh and blood
have said, "Well, you have enough to do here; this is your lot."
I believe, then, God is trying the man to see whether he is willing to begin that new work which is opening to him. Perhaps it
is a work in which nobody else has ever engaged; and when
you begin it, some excellent friend shrugs his shoulder, and
says, "O dear brother, how imprudent you are!" I think there
is no word in the English language that deserves more of my
esteem, and yet for which I have a greater and more insuffer-
able contempt from the misuse of it than the word "prudence."
Oh, the many times I have it whistled in my ears, "Prudence!"
—and this is the meaning of the word "prudence" according to
the translation I have given of it by these brethren,—*never act
upon faith.* If you can see your way clearly, that is to say, if
you are strong enough to do it yourself, do it, but never go
beyond your own strength; do not attempt anything in which
other people would differ from you in opinion. Along the cool
sequestered vale of life keep you the even tenor of your way.
If there is a giant Goliath, go to bed, and let giant Goliath defy
the hosts of Israel as he likes. If there are nations that need
help,—Macedonians that cry, "Come over and help us,"—tell
somebody else what the Macedonians said, and say, "What a
pity it is that nobody will go!" If Jesus calls, and duty, too,
just mind that you are so far off that you cannot hear the call;
like some militiamen I have heard of, who always say, when the
bugle sounds for them to come to drill, that they never heard it,
because they take wonderfully good care to be always so far
away that the sound cannot reach them. And there are many
such Christians as that, who always get out of the sound of
the bugle-note.

Most people like those things in which there are plenty of
great armies; but there are chosen men who always stand where
there is nothing to rest upon but the bare arm of God. This
seems to be the proof of the Christian when he can dare to say,
"This is the field of usefulness which God has put in my way;
though my strength is not sufficient, I have faith; here I am,
and I will do it." "Who art thou, O great mountain? Before
Zerrubbabel thou shalt become a plain." "Awake, awake,

Deborah; awake, awake, utter a song: arise, Barak, and lead thy captivity captive, thou sons of Abinoam." "Shake thyself from the dust; arise, and sit down, O Jerusalem! loose thyself from the bands of thy neck. O captive daughter of Zion!" for thy God is in the midst of thee, and if thou wilt but do and dare for him, when proved in the day of trial, thou shalt have his blessing upon thee, and that right early and abundantly.

Let us come to the closing question, and see WHAT HAS BEEN THE RESULT OF ALL THOSE PROVINGS THROUGH WHICH WE HAVE PASSED?

Well, I think *we have lost a good deal by our provings.* We have gained much, but we have had our heavy losses likewise. "What," says one, "lost anything by God's proving me?" Yes, brother, I will tell you one or two of the things you have lost. I think you have lost that habit of putting your trust so much in earthly things. So many trees have been cut down, that you had built on, that you begin to wish to build somewhere beyond the stars; you find that this world is not your rest. If you have lost that, you have lost something. Have you not also lost that habit of talking so positively about what you mean to do? A good thing if you have. You do not glitter so much, but there is more gold in you. You do not flash and sparkle, and make so much noise, but the waters run stiller because they are deeper. You have lost that habit of boasting in an arm of flesh.

As the result of your being proved, you have lost that disposition to invite trial. I know a Christian woman who had not any trouble for some time, and she was very troubled about having no trouble. She prayed to God to send her some; she will never pray that prayer again. She was like a child whom I heard crying in the street, and his mother opened the window, and asked him what he cried for; and when he said "Nothing," she said he should have something to cry for before long. There are many children of that sort; they think they cannot be children of God because they are not always living in hot water; but when they get the trial, they never think that again,—never. These are some of the things we have lost.

One has learned, by being proved, to lose that habit of treading quite so hard on the ground as we used to do. We used to tread on other people sometimes; by being proved, we tread more gently. We used to push and say, "If the man is in my way, I cannot help it;" now we walk a little more carefully, we do not wish to touch other people's sore places, because we know our own. I heard a dear brother say the other night that I comforted the doubters a great deal too much. I thought, if that dear brother had to go through some of the deep waters we ourselves have known in connection with this church, he would find the doubters want a great deal more comforting than he thinks; for, when one has been in the dungeon, and has not been able to read his own title clear, and when there have been times when sin and Satan have so prevailed over grace that one could only say, "O wretched man that I am, who shall deliver me from the body of this death?" then we have wanted something very sweet and very comforting. I do not think that a Christian knows much of doing business on the great waters if he does not feel, sometimes, as if he would give all he has to have as good a hope as the meanest lamb in Jesus' fold has. And we lose that habit of being so hard, and speaking so loftily, and these are blessed losses. Lord, send us many such losses!

Then, *we also gain much by being proved.* I cannot tell all that we gain. I never read a list of the ear-rings and the bracelets that the Israelitish women gained from the Egyptians; and I cannot, therefore, give you a category of all the golden jewels, and silver bracelets, and the rich ruby tiaras that Christians get from the depths of their tribulation. We get all sorts of choice things thus. Was it not Rutherford who said that he drank many sorts of God's wine, but the wine which was the sourest of all was the sweetest when it was down? And so assuredly it is. There are many sorts of bread that we eat, that are very delightful,—many breads of heaven; but that which is baked on the coals, just as the bread which Elijah ate was baked, that is the meal that makes us go in the strength thereof for forty days. All bread that comes from God is good; but that which the black ravens with their hoarse throats bring to us, that is the bread which is most fit for God's prophets. All our passages through the fiery furnace make us like swords when they are well annealed; they are ready to cut right through the bone, it makes us true Jerusalem blades thus to be put through the fire again and again. You and I will not cease from being tried until we get to heaven, and then it will be all over; and we shall sing, and this shall be the sweet note of it, "Thou hast proved us, O God; and blessed be thy name for it; before we were afflicted, we went astray; but now have we kept thy word."

There are many here who, I fear, if they were proved, would be found to be dross. Let such remember that God, by his grace, can transmute the vilest metal into the purest gold. One touch of the cross of Christ, one drop of his precious blood can turn a sinner into a saint. And however great and vile your sins may be, "there is life in a look at the crucified One." One glance at the bleeding Saviour, and your sins are forgiven. A simple act of trust in Jesus, and you are saved, and then, from that time forth, though you will have trial, you shall bless God for it; and we shall meet in heaven to praise the name of the Most High, world without end.

XII

LIMITING GOD

"They limited the Holy One of Israel."—Psalm 78 : 41.

MAN is always altering what God has ordained. Although God's order is ever the best, yet man will never agree therewith. When God gave forth the law it was engraved upon two stones. The first table contained the commandments concerning man and God, the second dealt with man and man. Sins against God are sins against the first table: sins against man are offences against the second table. Man, to prove constantly his perversity, will put the second table before the first, nay, upon the first, so as to cover and conceal it. What man is there among you that hath not in his heart often lamented sins against man, rather than sins against God? And which of you hath not felt a greater compunction for sins against your neighbour, or against the nation, than for sins committed against God and done in his sight? There are many transgressions of the first table of which we think so little, that perhaps we scarcely ever confess them at all, or if we acknowledge them, it is only because the grace of God has taught us to estimate them aright. One offence against the first table which seldom agitates the mind of an unconvicted sinner is that of unbelief, and with it, I may put the want of love to God. The sinner does not believe in God, does not trust in him, does not love him. He gives his heart to the things of earth, and denies it to his Creator. Of this high treason and rebellion he thinks nothing. If you could take him in the act of theft, a blush would mantle his cheek; but you detect him in the daily omission of love to God, and faith in his Son Jesus Christ, and you cannot make him feel that he is guilty of any evil in this. Oh! strange contortion of human judgment! Oh! blindness of mortal conscience, that this greatest of iniquities—a want of love to the All-Lovely, and a want of faith in him who is deserving of the highest trust—should be thought to be as nothing, and reckoned among the things that need not to be repented of.

Among such sins of the first table is that described in our text. It is full of evil to ourselves, and is calculated to dishonour both God and man, therefore let us be in earnest to cut it up both root and branch. I think we have all been guilty of this in our measure; and we are not free from it even to this day. Whether we be saints or sinners, we may stand here and make our humble confession that we have all "tempted the Lord our God and have limited the Holy One of Israel."

What then is meant by limiting the Holy One of Israel? In the first place, we limit the Holy One of Israel by DICTATING TO HIM. Shall mortal dare to dictate to his Creator? Shall it be possible that man shall lay down his commands, and expect the King of heaven to pay homage to his arrogance? Will a mortal impiously say, "Not thy will but mine be done?" Can it be possible that we should have the impertinence to map out the path of boundless wisdom, or should decree the footsteps which infinite grace should take, and dictate the designs which Omnipotence shall attempt? Startle! Startle at your own sin. Let each of us be amazed at our own iniquity. We have had the impudence to do this in our thoughts; we have climbed to the throne of the Highest; we have sought to take him from his throne that we might sit there; we have grasped his sceptre and his rod; we have weighed his judgments in the balances and tried his ways in the scales; we have been impious enough to exalt ourselves above all that is called God.

I will first address myself to the saint. Oh, heir of heaven, be ashamed and be confounded, while I remind thee that thou hast dared to dictate to God! How often have we in our prayers not simply wrestled with God *for a blessing*—for that was allowable—but we have imperiously demanded it. We have not said, "Deny thus to me, O my God, if so thou pleasest." We have not been ready to say as the Redeemer did, "Nevertheless, not as I will, but as thou wilt," but we have asked and would take no denial. Not with all humble deference to our Lord's superior wisdom and grace, but we have asked and declared that we would not be content unless we had that particular blessing upon which we had set our hearts. Now, whenever we come to God and ask for anything which we consider to be a real good, we have a right to plead earnestly, but we err when we go beyond the bounds of earnestness, and come to impudent demand. It is ours to ask for a blessing, but not to define what that blessing shall be. It is ours to place our head beneath the mighty hands of divine benediction, but it is not ours to uplift the hands as Joseph did those of Jacob, and say, "Not so, my father." We must be content if he gives the blessing cross-handed; quite as content that he should put his left hand on our head as the right. We must not intrude into God's almonry, let him do as seemeth him good. Prayer was never meant to be a fetter upon the sovereignty of God, much less a licensed channel for blasphemy. We must always subjoin at the bottom of the prayer this heavenly postscript, "Father, deny this if it be most for thy glory." Christ will have nothing to do with dictatorial prayers, he will not be a partaker with us in the sin of limiting the Holy One of Israel.

Oftentimes, too, we dictate to God with regard to *the measure of our blessing*. We ask the Lord that we might grow in the enjoyment of his presence, instead of that he gives us to see the hidden depravity of our heart. The blessing comes to us, but it is in another shape from what we expected. We go again to our knees, and we complain of God that he has not answered us, whereas the fact has been that he has answered the spirit of our prayer, but not the letter of it. He has given us the blessing itself, but not in the shape we asked for it. If ye ask, especially for temporal mercies, always take care to leave the degree of those mercies with God. Ye may say, "Lord, give me food convenient for me," but it is not yours to stipulate how many shillings you shall have per week, or how many pounds in the year. You may ask that your bread may be given you and that your water may be sure, but it is not yours to lay down to God out of what kind of vessels you shall drink, or on what kind of table your bread shall be served up to you. You must leave the measuring of your mercies with Him who measures the rain, and weighs the clouds of heaven.

And yet further, I fear that we have often dictated to God with regard to *the time*. As a church we meet together, and we pray God to send us a blessing. We expect to have it next week: it does not come. We wonder that the ministry is not blessed on the very next Sabbath day; so that hundreds are pricked in the heart. We pray again, and again, and again, and at last we begin to faint. And why is this? Simply because that in our hearts we have been setting a date and a time to God. We have made up our minds that the blessing must come within a certain period; and as it does not come, we do as it were spite our God by declaring we will stop no longer; that we have waited time enough; we will have no more patience; we will be gone; it is clear the blessing will not come. We waste our words we imagine by seeking it. Oh, how wrong is this!— What! is God to be tied to hours, or months, or years? Do his promises bear dates? Has he not himself said "Though the vision tarry, wait for it, it shall come, it shall not tarry." And yet we cannot wait God's time, but we must have *our* time. Let us always remember it is God's part to limit a certain day to Israel, saying, "To-day, if ye will hear my voice." But it is not our part to say to God, "To-day if thou wilt hear *my* voice." No; let us leave time to him, resting assured that when the ship of our prayers is long at sea, it brings home all the richer cargo, and if the seeds of supplication are long buried, they shall produce the richer harvest; for God, honour-ing our faith which he has exercised by waiting, shall multiply his favours and enlarge his bounty. Your prayers are out at interest at a great percentage. Let them alone. They shall come back—not only the capital, but with compound interest— if ye will but wait till the time runs out, and God's promises become due.

We have limited the Holy One in other ways, and we have done this with regard to *our prayers and efforts for others*. A mother has been anxious for her children's conversion. Her eldest son has been the object of her fervent prayer. Never a morning has passed without earnest cries to God for his salva-tion; she has spoken to him with all a mother's eloquence; she has prayed in private with him, she has used every means which love could suggest to make him think of a better world. All her efforts at present seem to be wasted. She appears to be ploughing upon a rock, and casting her bread upon the waters. Year after year has rolled on—her son has left her house, he has commenced business for himself; he begins now to display worldliness; he forsakes the house of prayer which his mother frequents. She looks round every Sabbath morning, but John is not there. The tear is in her eye. Every allusion in the minister's sermon to God's answering prayer makes her heart beat again. And at last she says, "Lo these many years have I sought God for this one blessing; I will seek no longer. I will, however, pray another month, and then, if he hear me not, I think I can never pray again." Mother, retract the words. Blot out such a thought from thy soul, for in this thou art limiting the Holy One of Israel. He is trying thy faith. Persevere, persevere while life lasts, and if thy prayers be not answered in thy lifetime, mayhap from the windows of heaven thou shalt look down and see the blessing of thy prayers descend on the head of thy child.

This has been the case, too, *when we have sought to do good to our fellow men.* You know a certain man in whose welfare you take an extraordinary interest. You have availed yourself occasionally of an opportunity of addressing him; you have pressed him to attend the house of God; you have mentioned him in your private devotions, and often at your family altar. You have spoken to others that they might pray with you, for you believed the promise, "If two of you shall agree on earth as touching any thing that they shall ask, it shall be done for them of my Father which is in heaven." But now months have rolled on, and your friend seems to be in a more hopeless condition than ever. *Now* he will not go to the house of God at all; perhaps some ungodly acquaintance has such power over him that your efforts are counteracted by his evil influence. All the good you can do is soon undone, and you are ready to say, "I will never use another effort; I will turn my attention to someone else. In this man's case, at least, my prayers will never be heard. I will withdraw my hand; I will not use unprofitable labour." And what is this but limiting the Holy One of Israel? What is this but saying to God, "Because thou hast not heard me when I wished to be heard—because thou hast not exactly blessed my efforts as *I* would have them blessed, therefore I will try this no more"? Once again attempt, and not once, but though a thousand times thou failest, try again, for God is not unfaithful to forget your work of faith and your labour of love.

While thus charging the people of God with sin, I have been solemnly condemning myself, and if a like conviction shall abide upon all my believing hearers, my errand is accomplished. *I will address myself now to those who cannot call themselves the children of God,* but who have lately been stirred up to seek salvation. There are many of you who are not hardened and careless now. There was a time when you were callous and indifferent, but it is not so with you at the present moment. You are anxiously saying, "What must I do to be saved?" and have been, perhaps, very earnestly in prayer during the last two or three months. Every Sunday morning's service sends you home to your knees, and you cannot refrain from sighs and tears even in your daily business, for you cry as one that cannot be silenced, "Lord, save, or I perish!" Mayhap Satan has been putting it into your heart, that since your prayers have not been heard is it now of no avail. "Oh," said the Evil One, "these many months hast thou prayed to God to put away thy sin, and he has not heard thee. Give it up; never bend thy knees again. Heaven is not for thee; therefore, make the best of this world; go and drink its pleasures; suck in its joys; lose not the happenings of both worlds; make thyself gay here, for God will never bless thee and save thee hereafter." And is this what he has said? Oh! listen not to him; he designs thy destruction. Hearken not to his voice. There is nothing he desires so much as that thou shouldst be his prey; therefore, be thou on thy watch-tower against him, and listen not to his cajoling. Hearken to me for a season, and God bless thee in the hearing, that thou mayest no longer limit the Holy One of Israel.

Sinner, what hast thou been doing, while thou hast said "I will restrain prayer because God has not as yet answered me." I say what hast thou been doing? Hast thou not been stipulating with God as to the day when he shall save thee? Is not the blessing of divine mercy worth waiting for? Knock, man, knock again and go not away. Who art thou that thou shouldst say to God, "I will have peace on such a day or else I will cease to supplicate?" Do you not think again that perhaps the cause of your present distress is that you have been dictating to God as to *the way in which he shall save you?* You have a pious acquaintance who was converted in a very remarkable manner. He was suddenly convicted and as suddenly justified in the sight of God. He knows the very day and hour in which

he obtained mercy, and *you* have foolishly made up your mind
that you will never lay hold upon Christ unless you feel the
same. You have laid it down as in a decree, that God is to
save you, as it were, by an electric shock, that you must be
consciously smitten, and vividly illumined, or else you will
never lay hold on Christ.

You want a vision. You dictate to God that he must send
one of his angels down to tell you he has forgiven you. Now
rest assured God will have nothing to do with your dictation.
With your desire to be saved he will have to do, but with your
planning as to how he should save you, he will have nought
to do. Oh, be content to get salvation anyhow if thou dost but
get it. Sinner, believe in Christ. That is God's command, and
thy privilege. Cast thyself flat on his atonement; trust thou
him and him alone, and if God choose not to comfort thee in
the way in which thou hast expected, yet be content to get the
blessing anyhow, so long as thou receivest it at all. Limit not, I
beseech thee, the Holy One of Israel. Cry thou this day, "Lord,
have mercy on me a sinner, and let it be not as I will, but as
thou wilt."

In the second place, we limit the Holy One of Israel by
DISTRUST. And here again I will divide my congregation into
the two grand classes of saints and sinners. Children of God,
purchased by blood and regenerated by the Spirit, you are
guilty here; for by your distrust and fear you have often
limited the Holy One of Israel, and have said in effect, that his
ear is heavy that it cannot hear, and that his arm is shortened
that it cannot save. *In your trials you have done this.* You have
looked upon your troubles, you have seen them roll like
mountain waves; you have hearkened to your fears, and they
have howled in your ears like tempestuous winds, and you have
said, "My barque is but a feeble one, and it will soon be shipwrecked. It is true that God has said that through tempests
and tossings he will bring me to my desired haven. But alas!
such a state as this was never contemplated in his promise; I
shall sink at last and never see his face with joy." What hast
thou done, fearful one? O thou of little faith, dost thou know
what sin thou hast committed? Thou hast judged the omnipotence of God to be finite. Thou hast said that thy troubles
are greater than his power, that thy woes are more terrible

than his might. I say retract that thought; drown *it* and thou shalt not be drowned thyself.

But says one, "I did believe this once, and I had hoped for an escape from my present predicament, but that escape has failed me. I did think that some friend would have assisted me, and thus, I imagined I should have come out of the furnace." Ah! and thou art distrusting God *because he does not choose to use the means which thou hast chosen* because his election and thy election are not the same, therefore thou doubtest him. Why man, he is not limited to means—to *any* means, much less to one of thy choosing. If he deliver thee not by calming the tempest, he hath a better way in store; he will send from above and deliver thee; he will snatch thee out of the deep waters lest the floods overflow thee. What might Shadrach, Meshach and Abed-nego have said? Suppose they had got it into their heads that God would deliver them in some particular way. They did have some such idea, but they said, as if to prove that they trusted not really to *their* thought about the deliverance—"Nevertheless, be it known unto thee, O king, we will not worship, thy gods, nor bow before the image which thou hast set up." They were prepared to let God have his will, even though he used no means of deliverance. But suppose they had confessed with flesh and blood, and Shadrach had said, "God will strike Nebuchadnezzar dead; just at the moment when the men are about to put us into the furnace the king will turn pale and die, and so we shall escape." O my friends, they would have trembled indeed when they went into the furnace if they had chosen their own means of deliverance, and the king had remained alive. But instead of this, they gave themselves up to God, though he did not deliver them. And, though he did not prevent their going into the furnace, yet he kept them alive in it, so that not so much as the smell of fire had passed upon them. It shall be even so with you. Repose in God. When thou seest him not, believe him; when everything seems to contradict thy faith, still stagger not at the promise. If HE hath said it, he can find ways and means to do it.

Trust in him, repose constantly on him, and limit not the Holy One of Israel. Do you not think that the Church as a great body has done this? We do not any of us expect to hear that a nation is born in a day. If it should be said that in a certain chapel in London this morning some thousand souls had bt converted under one sermon, we should shake our head incredulously, and say it cannot be. We have a notion that because we have only had drops of mercy of late, we are never to have showers of it; because mercy seems only to have come in little rills and trickling streamlets, we have conceived the idea that it never can roll its mighty floods like the huge rivers of the Western world. No, we have limited the Holy One of Israel; especially as preachers have done it. We do not expect our ministry to be blessed, and therefore it is not blessed. If we had learned to expect great things we should have them. If we had made up our minds to this, that the promise was great, that the Promiser was great, that his faithfulness was great, and that his power was great; and if with this for our strength we set to work expecting a great blessing, I trow we should not be disappointed. But the universal Church of Christ hath limited the Holy One of Israel. Why, my friends, if God should will it, ye need not ask where are to come the successors of such and such a man. Ye need not sit down and ask when such and such a one is gone where shall be another who shall preach the word with power. When God gives the word, great shall be the multitude of them that publish it; and when the multitude shall begin to publish, believe me, God can move thousands as easily as he can move tens.

And now I turn to the poor troubled heart, and although I accuse of sin, yet I doubt not the Spirit shall bear witness with the conscience, and leading to Christ, shall this morning deliver from its galling yoke. Poor troubled one, thou *hast said in thy heart, "my sins are too many to be forgiven."* What hast thou done? Repent thee, and let the tear roll down thy cheek. Thou hast limited the Holy One of Israel. Thou hast put thy sins above his grace. Thou hast considered that thy guilt is more omnipotent than omnipotence itself. He is able to save unto the uttermost them that come unto God by Christ. Thou canst not have exceeded the boundlessness of his grace. Be thy sins ever so many, the blood of Christ can put them all away; and if thou doubtest this, thou art limiting the Holy One of Israel.

Another says, I do not doubt his power to save, *but what I doubt is his willingness.* What hast thou done in this? Thou

'ove, the boundless love of the Holy One of
t thou stand on the shore of a love which
less. Was it deep enough and broad enough
ties of Paul, and doth it stop just where
..y thou art the limit, then; thou standest as the
...ung landmark of the grace of the Holy One of Israel! Out
upon thy folly! get rid of this thy mistrust. He whose love has
embraced the chief of sinners, is willing to embrace thee, if now
hating thy sin and leaving thy iniquity, thou art ready to put
thy trust in Jesus. I beseech thee, limit not the Holy One of
Israel by thinking he is unwilling to forgive. Are you really
conscious of the sin you are committing when you think God
unwilling to save? Why you are accusing God of being a liar.
Does not that alarm you? You have done worse than this, you
have even accused him of being perjured, for you doubt his
oath. "As I live, saith the Lord, I have no pleasure in the
death of him that dieth, but had rather that he should turn
unto me and live." You do not believe that? then you make
God to be perjured. Oh! tremble at such guilt as this.

"No, but," you say, "I would not accuse him; but he would
be quite just if he *were* unwilling to save me." I am glad thou
sayest that; that proves thou dost not accuse his justice. But
I still say thou art limiting his love. What doth he say himself?
hath he limited it? Hath he not himself said, "Ho, every one
that thirsteth, come ye to the waters, and he that hath no
money; come ye, buy, and eat; yea, come, buy wine and milk
without money and without price?" And thou art thirsty,
and yet thou thinkest that his love cannot reach to thee. Oh!
while God assures thee that thou art welcome, be not wicked
enough to throw the lie in the teeth of mercy. Limit not the
Holy One of Israel. "But, sir, I am such an old sinner." Yes,
but limit not God. "But I am such a black sinner." Limit not
the efficacy of the cleansing blood. "But I have aggravated
him so much." Limit not his infinite longsuffering. "But my
heart is so hard." Limit not the melting power of his grace.
"But I am so sinful." Limit not the potency of the atonement.
"But, sir, I am so hard hearted, and I feel so little my need of
him." Limit not the influences of the Spirit by thy folly or thy
stubbornness, but come as thou art, and put thy trust in
Christ, and so honour God and he will not dishonour thy faith.

If you will but now for half a moment consider how faithful God has been to his children and how true he has been to all his promises, I think that saint and sinner may stand together and make a common confession and utter a common prayer: "Lord, we have been guilty of doubting thee; we pray that we may limit thee no longer." Scout the thought, drive it far away, and now come, and at the foot of the cross renew your faith; in the sight of the flowing wounds renew your confidence and say, "Jesus, we put our trust in thee; thy Father's grace can never fail, thou hast loved us, and thou wilt love us despite our sins, thou wilt present us at last before thy Father's face in glory everlasting."

And now I address myself to a very small number of persons here present, for whose sorrowful state I feel the greatest pity. It has been my mournful duty, as pastor of so large a congregation, to have to deal with desperate cases. Here and there, there are men and women who have come into a state which, without meaning to wound them, I am free to confess, I think, is sullen DESPAIR. They feel that they are guilty; they know that Christ is able to save; they also doctrinally understand the duty of faith, and its power to bring peace; but they persevere in the declaration that there is no mercy for them. In vain you find out a parallel case; they soon discover some little discrepancy and so escape you. The most mighty promises lose all their force because they turn their edge by the declaration—"That does not mean me." They read in the Word of God that "Jesus Christ came into the world to save sinners;" they are sinners, but they cannot think he came to save them. They know right well that he is able to save them to the uttermost; they would not *say* they had gone beyond the uttermost, but still they think so. They cannot imagine that free grace and sovereign love can ever come to them. They have, it is true, their gleams of sunshine; sometimes they believe, but when the comfortable presence of God is gone, they relapse into their old despair. Let me speak very tenderly, and O that the Spirit of God would speak also! My dear brother and sister, what art thou doing? I ask thee, what art thou doing?—if thou art not limiting the Holy One of Israel? Wouldst thou dishonour God? "No," sayest thou, "I would not." But thou art doing it. Thou art saying that God cannot save thee, or if not saying that, thou art implying—that all the torture thou hast felt in thy conscience, and all the anxiety thou hast in thy heart, have never yet moved God to look on thee. Why, thou makest God to be the most hard-hearted of all beings.

If thou shouldst hear another groan as thou art groaning, thou wouldst weep over him; but thou thinkest that God looks on thee with cold indifference, and will never hear thy prayer. This is not only limiting—it is slandering the Holy One of Israel. Oh, come forth, I beseech you, and dare to believe a good thing of thy God. Dare to believe this, that he is willing now to save thee—that *now* he will put away thy sins. "But suppose, sir, I should believe something too good?" Nay, that thou canst not do. Think of God as being the most loving, the most tender-hearted being that can be, and thou hast thought just rightly of him. Think of him as having a mother's heart, that mourns over its sick baby; think of him as having a father's heart, pitying his children; think of him as having a husband's heart, loving his spouse and cherishing her, and thou hast just thought rightly of him. Think of him as being one who will not look on thy sins, but who casts them behind his back. Dare for once to give God a little honour. Come, put the crown on his head; say, "Lord, I am the vilest rebel out of hell, the most hard-hearted, the most full of blasphemous thoughts; I am the most wicked, the most abandoned; Lord let me have the honour now of being able to say, Thou art able to save even me; and on thy boundless love, thy great, thine infinite grace, do I rely."

XIII

ANGELIC PROTECTION IN APPOINTED WAYS

"For he shall give his angels charge over thee, to keep thee in all thy ways."—Psalm 91 : 11.

OUR text is a promise to pilgrims. You have set out upon the road to heaven: you have entered the narrow way by Christ, who is the gate at the head of the way, and now you are wondering how you will get on while you are on the road, and whether you will be preserved in the right way so as to endure unto the end. This promise comes to you with much of real heart-cheer: "He shall give his angels charge over thee, to keep thee in all thy ways."

My first remark is rather by way of implication from the text than in direct exposition of it. It is this, THERE ARE SOME WAYS WHICH ARE NOT INCLUDED IN THIS PROMISE, because they are not our ways, and they are not God's ways; but they are ways into which we may be tempted by Satan, and which we are jealously to avoid.

You know how, when the devil professed to quote this text to our Lord, he left out the latter part of it, "to keep thee *in all thy ways,*" because it would not have suited his purpose to mention that proviso. We, however, will begin with the words which the devil omitted, since the very fact of his omission of them seems to show how essential they are to a right understanding of the meaning of the text. O Christian, if you keep to the King's highway, you will be safe; but there are by-ways, and, alas! crooked lanes, down which you must not go; if you do go there, you will go at your own hazard. He who travels on the King's highway is under the King's protection; but he who takes to by-roads must protect himself, and the probability is that he will meet with robbers who will make him rue the day that ever he turned to the right hand or to the left.

So, first, we must take care that we never go *in the ways of presumption.* This is what Satan would have had Christ do. "Cast thyself down," said he, "for it is written, He shall give his angels charge over thee, to keep thee." This temptation to presumption is by no means an uncommon one. I have heard of it from the lips of men who were evidently not the children of God, or they would have resisted the temptation, and not have yielded to it as they did. They have said, "Well, we are God's children, so we may do as we like. We are saved, therefore we may live as we please;"—a dreadful inference from what, to other men, might be a precious truth. Oh beware of tempting the devil to tempt you! Beware, too, of tempting the Lord your God, as some do, who venture a long way into evil company, or into doubtful paths, under the mistaken notion that they are so prudent that they will not be overtaken as others might be,—that they are so sage, and withal so experienced, that they may go where young people must not venture, and may do a great many things which less-instructed Christians had better not touch. Where you think you are perfectly safe, there you are often most in danger. Horses frequently fall just at the bottom of the hill, when the driver thinks that it is unnecessary to rein them up any longer. When you are so foolish as to say, "Now I am out of the reach of temptation," you are in the very midst of temptation; and when you think you are not being tempted at all, you are being tempted the most by the very fancy that you are not being tempted.

O beloved friends, beware of presuming! Some have been so favoured in the dispensations of providence, so prosperous in everything they have undertaken, that they have thought they might speculate as far as ever they pleased; and, at last,—well, they have had very shady characters at the end of their lives. They have done once what they never ought to have done; and, because it succeeded, they have been tempted to do it again, and yet again. But, I pray you, sirs, never gather from the success of a wrong action that God is willing for you to repeat it; rather say, "God was very gracious to me in not punishing me that time, but I will never run such a risk as that again." I do not believe that Jonah, after having been once thrown into the sea, and been cast forth upon the shore by the whale, ever wanted to be flung into the sea again; he might not have felt certain about another whale coming along to carry him to land. If you have been miraculously delivered once from the great deep, do not put yourself into such a position again. Beware of all presumptuous ways, for God has not promised to keep you there.

And, brethren, you scarcely need to be told that you cannot expect to be preserved *if you go into sinful ways.* I trust that you do watch against the more coarse and vulgar sins to which others are prone, and that you will not be allowed to fall into them; but there is such a thing as falling by little and little. Mind, I pray you, the little evils. A man never falls into the great, unclean sins of lust all at once; it is usually by a long series of little familiarities that he reaches that terrible end. He is indecorous first, indecent next, and then, at last, criminal. Oh, keep back, keep back from the beginnings of evil. If you keep back at the very first, you will go no further; but if you slide just a little, you will find that this world is such a slippery place that you will surely fall, and fall frightfully, too.

I trust that no Christian man would practise dishonesty in his business; yet you know that it is very easy for one to do a wrong thing because it is "the custom of the trade." "They label this 100 yards, though it is only 90; but if I label it 90, I shall not sell it, and in the next shop it will probably be marked 110, so I must label mine a little more than it is." Well, if you do, recollect that you are a thief. Though it is the custom of the trade, you are a liar if you conform to it, and you cannot expect God's blessing upon you in doing it. Do you think that, in the day of judgment, God will say to men, "You are not guilty, for that deception was the custom of the trade"? By no means; what does the Lord care about the customs of your trade? Do right, at all hazards; if you do wrong, you do it at your peril, for you have no promise from God that he will keep you in such a way as that.

The man who professes to be a Christian must not expect God's angels to keep him if he goes *in the way of worldliness.* There are hundreds, and I fear thousands, of church-members, who say that they are the people of God, yet they appear to live entirely to the world. Their great aim is money-making, and personal aggrandizement, just as much as it is the aim of altogether ungodly men. The Kingdom of Christ, the needs of his Church, the wants of perishing souls, have a very slender place in their hearts; but they live wholly for themselves, only they try to conceal it under the plea of providing for their families. "Seek ye first the kingdom of God, and his righteousness; and all these things shall be added unto you," is a text from which we need to preach to professing Christians throughout London, and throughout the whole world.

There is also *the way of pride* which many tread. They must be "respectable"; they must move in "Society"—with a big S; and everything is ordered with a view to display. To be great, to be famous, to be esteemed, to keep up a high repute,—it is for this that they live. I do not believe there is any higher life, in this world, than the life of God which is given to everyone who believes on the Lord Jesus Christ. The highest life I aspire to is to live as Jesus Christ lived, and to walk as he walked; and that is the lowest kind of life with which any Christian ought to be contented.

There is also *the way of wilfulness* which I have known some follow. Very grievous is it to see some, whom we really think to be good men, shift their quarters apparently without any reason. They were doing very well, yet away they rush, for they cannot let well alone. Some brethren seem to be afflicted with a kind of perpetual fidgetiness. They are rolling stones, and gather no moss. They move from one position to another, not because there is any need for them to move, but just because they cannot stay still. They go away from their nest, and away from their home, and very often act in direct opposition to the order of God's providence. Oh, beware of that spirit of wilfulness! It is often wise, as the old saying puts it, to take advice of our pillow. He who does not sleep upon a thing may have to weep upon it. Better look before you leap. Always follow the cloud of God's providence, don't run before it; for, if you run before it, you may find it hard work to get back again.

One other way in which a Christian ought not to go is *the way of erroneous doctrine*. I know some professors who, as soon as a new heresy comes up, want to have taste of it. I confess that I never felt much temptation in that direction. I do not suppose, if you went into a chemist's shop, you would say to him, "I have heard of somebody being killed at Norwood by taking such-and-such a poison; I should like a taste of it." You would not ask him to take down his big bottles, and to give you a taste of all the deadly poisons he had in stock. "Oh, no!" you say, "we are in our right senses; we should not do such a foolish thing as that." Yet I know people who, as soon as ever there is any teaching spoken of as being erroneous, say, "We must have a look at that; we must have a taste of that;"—never satisfied except when they are tasting poisons. There is a period in life when a Christian man should obey Paul's injunction to the Thessalonians, "Prove all things;" but let him get that done as quickly as he can, and then let him get to the second part of the injunction, "Hold fast that which is good." Never hold anything fast till you have proved it to be good, but do not be everlastingly proving it. Some things do not need any proving; they bear upon their forefront their character. But others need to be proved; so, having proved the right things to be right, and the true things to be true, hold them fast, and turn not aside from them. These false-doctrine-makers and their disciples are the curse of the age in which we live. I implore you to abide in the good old paths. What you know to be true, that hold fast. Your father's God and your mother's God forsake not; as for the truths which God has taught you by his own Spirit, grapple them to you as with hooks of steel; for, if you go in the way of error, you cannot expect divine protection.

Now, secondly, THERE ARE WAYS IN WHICH SAFETY IS GUARANTEED. There is, first, *the way of humble faith in the Lord Jesus Christ.* You know that way, brother; so walk in it. Oh, to be nothing, and to let Christ be everything;—to confess our own guilt, and to be clothed in his righteousness! Keep to that safe road; for it is the King's highway, of which it may be said, "No lion shall be there, nor any ravenous beast shall go up thereon, it shall not be found there; but the redeemed shall walk there."

There is, next, *the way of obedience to divine precepts.* Do what God tells you, as God tells you, and because God tells you, and no hurt can come to you. The Lord told Moses to take by the tail the serpent from which he fled; he did so, and he was not bitten, but the serpent stiffened into a wonder-working rod. Obey the Lord in all things. Mind the jots and the tittles, for whosoever shall break one of the least of Christ's commandments, "and shall teach men so, shall be called the least in the Kingdom of Heaven; but whosoever shall do and teach them, the same shall be called great in the Kingdom of Heaven." Oh, to follow in the footsteps of the Lord Jesus Christ, step by step, and to keep closely to his footprints! It is in such ways that angelic protection will be afforded to us.

There is, also, *the way of childlike trust in providential guidance.* Happy is that man who always waits upon God to know what he shall do,—who asks the Lord ever to guide him, and who dares not lean upon his own understanding. Watch the Lord's providential leadings; wait for divine guidance. It is far better to stand still than to run in the wrong road. Pause a while, and pray for direction, and do not move until you hear the voice behind you saying, "This is the way; walk ye in it."

There is, too, *the way of strict principle and stern integrity.* Travelling along that road will often involve a good many losses and crosses, and much reproach, and sometimes it will even appear to destroy your usefulness. But I charge you— young men especially—never violate any principle which you profess to hold. I believe that it has been a lasting blessing to some, whom I know, that they have scorned to trim their sails, even in the smallest degree, to please any living soul. Do you the same. "Be just, and fear not." Keep to a cause that is despised if you believe it is a right one, and love it all the more because it is despised. Ask not what will pay; care not for the flatterer's smile. Pursue truth even though she may go along very rough roads; she will always repay you in the long run. Cling to her, and win her smile; then the frowns of the whole world need not cause you a moment's thought. The way of principle is the way of safety; God's angels will keep you if you keep to that road.

And I am quite sure that *the way of consecrated service for God's glory* is another of these safe ways. It is well when a man says, "I choose my path by this rule,—how can I best serve my God? Having judged whether there is any principle in- volved, and having a fair choice between this and that, I say to myself, 'In which way can I hope to be the more useful? In what course of life can I best glorify God?" That is your way to heaven, Christian,—the way in which your Master can get the most glory out of you; and, if you walk in that way, you may depend upon it that you will be protected by his sovereign power.

And once again, there is *the way of separation from the world, and close walking with God.* No man ever suffered any real injury through keeping himself aloof from the ways of ungodly men; and, on the other hand, no man ever failed to be a gainer by close and intimate fellowship with God. "Enoch walked with God," and he gained, not only escape from the pangs of death, but also the testimony that "he pleased God." O Christian men, could not more of us choose this blessed path, and walk in it continually?

But I must pass on to note, in the third place, that THESE RIGHT WAYS WILL LEAD US INTO DIFFERING CIRCUMSTANCES.

Sometimes, *the right way will lead us into very stony places,* positions of great difficulty; yet here is the promise to meet that emergency, "They shall bear thee up in their hands, lest thou dash thy foot against a stone." A way is none the less right because it is rough. Indeed, often it is all the more sure to be the right way because it is so displeasing to flesh and blood.

Sometimes, also, *the right way may be very terrible with temptation.* If your path is so beset, do not, therefore, imagine that it is a wrong way, because the Psalmist goes on to say, "Thou shalt tread upon the lion and adder." Lions and adders will come to you, temptations will threaten to devour you even while you are in the right road; but, then, you are promised that, as long as it is the right road that you are in, you shall get the victory over the lion and the adder. The temptation may be of so mysterious a character that you cannot understand it. It may be like a dragon; but, if so, here is your comfort, "the young lion and the dragon shalt thou trample under feet."

And remember that even if the road is not stony, and if no lion attacks you, *you will be kept from the perils of the smooth and easy roads.* You will always need divine and angelic keeping, for God would not have charged his angels to keep his people in all their ways if they did not need protection in *all* their ways. Some of you are just now prospering in business, but your way is not any safer than the way of the man who is losing his all; indeed, yours may not be as safe as his. To you who are in robust health, I venture to say that your path is more perilous than the path of the man who is always ailing; and to all of you I say, do pray for angelic keeping.

Now we come to the fourth point, WHILE WALKING IN ALL RIGHT WAYS, BELIEVERS ARE SECURE. "He shall give his angels charge over thee, to keep thee in all thy ways."

O Christian man, if you have not violated your conscience,— if you have not forsaken the path of communion with your God, think what high privileges are yours! First, *God himself concerns himself about you.* He charges his angels to take care of you. David, when his soldiers went to battle against his rebellious son, Absalom, specially charged their leaders to deal gently with the young man, Absalom, for his sake; but he charged them in vain. In a far higher sense, God charges his angels to guard his saints, and he does not charge them in vain. This is not a mere general command; it is a sort of imperative personal charge that God lays upon his angels: "Take care of my children; they are in my road,—the King's high road of rectitude. Watch over them; and do not suffer them to be hurt."

Next, *you have mysterious agencies to protect you:* "He shall give *his angels* charge over thee." We speak of dragons, but we do not know much about them; and we do not know much about angels, but we feel sure that angels can overcome dragons, for they are more than a match for devils; and if mysterious temptations come to you, there shall also be mysterious defenders to thrust them back. You have more friends, poor Christian, than you know of. When you are fighting the battles of God, you may hear a rush of angels' wings at your side if you only have your ears divinely opened. If all men forsake you, God can send angels, though you see them not, to strengthen you in some secret manner that I cannot fully explain. "Behold, the mountain was full of horses and chariots of fire round about Elisha," the prophet who dared to be true to his God, and to serve him faithfully.

And as angels are on our side, *so are all things, visible and invisible.* Why believers, the very stones of the field are in league with you, and the beasts of the field are at peace with you. Wherever you go, you have friends ready to help you. It is true that you have enemies among the wicked, but their weapons shall not prevail against you; and wherever there is a messenger of God,—be it wind, or storm, or lightning, or hail,—it is your friend. The very stars in their courses fight for you. The forces, terrific and tremendous, which at times shake the world, are only your Father's flaming swords unsheathed to protect you. Sing then, ye saints of the Lord, for everything is on your side. "Ye shall go out with joy, and be led forth with peace: the mountains and the hills shall break forth before you into singing, and all the trees of the field shall clap their hands."

What a very sweet thought is suggested by the word "thee" in our text! It teaches us that *each one of the saints is personally protected:* "He shall give his angels charge over *thee,* to keep *thee* in all *thy* ways." God takes a personal interest in every traveller along the right road, and charges his angels to keep him. Perhaps you say, "I do not read the text, sir, as referring to me." Well, I think you should do so. When you read the precept, "Thou shalt not steal," do you suppose that it refers to you? "Oh, yes!" you say, "I would not like to suggest that it did not mean me; I would not plead exemption from the precept." Well, then, my dear brother, do not seek to be exempted from the promise. Just as you feel sure that the precept applies to you, so, as a child of God, feel sure that the promise applies to you.

This protection is perpetual, as well as personal; God's angels are "to keep thee *in all thy ways;*"—in thy ups and thy downs, in thy advancements and thy retirings;—to keep thee when thou art asleep, and when thou art awake;—to keep thee when thou art alone, and when thou art in company;—to keep thee if thou hast to preach, and to keep thee if thou hast to hear;—to keep thee if thou hast to serve, and to keep thee if thou hast to suffer. Thou always needest keeping, and thou shalt always have it, for the angels are charged "to keep thee in all thy ways."

Note just one more point, that *all these privileges come to us by Jesus Christ,* for Christ is that mystic ladder which Jacob saw, up and down whose wondrous rungs the angels came and went. The commerce between the saints and heaven is kept up by way of the person of the Lord Jesus Christ. Oh, what joy is this! If Christ is yours, angels are yours, and all the principalities and powers in the heavenly places will delight to take care of you.

Now, if anyone here is going home to a lonely room, I should like you to feel that you are not going there alone. Father and mother are away in the country, perhaps, and some of you young people feel quite alone in London; but, if you are believing in the Lord Jesus Christ, you are not alone, for the Lord of all the holy angels is with you, and an innumerable company of blessed spirits is round about you. Take comfort from this glorious truth. God's mysterious angelic agency, which you see not, and hear not, but which is most true and real, will form a cordon round about you to protect you in the midst of the temptations of this great city; and if you be but faithful to him, and keep in his ways, nothing shall hurt you between here and heaven. There may be many darts hurled at you, but the great shield of faith shall turn them all aside, or quench them for ever. You will have to encounter many temptations and trials, but you will be preserved amid them all. Those devils are great cowards; so, when God once takes entire possession of a man, he need not fear even though all hell were let loose upon him. "If God be for us, who can be against us."

There are two or three thoughts which I think are worth remembering. The first is this. Dear brethren, we see, from this text, that *the lowest employment is consistent with the highest enjoyment.* The angels are our nurses: "they shall bear thee up in their hands," just as nurses hold up little children who are not able to stand by themselves. Those angels continually behold God's face, and live in the perfect bliss of heaven, yet they condescend to do such humble deeds as these. Be like the angels in this respect; teach an infant class in the Sunday-school, yet keep your face bright with the light of God's countenance. Give away tracts, go and visit among the poor, look after fallen women, or do any other work for the Lord that needs to be done. Never mind what it is, but remember that the employment is all the more honourable because it appears to be so commonplace. Never was Christ grander, methinks, than when he washed his disciples' feet; certainly, never are we more like him than when we also are willing to wash their feet, or render any lowly service that they may need.

The next thought is, *as angels watch over us, how cheerfully ought we to watch over one another!* How gladly you, who are older in divine life, ought to watch over the younger ones of the Lord's family! If God enables you to have any of the joy of angels over repenting sinners, mind that you take some of the care which angels exercise over those who walk in God's ways. Watch over one another. "Bear ye one another's burdens and so fulfil the law of Christ." Visit each other in your sicknesses; seek to bring back to Christ and the church all the backsliders whom you can find; labour for the good of one another; for, in this way only, can our task be done, and you shall be like the angels if you bear up the feeble ones in your hands lest they trip up and fall to their grievous hurt.

Then, next, *how safe and happy we ought to feel when we know that God has charged the angels to take care of us!* Do not be so nervous, my dear sister, the next time there is a little storm, or even a great storm. Do not be afraid, my dear friend, when sickness comes into your house. Remember the promise that precedes our text: "Because thou hast made the Lord, which is my refuge, even the most High, thy habitation; there shall no evil befall thee, neither shall any plague come nigh thy dwelling." But suppose it should seem right to the Lord to let the plague come to you, and suppose you shall die of it, well, you will the sooner be in heaven. Wherefore, comfort one another with the reflection that all is well with you as long as you keep in the way of duty.

And, lastly, *how holy we ought to be with such holy beings watching over us!* If the angels are always hovering round you, mind what you are at. Would you have spoken as you did when you were coming in at that door yonder, if you had seen an angel standing by your side, listening to what you were saying? Oh, no; you are wonderfully decorous when there is somebody near whom you respect! How often your glib tongue is checked when there is some Christian man or woman, whom you highly esteem, within hearing! How many a thing is done that would not be done under the eye of one whom you love! Whether we are alone or in company, let us not sin, because angels are ever watching us, and the angels' Lord is also watching us. May he graciously keep us in his holy way; and if we are so kept, we shall be preserved from all evil while we are here; and, at last, we shall see his face with joy, and abide with him for ever.

XIV

BLESSED DISCIPLINE

"Blessed is the man whom thou chastenest, O Lord, and teachest him out of thy law; that thou mayest give him rest from the days of adversity, until the pit be digged for the wicked. For the Lord will not cast off his people, neither will he forsake his inheritance. But judgment shall return unto righteousness: and all the upright in heart shall follow it."—Psalm 94: 12–15.

THERE are times when the wicked seem to have things all their own way. This earth is not the realm of final justice; we are not yet standing before the Lord's great judgment-seat. God permits many things to be for a while in confusion. They who are highest with him are often lowest with them; and those for whom he has no regard seem to heap up the treasures of the world till their eyes stand out with fatness, and they have more than heart can wish. Let no child of God be astonished at this arrangement. It has often been so in the past, and it has been the great enigma that has puzzled the world. The children of God have also sat down, and looked into it; but it has been even to them a great deep which they could not fathom. They have sighed over it, but their sighs have not altered the facts.

It is still true that often the wicked triumph, and the servants of iniquity delight themselves in the high places of the earth. The righteous need not wonder that they suffer now, for that has been the lot of God's people all along, and there have been certain times in human history when God has seemed to be altogether deaf to the cries of his suffering people. Remember the martyr-age, and the days of the Covenanters, who were hunted upon the mountains like the partridge. You must not wonder if the easy places of the earth are not yours, and if the sentinel's stern duties should fall to your lot. It is so, and so it must be, for God has so ordained it.

To comfort any of the Lord's children who have begun to worry themselves because things do not go with them as they desire, I have selected this text, and I pray the Lord to bless it to them.

First, I shall ask you to notice that GOD'S CHILDREN ARE UNDER TUITION.

Other children may run about, and take holiday; they may wander into the woods, and gather the flowers, and do very much what they like; but God's own children have to go to school. This is a great privilege for them, although they do not always think so. Children are not often good judges of what is best for themselves. No doubt, we should like to play the truant, we should be very glad to put away our school-bags, and quit the school-house, and go out by ourselves, and wander at our own sweet will; but our heavenly Father loves us too well to let it be so with us. Because we are his children, therefore he will have us trained and prepared for that high destiny which awaits us by-and-by.

Note how this tuition is described in our text; the very first word concerning it is, "chastenest." "Blessed is the man whom thou chastenest, O Lord, and teachest," as if the chastening were the primary part of the teaching, as if it occupied so large a share of it that it was put first: "Blessed is the man whom thou chastenest, O Lord, and teachest." In God's school-house the rod is still extant; *with the Lord, chastening is teaching.* He does not spoil his children; but chastens them, aye even unto scourging, as the Apostle puts it. His chastening is the most severe with those whom he loves best: "Whom the Lord tenderly loveth he chasteneth, and scourgeth every son whom he receiveth." Some of us know what it is to have this teaching by chastening. I have often told you that I am afraid I have never learnt anything of God except by the rod; and, in looking back, I am afraid that I must confirm that statement. I have forgotten some of the gentle lessons; but when they have been whipped into me, I have remembered them. I met with a friend, the other day, who said that it was the very reverse with him. He could not remember any benefit that he had ever gained by chastening, and he thought that all the good he had received from the Lord had come to him by tenderness and prosperity. I did not controvert with him about the matter, for the experiences of God's people may differ; but this I know, that some of us have learnt much from the Lord's chastening rod.

For instance, we have learnt the evil of sin. "Before I was afflicted I went astray; but now have I kept thy word." There are some sorrows that come evidently as the result of our own folly. We have to reap the harvest of the seed that we sow; and by this process we are made to see that it is an exceedingly evil and bitter thing to sin against God. This is an important lesson; I wish that more had thoroughly learnt it. I wish that some Christian professors had anything like a true idea of the exceeding sinfulness of sin; but I believe that instruction upon this point often comes from the chastening hand of God.

Our chastening teaches us the unsatisfactory nature of worldly things. We can easily become attached to the things which we possess. It is a very difficult thing to handle gold without allowing it to adhere to your fingers; and when it gets into your purse, you need much grace to prevent it getting into your heart. Even our children can soon grow into idols, and our health and our comfort may make us forget God. I never knew affliction and trial make us do that; but when the gourds are taken away, then the sun shines on us. How often has God shaken all the leaves off our trees, and then we have seen the heavens which we never saw when all the leaves were green! By losing this, and losing that, we are made to feel that all the things which we possess perish in the using, and are such temporary joys that we cannot hope to fill our hearts with them.

Do we not also learn by affliction our own frailty, and our own impatience? We are wonderfully patient when we have nothing to suffer, as we are all great heroes and very courageous when there is no fighting to be done. We sometimes say to one another, "What a mass of faith that brother has! What a vast mountain of faith that sister possesses!" We are all almost inclined to envy them; but we remember the fable of the stag which had such magnificent antlers that he said to himself, as he looked at his fine figure in the water, "It is most absurd for us stags to be afraid of dogs. The next time I hear a dog bark, I will just toss him on my horns, and there will soon be an end of him." Yes, so he thought; but just then the baying of a hound was heard in the distance, and the boastful stag took to his heels, and ran as fast as the rest of the herd did. So it is often with those who seem to have great faith when they do not want it; but when they do need it, where is it? Stretch some men upon a bed of sickness for a week or two, and see whether they will be able to hector at the rate they now do. They would sing another song, I warrant you, if once they had such a twist of pain as some of us have had to endure, and the beads of perspiration stood on their brow while they tried to bear it. Ah, yes, we find how great our weakness is when first one thing is taken away, and then another, and the chastening hand of God makes the blows to fall thick and heavy upon us!

Do we not then learn also the value of prayer? I said to this friend to whom I have referred, "Did you not pray much more under your affliction than you did before?" "Oh, yes!" he replied; "I grant you that 'Trials give new life to prayer'." Do we ever pray in such dead earnest as when everything seems to be sinking from under our feet, and our sweetest cups are full of bitterness? Then we turn to God, and say, "Show me wherefore thou contendest with me." I do not think that we ever pray with such fervour of supplication in our prosperity as we do in our adversity.

And then how precious the promises become! As we only see the stars when the shadows gather at night, so the promises shine out like newly-kindled stars when we get into the night of affliction. I am sure that there are passages of Scripture which are full of consolation, the depths of which we do not even imagine yet, and we never shall know all that is in them till we get into the deeps of soul-trouble which correspond with them. There are points of view from which scenery is to be beheld at its best; and, until we find out those points of view, we may be missing the sight of some of the most beautiful objects in nature. God leads us one way and another by our chastisements to understand and prize his promises.

And, oh, how should we ever know the faithfulness of God if it were not for affliction? We might talk about it, and theoretically understand it; but to try to prove the greatness of Jehovah's love, and the absolute certainty of his eternal faithfulness,—this cometh not except by the way of affliction and trial.

I might talk on for ever about the sweet uses of adversity, and not exhaust the subject. You experienced people of God know even more than I do about this matter, for some of you have done business on deeper waters than my barque has yet ploughed; and yet, methinks, my keel has passed over the deep places of the sea of trouble, and there may be deeper depths before me still. I have probably said sufficient to prove to you that chastening is a divine way of instructing us. You will find that, if you want the most Christ-like saints, and the most deeply experimental believers, and the Christians who are best acquainted with the Word of God, you must look for them among those who are the most intimately acquainted with the fiery furnace and its burning heat.

If you read the text through, you will notice that the rod is not without the Word. I call your special attention to that: "Blessed is the man whom thou chastenest, O Lord, and teachest him out of thy law." The rod and the Book go together; the rod drives us to the Book, and the Book explains the meaning of the rod; we must have them both if we would be fully instructed in the things of God. *The Word of God is our school-book*. At first, it is our primer; and when we get furthest advanced in grace, it will be our profoundest classic; and all the way along it will supply us with our choicest poetry and everything else that we desire.

We look to the Bible for comfort when we are chastened; we turn over its pages, and seek to find a passage which fits our case, and ministers relief to our necessity. Have you not often done so? Why, this Book is something like the whitesmith's bunch of keys! Perhaps you have lost the key of your drawer, and you cannot get at your things. You send for the smith, and he keeps on trying different keys till at last he finds one that exactly fits the wards of your lock. So, if you keep on fingering away at the promises, you will come at last upon one that was made on purpose for your case. Perhaps your lock is one with very peculiar wards; you never could make out why it was shaped just as it is; but now that you have found the key that opens it, you understand that both lock and key were made to fit each other.

The word of God is not only used at such times for comfort, but also for direction. How frequently you have been unable to see your way! You have wished that there was some prophet of God with the Urim and Thummim, that he might tell you what to do. The great guiding principles of God's truth, his Law and his Gospel, faith in him and in his providential care, have furnished you with a direction quite as clear as if some prophet had plainly told you what to do. You have sought the direction of the Word of the Lord when you have gone to enquire in his temple, he has answered you out of the secret place of thunder, and you have known without doubt the way that you should take.

At such times, too, we have proved, the power of the Word of God. When your vessel is sailing along very smoothly, the Word of God may grow to be a dead letter with you; but when the waves are rolling mountains high, and dashing over you, and you are soaked through and through, and fear that the deep will swallow you up, then you begin to test the promises, and to prove the power of the Word of God. When its inexpressible sweetness reaches your heart, then you can indeed feel that you have been taught out of God's Word. You see how the two things go together: "Blessed is the man whom thou chastenest, O Lord, and teachest him out of thy law."

That leads me to say that, according to our text, *God himself is our Teacher.* He is not satisfied with giving us a Book, and smiting us when we are inattentive to its teachings; but he himself teaches us. Was there ever a teacher so full of wisdom, a teacher who understood his pupils so well, a teacher so altogether master of the whole art of tuition? Was there ever a teacher so patient, so able to apply his lessons to the heart itself, so full of power to give understanding as well as to make the thing clear to the understanding when it is given? Happy people who have God to be their Tutor! Happy pupils, even though, when the school-bell rings, you have half a mind to stay away, and play with yonder children who do not belong to your school, yet happy are you if you are truly God's scholars. Even if, every now and then, your days are spent in weeping, and your lessons are so badly done that they bring the rod upon you, yet are you happy children. "Blessed is the man whom thou chastenest, O Lord, and teachest him out of thy law."

Now upon our second point I will say a little. We have had God's children under tuition; now let us think of GOD'S CHILDREN EDUCATED. The Lord has chastened and taught his child for this purpose: "That thou mayest give him rest from the days of adversity, until the pit be digged for the wicked." "What!" you ask, "chastened to give us rest? It is usual for

chastening to break our rest." Yes, I know that it is so with
other chastenings; but in very deed this is the way in which
God gives rest to his people.

First, *we learn to rest in the will of God.* Our will is naturally
very stubborn; and when we are chastened, at first we kick out,
like a bullock unaccustomed to the yoke; but by degrees we
feel that we *must* bear the yoke. We then go a little further,
and we feel that we *ought* to bear it, even though God should
lay upon us anything he pleases, and we should feel it very
galling. By-and-by, the yoke begins to fit our neck, and we
come even to *love* it. I do not suppose that many of us will
ever get like Samuel Rutherford, when he said that he began
to wonder which he loved best, Christ or his cross, for the cross
had brought him so much blessing that he was quite in love
with it. No, we have not reached that point yet, so that we
love our cross; still, we can say this, that we have learned that
it is—

> *"Sweet to lie passive in his hand,*
> *And know no will but his."*

If we struggle against God's will, we only increase our sorrow.
Our self-will usually lies at the root of our greatest griefs. Give
way, and thou hast won; yield to God, and thou hast obtained
the blessing thou dost desire. The bitterness is gone out of thy
grief when thou consentest to be grieved if God will have it so.

We make advances in our spiritual education when *we learn to
rest after our afflictions.* When any trouble is over, great delights
often come to us. It is with us as it was with our Master;
he had been with the wild beasts; worse still, he had been
tempted of the devil; but angels came, and ministered unto
him. There is, to a believer, sometimes, a wonderfully clear
shining after the rain. Perhaps there is no happier period of
life than the state of convalescence, when the sick man is
gradually recovering his former strength after a long illness.
So God gives surprising peace to his people when he takes away
their troubles, but he also gives them a great measure of peace
in their troubles. Thus, for another lesson, *we learn to rest in
adversity.* The Lord chastens us in order that we may learn
how to stand fast, and bear up bravely while the trouble is yet
upon us.

I have often had to notice the singularity of my Lord's loving-kindness and tenderness to myself in the time of need. I do not say that it is singularity for him, for he is often doing it; but the singularity lies in the fact that the Lord does it when nobody else could or would do it. He gives us comfort when nobody else is either willing or able to render any comfort to us. This very afternoon, I have had a remarkable instance of how good cheer is sent to me by my gracious God just when I most need it. I was heavy and sad at heart, and there came to my door, to see me, a foreign gentleman, an officer of considerable rank in the Italian army. He spoke to me in very good English, but I cannot tell you all that he said to me, though it was most cheering and kind. I asked him why he should come so far to see me. He spoke of me as though I were a great man, and I assured him that he was quite mistaken, for I was nothing of the kind. As we walked along, and talked, he said, "But you are the greatest man in all the world to me." "Why is that?" I asked; and he answered, "I was a Catholic, and a bad Catholic, too. I did not rightly know anything about the Lord Jesus Christ, and I was fast becoming an infidel; but I met with a sermon of yours in Italian, by reading it I was brought into the light and liberty of the Gospel; I found the Saviour, and I felt that I must come, and tell you about it." Then he further cheered and encouraged my heart by letting me see how much he knew of our Lord Jesus, and he had learnt it all from nothing but the Bible itself, which he had read after being guided to it by a stray sermon of mine. "Well," I thought, "my Master sends this man all the way from the South of Italy to come just at this particular time, when I was sorely needing just such a comforting message." Why should he do so? Only that he likes, when his children have to take bitter medicine, to give them a piece of sugar after it. Therefore, my brother, be you willing to take your medicine, else there may come a sharp chastening with it. Oh, for grace so to suffer, and so to endure, that we may just give ourselves up into the hand of the ever-blessed One, and thus he will perfect in us the tuition of his wonderful Word! Then shall it be true that the Lord has taught us to rest even in the days of our adversity.

I must now go on to the third point, which is, that GOD'S CHILDREN ARE STILL DEAR TO HIM. We have thought of them at school, chastened and instructed, and we have seen them learning a few lessons. Now let us notice how dear they are to their Lord at all times, for the text says, "The Lord will not cast off his people, neither will he forsake his inheritance."

First, then, *the Lord will not cast off his people.* Sometimes you are cast down; but you are never cast off. Sometimes others cast you off; but the Lord will not cast off his people. Sometimes you are cast into the furnace; yes, it may be so, but in the furnace you are not cast off. Metal put into the furnace is not thrown away; had it been worthless, it might have been left on the heap with the slag; but it is put into the furnace because it is of value. When you are put into the furnace, and into the greatest heat that can be obtained, it is that the Lord may take away your dross, and purify you for his service.

> "*In the furnace God may prove thee,*
> *Thence to bring thee forth more bright;*
> *But can never cease to love thee:*
> *Thou art precious in his sight:*
> *God is with thee,*
> *God thine everlasting light.*"

Then, further, *the Lord will not forsake his people,* for it is added, "Neither will he forsake his inheritance." He chose them to be his inheritance, he has bought them as his inheritance, and he will never forsake them. Still shall you be supported by the Lord, but never forsaken by him; still shall you be owned by him, but never forsaken. Still shall you be kept, defended against all comers, and preserved to be the Lord's own people, for he will not forsake his inheritance.

I do not feel as if I need say much more upon this theme; but it is enough for me, I think, just to remind you of those precious words of our great and gracious Father, which are many times repeated in his Word, "I will never leave thee, nor forsake thee," and leave them with you, his children. Take them, and feed upon them. God give you to know the full comfort of them!

So I shall close with this fourth point, God's people will be righted in the end: "Judgment shall return unto righteousness: and all the upright in heart shall follow it."

Just now, *judgment has gone away*. It has gone up to its own land; judgment is within the veil, but there are reasons for its absence from us. Judgment has gone away, perhaps, that it may try the faith of God's people. The Lord does not to-day strike down the profane, nor slay the hypocrite, as he might if he dealt with them in strict justice. Judgment has gone out of the world for a while, though it watcheth and recordeth all things. It is gone partly for our trial and testing, that we may learn to trust an absent God and Saviour. Judgment is also gone away in order that mercy may be extended to the ungodly, that they may live, and that they may turn to God; for he willeth not the death of any, but that they may turn unto him and live. Judgment has gone up to the throne for a while until the wicked shall have completed the full measure of their sin, "until the pit be digged for the wicked." Not yet is the iniquity of the Amorites full; and judgment has gone away and will stay away until it is.

Do not be in a hurry, child of God; the Lord has timed his absence. Hearken to his next word: "*Judgment shall return unto righteousness*." You shall hear the trumpet soon; you shall hear the sound of that blast, "the loudest and the last," telling you that the day of the great assize has come, and that the Judge has arrived, to right all wrongs, to punish all iniquity, and to reward all virtue, and all true, faithful service. "Judgment shall return." We cannot tell how long it will linger, but it will return. Christ will come again. As surely as he ascended into heaven, he will so come in like manner as he went up. He shall judge the earth in righteousness, and his people with his truth. Behold, he cometh! And when he comes, judgment shall return unto righteousness.

And what then? *Judgment shall be welcomed by the godly*. When it comes, "all the upright in heart shall follow it." The chariot of righteousness shall lead the way, and all the people of God shall follow it in a glorious procession. Then shall they receive their Lord's commendation, "Well done, good and faithful servants." They shall follow it, as they wear their golden crowns, nay, as they cast them at the foot of the throne, saying, "Thou art worthy, O Lord, to receive glory, and honour, and power." Saints will follow the chariot of judgment, coming forth from their concealment, and shining as the sun in the kingdom of their Father. They shall come from the places where slander has banished them, and show themselves again, and God shall be glorified in them. Now you who love the Lord, be not in a hurry to have all this fulfilled. Leave your cases in the dear hand of him who will ere long judge all righteously.

I have done when I have reminded you that he is accursed who has never felt the chastening hand of God, or sat at his feet to learn of him; but he is blessed indeed who yields himself entirely up to be the disciple of the Lord. May it be so with every one of you, for our Lord Jesus Christ's sake!

XV

THE KING AND HIS COURT

"Mine eyes shall be upon the faithful of the land, that they may dwell with me: he that walketh in a perfect way, he shall serve me."—Psalm 101: 6.

DAVID is going to be king, and these are the resolutions that he makes before he ascends the throne. He meant that he would look out the best men in the nation, and that he would take care of them, and give them offices about his court, that so he might have his work well done, that his people might be judged by wise and righteous men, and all the affairs of state should be managed by those who were faithful to God. This was a very proper thing for him to do. I wish that those who are not kings, but who are placed in any position of influence, would have their eyes upon the faithful of the land. Good men should patronize good men; those who have it in their power should, to the utmost of their ability, advance those whom they know to be upright and true and gracious men; but we are not going to talk about David now, but about the Son of David, "great David's greater Son," the King of kings and Lord of lords. There is no doubt that in his Kingdom his eyes are upon the faithful. He looks upon the faithful among his people, he takes them into communion with himself; and he uses them as his servants in conspicuous and remarkable ways.

First, then, WHO ARE THESE FAITHFUL MEN to whom Jesus, our King, will have respect at all times?

I answer, they may be known in part by this mark, they are *true in their dealings with God.* A man who is not honest to God is honest to nobody; he who will rob his God will soon rob his fellow-men. Now, I mean by being truthful and upright to God just this, that we walk before him in deep sincerity of heart. To make a profession of being what we are not, is not being among the faithful of the land; and to come before God with prayers which are no prayers, but only the skins and shells of prayers, is not being faithful before God. To profess to sing his praises, when we are only uttering words without heart, is to make ourselves as sounding brass and a tinkling cymbal in the ears of God. We are not accepted with him if our heart is not true. A man who is faithful before God will not go in his religious expressions beyond his religious experience; he will always be afraid of stretching his arm farther than his sleeve will reach. If he has not felt certain changes, he will not profess to have felt them; he would rather err on the side of doubting and distrusting himself than on the side of boasting and claiming for himself what he really does not possess.

I think that it is a most important thing to be very true and thorough in our private walk with God. If thou art backsliding, it is well to know it. If thou art making but small progress, it is well to confess it. If thou art an idler, it is well to admit it. If thou hast become lukewarm, it is well to know it; nothing is more dangerous than to be saying to thyself, "I am rich, and increased with goods, and have need of nothing," when all the while thou art "wretched, and miserable, and poor, and blind, and naked."

God has his eyes upon the faithful of the land, those who are faithful to himself, who do not attempt to deceive themselves with religious professions which they cannot support. How many a man has become a bankrupt by a lavish expenditure which exceeded his income! He said that he "must keep up appearances," and he did keep up appearances till they became his ruins. God grant that you and I may never try to keep up appearances before him! Be what you would seem to be; and in the presence of God never seem to be or dream of seeming to be what you are not. Thus I think we, first of all, know the faithful by their upright dealing with God.

This will lead them to be *true in their dealings with men.* I have heard, at times, of professing Christians who are no more straight in business than worldlings are. It is a shame to you of whom this can be said; and it is a disgrace to the church to which you belong. It brings dishonour upon the Lord Jesus Christ if any of you profess to be his servants, and yet lie and cheat, or, what is much the same thing, puff your goods beyond what can honestly and fairly be said of them, or sell them under false names, deceiving the people who purchase of you. I am not going into all the tricks of trade. That man is not faithful in God's esteem who is not upright, honest, true to a hair's breadth, in his dealings with his fellow-men. We must stand to our bond even though we lose by it. We must be true to the word we speak though it be to our own hurt. God grant that his Spirit may work in us, not only the ordinary integrity which may be found in many a natural man, but something deeper and more thorough than that, in all our dealings in business, in the family, and everywhere else, for the eyes of the King are upon the faithful of the land!

Now such people will, in the next place, always be *true in their dealings with men on God's behalf.* I think this passage bears very pertinently upon the minister, and upon the Sunday-school teacher, and upon the Christian worker. The eyes of Christ are upon the faithful of the land. If I come here, and teach you what I do not believe, or if I conceal what I do believe, or if I tell you something which has in it a suppression of truth, or if I preach to you orthodox doctrine while in my own heart I believe something different, remember that I cannot be said to be one of the faithful of the land. And if I, as a minister, sit still, and see the Gospel of Christ trampled in the mire, and hold my tongue for fear of shame and contempt, I cannot be called one of the faithful of the land. If you, dear Sunday-school teachers, in your instruction of the children, keep back from them anything they ought to know, or if, in telling them what they ought to know, you do not press it home upon their consciences, if you do not pray with them, if you do not long for their conversion, you are not faithful to their souls on God's behalf, and the eye of Christ will not be fixed upon you with approval.

It is a very hard thing always to be faithful with men on God's behalf. I know that it is so even in visiting the sick; one is tempted to begin to comfort some of them when they ought not to be comforted, to say very soft and gentle words to them because they are ill, when, perhaps, they have never felt their need of a Saviour, and never been awakened to any sense of spiritual need. I remember one who was greatly condemned for the action that he thought it right to take. Two or three of us had been to see a sick and dying man, and he always welcomed the visitors, and we prayed with him, and told him the Gospel, but we were all under the impression that we had produced no effect whatever upon his mind, and that he was passing into another world without any knowledge of his lost estate, and without any repentance or faith in Christ. The good man to whom I refer,—he is now in heaven, but I well remember the reproach that he suffered for what he did,—he stood at the foot of the bed, and he said, "Friend, you are a deceived man; you are dying, and you have no well-grounded hope. You always say, 'Yes, yes, yes,' to all we say; but my inmost thought of you is that you are without God, and without hope, and if you die as you are, you will be lost for ever." The man's wife was thunderstruck, so was he; but when we went to visit him the next day, you should have seen the change that God had wrought in him. There was a broken-hearted man crying for mercy, a man in sore trouble and distress of soul. The faithful messenger of God had told him the naked truth; it pained him to do it, but he had been more faithful to the sick man than others who had spoken very kindly to him. Oh, I believe, if we are faithful, so that we are clear of the blood of all men, faithful to the truth, faithful to our own consciences, faithful to the consciences of those with whom we have to deal, then we are among the number of whom the text says, "Mine eyes shall be upon the faithful of the land, that they may dwell with me."

Have you and I been faithful to our own children, and faithful to our own parents? Wives, have you been faithful to your own husbands about their souls? Do you not think that some of us might go home to-night, and pour out floods of tears before God as we confess, "No, we have not been faithful as we should have been to what we know of the Gospel, and to those to whom we were bound to teach it"? Christ has a special eye of love for those who are faithful in their dealings with God, faithful in their dealings with man, and faithful in their dealings with the souls of men on God's behalf. Oh, that we may be amongst that happy company!

Then, observe that these faithful men are *thorough in all that they do*. If you read the second part of our text, you will see that the Psalmist also says, "He that walketh in a perfect way, he shall serve me." May I be permitted to say, especially to you who are commencing the Christian life, that if you wish to live near to God, and to be greatly used of him, it is important that you should begin as you mean to go on, by endeavouring to walk in a perfect way? There are some who trifle at first with their own convictions. I cannot help quoting myself, at the risk of being called egotistical. When I was converted to the Lord Jesus Christ, and made to rejoice in him, I read the New Testament for myself. I had no friend, and no relative, who was a baptized believer; I come of a stock in which infant baptism has been long religiously observed. I read the Scriptures, and I saw there that the believer only was to be baptized. That truth came to my conscience; but the suggestion which came to me from friends was, "Well, it really is a pity to introduce this matter, for all those around you think differently." I have never ceased to thank God that I was thoroughly honest to my convictions about the ordinance.

Do any of you think it a trifle? Very well, waive that point for the moment ; but when a man is not honest to his convictions about a trifle, the next thing is that he is not honest to his convictions about something else, and so he gets off the lines ; and if you begin to go a little aside, for the sake of peace, or to prevent disturbance, or to please your friends, you have taken a way of life which will lead you I cannot tell where. Be you determined that, if others do as they please, you are not accountable for their action ; but you will do what you believe to be right. If you are a Christian, go through with it ; be a follower of Christ in every respect as far as the Word of God and your own conscience lead you. I found that the habit of beginning to think for myself, and to follow my convictions was useful to me, and it has been useful to me to this day ; and at this moment, before the living God, I am able to stand on my own feet, to lean neither on this man nor on that, but only on that eternal arm which will support any man and every man who, in the sight of God, determines to follow the truth wherever it may lead him.

Now, I earnestly pray every Christian person here, especially in the beginning of life, to look well to this matter, for the joy of your life, the peace of your life, the inward rest of your life, will much depend under God upon your being faithful to your convictions in every point as God shall help you. The great King himself seems to say to-night, "Mine eyes shall be upon the faithful of the land, that they may dwell with me: he that walketh in a perfect way, he shall serve me. He is the man whom I will pick out for my servant. I will put him here, or I will place him there, where I am unable to station some others because they are not clear and straight in their conduct, and because they are not to be depended upon for loyal obedience to their Lord and Master."

But now, secondly, I want to answer this question, WHAT WILL THE KING DO WITH THEM? David says, "Mine eyes shall be upon the faithful of the land," and David's Son, the Lord Jesus Christ, says the same. What does he mean?

Well, first, *his eye of search will seek them out.* That dear brother who is faithful to God is only a young apprentice; but he has been faithful in not breaking the Sabbath. Nobody knows about him, dear young man, but the eyes of the Lord are upon him. There is a working-man who, the other day, in the midst of a swearing company, rebuked the blasphemer, and spoke up for Christ. That noble action is not recorded in the newspaper, and never will be; but God's eye is upon the faithful of the land. There is a poor woman who, the other day, lost a good deal by being straight and honest. No one will report it; nobody will put her down in the legion of honour. Aye, but God's eyes are upon the faithful of the land! And when you, through the grace of God, are led to follow Christ faithfully, quite alone, not wishing to be seen, doing in secret what only God himself knows, it is reward enough for you that the Lord Jesus Christ sees what you do, and he himself will one day reward you openly.

But there is more than that. When the King says, "Mine eyes shall be upon the faithful of the land," it means that *his eye of favour will cheer them.* The King would first search them out, and then he would bring them forward; he would promote their interests, he would see that the faithful men were not thrust into a corner and neglected, he would have an eye to cheering them as they had an eye to pleasing him. I believe that God greatly favours and blesses those whom, by his grace, he makes to be faithful. If you are unfaithful, your unfaithfulness will come home to you sometime or other; I mean, if you are a child of God, for there is discipline in the house of the Lord. I am not talking now about the punishments of the law; the children of God are not under the law; I am speaking about the discipline of the Gospel. You are saved; by free, rich, sovereign grace you are saved, and you are made a child of God. From the moment of your new birth you come under the discipline of the great Father's house; and if you are unfaithful, your unfaithfulness will deprive you of many a comfort and many a joy. It will dog your footsteps, and track you when you least expect it. Look at David. After his great sin, he was never the man that he had been before; and many were the griefs and pangs of heart which he brought upon himself by that one terrible fall. The Lord grant that we may be kept faithful, so that God's eye of approval may rest upon us, and that we may joy and rejoice in him from day to day!

But then the text, after saying, "Mine eyes shall be upon the faithful of the land," adds, "that they may dwell with me." *The faithful shall dwell with God.* Oh, this is a choice privilege! When grace makes a man faithful, God rewards his faithfulness by permitting him to dwell in close communion with his Lord. It is a wonderful thing to me that, if we have any good works, God always works them in us, and then he rewards us for them as if they were our own. He gives us grace, and then smiles on us because of the grace that he himself gives. So, if he makes a man faithful, he then rewards him for it according to his grace, and says, "He shall dwell with me."

I think I see David carrying out this resolution. There is a poor but honest man away down there in Bethlehem; and David hears of his strict integrity, and sends him a letter. "Come to Jerusalem," says the king, "I will make a courtier of you, I will make a friend of you. You are the sort of man I want, come and dwell with me." He hears of another poor man, over yonder, who has been ridiculed because he stood up for Jehovah, the God of Israel, when others were inclined to worship some false god. "Come up to Jerusalem," says he, "come to live with me. You are my sort of company, for you are one of the faithful ones." Now, that is what the Lord Jesus Christ says to us. He calls us as sinners, but he communes with us as saints. He washes us when we are guilty; but after we are washed, and he has made us upright in his sight, then he takes us to dwell with him, he delights in opening his heart to us, and in permitting us to open our heart to him.

Now, if any of you are not faithful to Christ, I can tell you that you will not be able to commune with him. If you have done a wrong thing in business, or if you have held your tongue, and not been faithful in testifying for Christ, when you go on your knees at night, you will not be able to find yourself so led out in prayer as you were before when you were true to him. And when you turn to the Scriptures, instead of finding them speaking to you, they will seem as if they were dumb, no voice of comfort will come from them. But if you have been faithful and true, and out and out for Christ, then you shall dwell with him, you shall abide in him, and his word shall abide in you.

Then it is added, "he shall serve me." *The faithful shall be Christ's servants.* I do not know which is the greater privilege, "He shall dwell with me," or, "He shall serve me." Perhaps the second is the higher. Have you ever thought, beloved friend, what an honour it is to be permitted to do anything for God? For God to bless us, is great condescension on his part; but for him to permit us to be of any use to him, this is a wonderful honour from his right hand. I believe that there is more honour in being allowed, for the glory of God, to teach a little Sunday-school child the way of salvation, than there would be in ruling the whole German Empire if it was done for the glorification of self. The honour does not lie in the act so much as in the motive; and if the motive be, "I did it unto the Lord," then I stand in the same rank with angels, ay, in a line with those wonderful living creatures that John saw in the Revelation, who reveal the glory of God and continually do him service.

The Lord will not have you as his servant if you are not faithful, if you do not give yourself up to the truth and to be true through and through. It is not God's way to send forth his truth by untruthful men. If there is a lie in thy left hand, the truth in thy right hand will seem to have lost at least half its power. Like the hoard of Achan hidden away in the tent, which robbed all Israel of the victory at the gates of Ai, so will you find that anything which is untrue, hidden away in your life or your conduct, will deprive you of victory when you go out in the service of God. "He shall serve me," says Christ; and he will not accept the service of those who are not true to him.

Thus I have spoken of a very necessary practical truth, and I am going to close by trying to answer one more question, HOW MAY WE GET AMONG THESE FAITHFUL ONES?

Perhaps we can truly say, God helping us, we hope that we are among them. If so, as we read, "it is he that hath made us, and not we ourselves." If there be any faithfulness, if there be any uprightness, unto God be the glory of it all. Pray that you may never lose your faithfulness, but that you may be kept even unto the end. Remember that passage in Jude's Epistle, "Now unto him that is able to guard you from stumbling." So it is in the Revised Version, and it is an improvement and nearer to the original than our old text; for while it is a great mercy to be kept from falling, it is a still greater favour to be guarded from stumbling, so as to walk with careful, steady progress in uprightness before God all your life.

But now I speak to others who are not as yet faithful. You say, "How are we to get among the faithful?" Well, I should say, first, so far as you may be, and so far as your light goes, be faithful to-night, *be honest in confessing sin.* Before you sleep, put yourself before God just as you are. Have you hitherto neglected religion? Confess it. Or have you pretended to possess religion when there was no truth in your profession? Confess it. What has been your sin? Confess it. Kneel by your bedside, and there, God alone seeing you, unveil your heart before him. You say that he knows all about you; that is true, and that is a reason why you should be the more explicit in your confession to him. Speak freely to God, and make him, as you ought to make him, your only "Father Confessor." Tell him that you are lost, tell him that you are hard-hearted, tell him that you are unfeeling, tell him that you desire to be converted, but that it is only a faint desire as yet, tell him all about yourself; in a word, begin to deal with God on the straight. If you have not done so already, I pray God that you may do so to-night, and I beseech you to go as far as you can in this matter. Reveal your poverty, your filthiness, your sin, your nakedness, your desert of hell; only do all honestly, as in the sight of God. What a wonderful thing it is that men do not like to act thus; yet, when the grace of God enables them to do it, they are already on the road to salvation. When the man comes before God, with a rope round his neck, confessing that he deserves to die, then there is this blessed text to comfort him, "If we confess our sins, he is faithful and just to forgive us our sins, and to cleanse us from all unrighteousness."

Well, then, next, *be anxious to have a new heart and a right spirit.* May God make you thus anxious to-night! Remember that there is evil in us by nature. "All have sinned, and come short of the glory of God." "The heart is deceitful above all things, and desperately wicked;" and before we can be faithful we must be born again. No man will ever be true until the God of truth has truly renewed him. Our tendency is to lean either this way or that; to stand upright is a gift of divine grace, and none but the Holy Spirit can bestow it upon us. Oh, that we might have a deep anxiety to undergo that wondrous change, that radical and total change of heart which the Saviour described when he said to Nicodemus, "Ye must be born again"! Go to the Lord with David's prayer, "Create in me a clean heart, O God; and renew a right spirit within me." Plead that Old Testament promise, "A new heart also will I give you, and a new spirit will I put within you: and I will take away the stony heart out of your flesh, and I will give you an heart of flesh."

Then, supposing that you have come thus far, I earnestly entreat you, if you would be found among the faithful of the land, *be sincere in all your dealings with the living God.* If you mean to pray, do pray; if you believe in Jesus, do not simply say that you believe, but believe; if you repent, do not merely talk of repentance, but repent. Let everything be thorough and downright. May the Spirit of God save you from getting the imitation of spirituality, which will damn you, and may he give you the reality of spiritual life, which will effectually save you!

I believe that there are many who are very much injured by being led to profess religion when they do not possess it. There is a Revival meeeting, there is a room for converts, they get in there, they are pressed, they are exhorted, they are entreated, they think that they are sincere; in a certain measure they are, but there is no sense of guilt, no loathing of sin, no true repentance, no wounding, and hence no healing, no stripping, and hence no clothing. The whole thing is but a mere sham; and they go away, and are themselves deceived, and afterwards return to their old sins, and are worse than they were before. If you have not eternal life, do not pretend that you have it. I charge you before God, who shall judge the quick and the dead, in the day of his appearing, never cheat yourself in this matter, for you are the only person that you can really cheat for long. God himself you never can deceive. Make clear, clean, sharp, distinct, decided work of this matter; or rather, may God the Holy Ghost work this miracle of mercy in you, for Christ's name's sake!

Lastly, if thou wouldst be among the faithful of the land, *depend continually upon the Lord Jesus and his Word* to make and keep thee faithful. Every day wait upon him for fresh anointing and renewed power; and daily live unto him, and for him, laying thyself out to honour him who has redeemed thee. Thy only hope is in his precious blood; then let the object of thy existence be to glorify him alone. If this be so, thou shalt be among the faithful of the land, and thou shalt dwell with the King, even with the King of kings, and thou shalt serve him for ever and ever.

Are you not glad to hear this, you great sinners? Jesus is as able to pardon you now as he was to save the dying thief; and you who have hard hearts, he is able to give you new ones to-day, as he gave them to those of old. And oh, you children of God, I pray you, do not act as if David had a great God, and you had a little God! Do not act as if, in the trials of the olden times, God made bare his arm, and that now he will hardly put out his little finger. Do not treat him as if it could be so. God still hears prayer; if he does not work miracles, he does the same thing in some other way which is even better. He delivers us still; he feeds us still; he leads us still; he guards us still; he is the same as ever he was.

Oh, if you would but trust him! Abraham's God is your God, and he can help you in the day of battle. Joshua's God is your God, and he says to you, as he did to Joshua, "I will not fail thee, nor forsake thee." Oh, do believe it! Jesus Christ, my grandfather's Jesus Christ, my father's Jesus Christ, is my Jesus Christ. Look back on all the godly people you have ever known, and think of what the Lord did for them, and then remember that his arm is not shortened, his ear is not heavy, his love is not diminished, his wisdom is not turned to foolishness. He is still able and willing to bless you, as in all the ages that have gone by. Trust him, ye saints; trust him, ye sinners; and the Lord bless you all, for Jesus Christ's sake!

XVI

OUR HEAVENLY FATHER'S PITY

"Like as a father pitieth his children, so the Lord pitieth them that fear him."—Psalm 103: 13.

WHAT a blow this is for pride! Then, God's children are pitiable objects; notwithstanding that he hath crowned them with glory and honour; hath given them perfection in Christ Jesus; hath breathed into them the breath of spiritual life; hath set their feet upon a rock, and established their goings; yet they are, and they ever will be, so long as they are here below, pitiable objects. It is like tolling the death-knell of all our pride, to talk about God pitying us.

Why, my brethren, we shed our pity profusely upon the ungodly; we are often pitying the wicked, the profane, the blasphemer, and Sabbath-breaker; but here we find God pitying us. Even David, the mighty psalmist, is pitied; a prophet, a priest, a king, each of these shall have pity from God, for "he pitieth them that fear him," and finds good reasons for pitying them, however high their station, however holy their character, or however happy their position. We are pitiable beings. Oh! boast not, believer; be not thou loud in praise of thyself; put thy finger on thy lips, and be silent when thou hearest that God pities thee. The next time carnal security would creep in, or fleshly conceit would get the upper hand of thee, remember that, whilst thou art boasting, God is pitying; and whilst thou art triumphing, he is looking down upon thee with a pitying eye of compassion, for he findeth reason for compassion, when thou canst only see cause for glorying.

Our subject then, will be a review; a review of our lives, if we are the Lord's children, and fear him. I hope it will be profitable to us; it will not be profitable through the newness of the thoughts, but rather by "stirring up your pure minds by way of remembrance," to look back upon all the way whereby the Lord your God hath led you. "Like as a father pitieth his children, so the Lord pitieth them that fear him."

Notice THE DISPLAYS OF THIS PITY: "Like as a father pitieth his children, so the Lord pitieth them that fear him." When does a father display his pity towards his child? I answer,— on many and divers occasions.

Sometimes, *the father's pity is bestowed upon the child's ignorance.* He himself knoweth a thing, which to his child is a profound mystery; he himself knoweth a certain truth, which is to him an axiom and an element of his knowledge; but to his child it seemeth like the apex of the pyramid of knowledge, he wondereth how he can ever attain to so high a pitch of learning. And, oh, how foolish are the child's surmises! How long he is guessing at truth, and how mistaken are the axioms which he founds upon his mistakes of thought! And how the father pities the child if he falls among bad companions, who teach him errors; who, instead of filling his mind with truth, fill it with falsehood! When he cometh to his father with all those strange stories, with which wicked men have filled his little ears, the father pities him, that he should be so ignorant as to be carried away by every wind of tattling, that he should receive every talker into his confidence, and believe everything because man hath said it; taking every man's opinion, and believing what any man declares to be right!

So, when, in the plenitude of our supposed wisdom, we think ourselves infallible, God looketh down on our wisdom as being childish folly; when, in the glory of our wondrous eloquence, we talk great things, God looketh down upon us as upon the prattler, who talketh fast, but talketh foolishly. And, often, when we come before our fellows, and spread before them wondrous discoveries that we have made, he that sitteth in the heavens doth not laugh in derision, but he smileth in compassion, that we should think ourselves so wise in having discovered nothing, and so supremely learned in having found out untruths.

And how God must pity his dear family when he finds them led astray by false doctrine and error! How many there are of God's people, who go up to houses of prayer, so-called, where, instead of hearing the truths of the Kingdom of Heaven, they are taught all kinds of strange things; where they hear "another gospel, which is not another, but there be some that trouble them;" where all the isms and fancies of man are preached, instead of the truth of God, in all its discrimination, in all its power, in all its constancy and everlastingness, and the power of its application to the soul by the Spirit of God is sought for. How God pities some of his children, who are thus led astray! One of them, perhaps, says of their minister, "Is he not intellectual? Is he not a wonderful minister? Though he said nothing about Jesus Christ, to-day, yet it was such a clever discourse! It is true, he did not preach God's Gospel; but, then, see how beautifully he cleared up that point of metaphysics! It is quite certain that he did not lead me to hold more fellowship with my Redeemer; but then how excellent was that distinction which he drew between those two similar terms which he employed! I never heard a man so clever as my own minister; I cannot go and hear any of those vulgar preachers who talk to their hearers in a way that servant girls and mechanics can understand."

God pities his children when they are in this position. He does not pity them when they hear the truth,—when they have real Gospel fare, however roughly the meat may be carved, and however it may be served up on the coarsest platter that human speech can supply. He pities them not, when they get such spiritual food as that; but he does pity them when they are misguided; when they are carried away by "philosophy, falsely so called;" being misled by the seeming wisdom of man, which, after all, is but folly, having nought of wisdom in it; the highest wisdom being that of believing what God has said; receiving God's truth simply as God's truth, and asking no questions about it. God pities his children, however, in all their ignorance; he is not angry with them, nor doth he speak sharply to them; but he leadeth them on by his Spirit, until they understand his truth, and receive his Word.

It were well, however, if there were nothing else but ignorance to bear with; but the parent often has something worse than that to suffer from his child, he has to endure *the frowardness and waywardness of human nature.* There is the continual uprising of evil passions; the perpetual proneness to disobedience; the frequent wandering from the path of righteousness; and, oftentimes, the father has to pass that by with, perhaps, just a little admonition, but without a frown, without a sharp word, without a blow; he has to say. "My child it is all forgiven you;" and though his temper may be sorely tried, yet he has patience with his child, for he pities the child's froward-ness; he knows, too, that he was once a child himself, and then he did the same as his child is now doing; and, therefore, doth he have patience with his child, and he pities him. My brethren, what pity has the Lord had upon you and me, in all our wanderings! How often have we gone astray; and yet, compared with our wanderings, how seldom had we been chastised! How frequently have we broken his command-ments, and rebelled against his covenant; and yet how light have been the strokes of chastisement, compared with the weight of our guilt; and how seldom hath he afflicted us, compared with the frequency of our transgressions! How hath he had patience with all our shortcomings, and hath bidden his hand be still, when, if it had been like ours, it would have risen in hot anger to smite us to the dust! Truly, he hath pitied us, "like as a father pitieth his children," only with a far greater patience. Even as he is himself infinitely greater than all earthly fathers, so hath his pity been more continuous, more patient, and more longsuffering, than the pity of any human parent who has ever breathed.

And as a father pitieth his child, not only in all his froward-ness, but *in all his actual transgressions, and downright sin,* when he grows from the mere wish to do evil up to the actual com-mission of the crime,—like as a father still pitieth his child, even when his follies have ripened into the worst of guilt, so hath God pitied us when we have gone into gross sin before our conversion; aye, and some of us even after it. When we have gone astray like lost sheep, have broken the hedges of his commands, and have gone rambling over the dark hills of transgression, still hath he had pity upon us. It is amazing how far a father's pity will go towards his child, even when he has transgressed never so much. There are some who have shut the door in their children's faces, and bidden them never enter their house again, nor come near them; they have ceased to speak of them, for they have determined that they would never take their names on their lips again, nor consider them their children. But such fathers are, I trust, very few in number; it is rarely that we meet with them. A father usually endureth much, and endureth long. After he hath had the peace of his home destroyed, and his grey hairs almost brought with sorrow to the tomb; after his family has been made a wreck, and he has lost almost everything he had, by the profligacy of his son,—still his love, tenacious to the last, holdeth to his boy, and will not let him go. And even when others speak harshly of him, the old man palliates his son's guilt,—perhaps a little foolishly; but if he can find an excuse for him, he does; he will not have it that his son is worse than others, and he will allow no man to make his son's guilt appear greater than it is; but he will, as far as he can, try to make it seem less.

Our Heavenly Father is not foolishly pitiful, but he is pitiful. Aye, and he is better than that; he is wisely pitiful over the most erring of his children. Our God is constant in his affection, and merciful towards his children; when they go astray, he pities all their guilt and sin. It is true, he takes the rod into his hand, and sometimes causes them to weep bitterly by reason of the soreness of his chastisement. He applieth the rod to their very soul, and bringeth the iron into their inmost spirit; he maketh them smart, and cry, and groan, and sigh; but all he doth is in pity, because he is determined to save them. He will not let them go unpunished, because he pities them for their folly and their sin. Just as the physician will not let the man go without his medicine, because he pities him in his disease; so God will not let his children go without his chastisement, because he pities them in their sin. And mark, too, even that chastisement is one of pity; there is not one twig too many in the rod, nor one stroke over the right number, not one drop of gall too much, and that drop is none too bitter; the affliction is all measured out, and weighed in balances and scales, all given as it should be,—no more than there is a needs-be for. God pitieth his children in all their chastisement, and pitieth them in all their guilt and wanderings; and he will not let them go away from him altogether, nor will he suffer them to perish, for he pities them still.

God also pities his children *in sickness*; that is a time when a father pities his children very much. It does not say, "Like as a mother pitieth her children, so the Lord pitieth them that fear him;" and I think the reason is this; not because a mother's pity is less intense, and less affectionate,—for it is more so, by far,—but because it is sometimes less effectual than the father's.

A mother may pity her child, yet she may not be able to preserve it from an enemy. The mother may pity her child when it is sick, but she may be alone in the house, and she may not be able to travel far enough to find a physician; and, therefore, God has put in, not merely the affection, but the strength of pity: "Like as a father pitieth his children, so the Lord pitieth them that fear him." On the bed of sickness, the strength of pity is proved by Christ upon God's people. He does not stand, as the mother would, to weep over the child, but he does more than that; he does give true compassion, he does sympathize; but, more than that, he heals! He makes the wounded spirit whole; he removes the aching pain from the conscience, binds up the broken heart, makes the weak to be strong, and the faint one to rejoice! He gives us the strength of pity; and some of us can remember that strength of pity when, in our sickness, we lay tossing in our beds, with hardly power to pray; when we said our heart and our flesh had failed us, and we must die; when our brain was racked with discordant thoughts, and reason seemed to have left its throne, and blank despair held carnival within our brain, which, for a while, was under the dominion of the Lord of Misrule, and revelry was kept up there perpetually. It was then, when we could do nothing, that Jesus came to us, not merely with the faint whispers of compassion, but with the strong voice of healing, bade our fears be still, comforted our aching heart, and then made our flesh leap for joy, because our spirit, its twin-sister, which had been broken on the wheel, was delivered from the tormentor, and made perfectly whole.

And your Heavenly Father pities you who are his children under all your *manifold trials*, of whatever kind they are, and from whatever quarter they proceed. Thus, when persecuted, you have had his pity; when the jeer and taint of the ungodly have been cast upon you; and when worse than that has been attempted against your person. When you have had to bear the brunt of poverty, you have had God's pity shed upon you; and you have had a pity, too, that was not barely that of words, you have had the pity of help; he has given you your bread in your extremity, and made your water sure when the brook was dry. Ye who have lost your friends, and have had to weep over numerous bereavements; ye who have mourned

over your family, who have been swept away one after another;
not once have you been bereaved without the pity of your God;
never once has the clay fallen on the coffin lid, with the sad
message, "Ashes to ashes, dust to dust," without the pity of
your God falling on your heart, like gentle dew from heaven.
He hath ever pitied thee in thy low estate; he hath been ever
with thee in all thy varied troubles, and hath never left thee.
"'Mid scenes of confusion, and creature complaints," he hath
kept by thy side, and led thee all thy journey through; and
here thou canst raise thine Ebenezer, and write the words of
our text upon it, "Like as a father pitieth his children, so the
Lord pitieth them that fear him, and he hath pitied me up to
this hour."

Yet once more, sometimes God's people have wrongs; and a
father pities his children, *if they have wrongs that are unrevenged.*
I know a father, who sometimes says, "If you strike me, you
may strike me again, and I will turn to you the other cheek,
and you may smite me as long as you please. But," says that
good man, and he is a peace man, too; like myself, a thorough
peace man, though a little inconsistent, "strike my children,
and I will knock you down, if I can! I will not have you meddle
with them. If you hit me, I will not resist you; you may do
what you please with me; but if you smite my children, that
I never can endure. I love them so, that I should break
through every principle to resent it; so strong is my natural
affection for them, that though I might conceive myself to be
wrong in what I did, I should do it, most certainly." Depend
upon it, there is nothing brings a man's wrath up like touching
his children; and the same thing is true of God. You may
curse him, and he will not be so wroth with you as if you touch
his children. The prophet Zechariah declared to his ancient
people, "He that toucheth you, toucheth the apple of his eye."
If any of you want to know the shortest road to damnation, I
will tell it to you; despise God's little ones; treat God's people
ill, and you will damn yourself by express. Remember our
Lord's words, "But whoso shall offend one of these little ones
which believe in me, it were better for him that a millstone were
hanged about his neck, and that he were drowned in the depth
of the sea."

There never was a wrong done to one of God's people that

God did not avenge; there has never been an ill deed done towards them yet but he hath punished the doer of it. Though he suffered Assyria to break Israel in pieces, yet let Assyria speak, when she riseth from her tomb, and tell how terribly God hath shivered her with a rod of iron, because she vaunted herself against the people of the Most High. Let old Rome testify that on her still rests the blood of the martyrs. Behold, our God hath broken her empire in pieces; the Roman emperor has ceased to exist, and his gaudy pomp is gone; aye, and modern Rome, too, hath an awful doom yet to come; she, above all other cities, hath a fearful future before her; she, that is wrapt in scarlet, and sitteth on the seven hills, the whore of Babylon, drunk with the blood of the saints, shall yet meet the doom foretold in the Revelation. Lo! God hath said it; she shall be rent in pieces, she shall be burnt with fire and utterly consumed.

And now I want you briefly to notice THE SPIRIT OF GOD'S PITY.

There are different sorts of pity. Some I would not have at any price whatever. Did you ever see *the pity of contempt*? Have you not often seen a gentleman watching a poor man doing something or other, and then saying to him, "Poor fellow, I do pity you"? Have you never seen a very respectable aristocrat, who has never heard anything but the most "proper" kind of preaching, turn on his heel, and go out of a chapel door, saying, "Well, I do pity people who can listen to such stuff as that"? We have often seen that pity of contempt. But that is not God's kind of pity; he never pities his people in the way of contempt; a father never so pities his children. Sometimes, when a boy is writing a copy, a stranger goes through the school, and says, "Well, he is an ignoramus;" and he pities him, perhaps; but there is a sneer with his pity. But the lad's father comes into the room; the boy has just got into pot-hooks and hangers, and the father thinks he makes them very well for such a little boy. He pities him, perhaps, that he is not able to write better, but there is no contempt with his pity. Nor is there any contempt with God's pity; he sees what we are, and pities us, but there is not a solitary grain of contempt for any of his people in his pity.

Other people's pity is *the pity of inaction*. "Oh, I do pity you

very much!" says a person to a sick woman; "your husband is
dead, your children have to be supported, and you have to work
hard. Well, my good woman, I pity you very much; but I
cannot afford to give you anything; I have so many calls
upon me." How much pity there is of that kind in the world!
You can get pity of that sort, in abundance. If you lift the
knocker of the first door you come to, you will get plenty of
pity of that kind; pity is the cheapest thing in the world, if
that is all. But God's pity is not pity of that sort; it is not the
pity which is mere pity, it is not the pity of inaction; but,
when his heart moves, his hand moves too, and he relieveth all
the wants of those he pities.

And let me say, again, God's pity is not *the pity of mere
sensitiveness*. The other day, a gentleman, talking of accidents,
said, in my hearing, "I saw a boy running down a lane, where
a cab was coming at a very rapid rate; I saw that the boy must
be crushed under the horse's feet, or under the wheels; I stood
for a moment thunderstruck, and then I saw him crushed to
pieces under the wheels! I ran down the next street in a moment;
I was so sensitive, I could not bear the sight." Instead of seeing
what help he could give, he ran away. "Yet," he said, "I did
not do that from any want of sympathy, or any lack of pity;
and when I stopped myself, I thought it useless to go back,
for I am so sensitive that I naturally avoid every sight of
misery." That is not God's way of showing pity; his pity is
not the pity of the stranger who ran away. If that had been
his own boy, he would have stopped, and seen what was the
matter, and tried to render assistance; but God's pity is the
pity of the father; it is not the pity of the mere sensation of the
moment, but the pity which desires to do something to relieve
his children in distress.

> "*The pity of the Lord,*
> *To those that fear his name,*
> *Is such as tender parents feel;*
> *He knows our feeble frame.*"

Then, tried believer, take your case before your God to-night
in prayer. He is a God of pity, and not a God of mere pity.
Go to him now if you are poor; tell him all your care, and see

if he will not help you. Go and tell him that your spirit is depressed, and see if he will not cheer you; tell him that your way is hedged up, and that you cannot find your path, and see if he will not direct you. Tell him you are ignorant, and know nothing, and see if he will not teach you; tell him you have fallen, and see if he will not set you on your feet, take you by the arm, and teach you to go; tell him you are black by reason of your falls, and see if he will not wash and cleanse you; tell him that you cut yourself against a stone when you fell, and see if he will not bathe your sores; tell him you are distressed because you have sinned, and see if he will not kiss you with the kisses of his love, and tell you he has forgiven you. Go and try him, for his pity is a heavenly pity; it is the very nard of Paradise, that healeth sores effectually.

I close, by noticing THE PEOPLE WHOM GOD PITIES. Who are the objects of God's pity? "The Lord pitieth *them that fear him.*"

Some of you, he does not pity at all; you that do not fear him, but trifle with him,— you that hate him,—you that despise him,—you that are careless about him,—you that never think of him,—you have none of his pity. When you are sick, he looks upon your sickness as something that you deserve; when you go astray, he looks upon your wandering as a mere matter of course of your guilty nature; and he is angry with you,— wrathful with you. Your afflictions are not strokes of his rod, they are cuts of his sword; your sins are not things that he overlooks; but if you die as you now are, guilty and unsaved, remember that, even when you are cast away by God, justice shall look upon you with a tearless eye, and say to you, "Ye knew your duty, but ye did it not." And the stern voice of God shall, because you have been desperately guilty, drive you away from his presence for ever. Think not that this text will afford you any consolation in this life, or in that which is to come. Ye shall not have even a drop of water to cool your tongues in hell; no pity shall be shed upon you there. If you could have pity bestowed upon you in the regions of your punishment, it might fall like a shower of gentle rain upon your tongues. But God bestoweth no pity upon you that love him not, and fear him not, and turn not from the error of your ways.

Oh, that you would but fear him! Would to God that he would make you fear him now! Oh, that ye would tremble at his presence; and, then, oh, that ye could know yourselves to be his children, and fear him as children do their parents! Oh, that ye did reverence his name, and keep his Sabbaths! Oh, that ye did obey his commandments, and have his fear ever before your eyes! Then should your peace be like a river, and your righteousness like the waves of the sea. Oh, that you were wise to bow yourselves before him, and to confess your guiltiness! Oh, that you would come, "just as you are, without one plea," to Jesus Christ! Oh, that you were stripped of every rag of self-righteousness, and clothed in the righteousness of Christ! Then you would have Christ as your Saviour, and you might rejoice that, henceforth, he would pity you in all your sicknesses, and in all your wanderings; he would pity you here, and at last lead you up to be where pity shall be unneeded, in the land of the blessed, in the home of the hereafter, where the weary rest, and the wicked cease from troubling.

But they do not cease from trouble; in hell, they are troubled without pity. Seeing that they would not turn at God's reproof, and would not heed his warnings, but cast his truth behind their back; seeing that, being often reproved, they hardened their necks, they were therefore, "suddenly destroyed, and that without remedy." Seeing that they have destroyed themselves; seeing that they have rejected the invitations of the Gospel; seeing that they have despised the Son of God; seeing that they have loved their own righteousness better than Christ's, and preferred hell to heaven, the penalties of iniquity to the reward of the righteous; therefore, without pity, they shall be shut away, for ever, from the regions of happiness, and banished from the presence of him who pitieth them that fear him, but punisheth them that fear him not. The Lord save us all from such a terrible doom as that, for Jesus' sake!

XVII

"THERE *IS* FORGIVENESS"

"But there is forgiveness with thee, that thou mayest be feared."—Psalm 130: 4.

HAVE you noticed the verse which comes before the text? It runs thus, "If thou, Lord, shouldest mark iniquities, O Lord, who shall stand?" That is a confession. Now, confession must always come before absolution. "If we confess our sins, he is faithful and just to forgive us our sins." If we try to cloak our sin, "if we say that we have no sin, we deceive ourselves, and the truth is not in us," and no pardon can come from God to us. Therefore, plead guilty, plead guilty. Thou oughtest to do it, for thou art guilty. Thou wilt find it wisest to do it, for this is the only way to obtain mercy. Cast thyself upon the mercy of thy Judge, and thou shalt find mercy; but first acknowledge that thou needest mercy. Be honest with thy conscience, and honest with thy God, and confess thine iniquity which thou hast done, and mourn over the righteousness to which thou hast not attained.

You notice that this confession is recorded with a kind of grave astonishment: "If thou, Lord, shouldest mark iniquities, O Lord, who shall stand?" This is as much as for the Psalmist to say, "I am sure that I cannot, and who can?" And if God shall deal with us according to our iniquities, where shall we stand, and who among us shall stand anywhere? I dare not stand to preach if God shall judge me according to my iniquities. You dare not stand to sing; what have you to do with singing if God is marking your iniquities? I wonder that men can stand at their counters, and stand at their work, while their sin is unforgiven. And then how shall we stand in the day of judgment? The best saint on earth, if he stands in his own righteousness alone, and is judged according to his own offences, why, the justice of God will blow him away like the chaff, or consume him as with a flame of fire.

It is a dreadful fact that this "if" is no "if" to those who are not believers in Christ, but it is a matter of terrible certainty. God does mark the iniquities of you who are unbelievers. Although as yet he does not visit them upon you, else you could not stand, yet he sees them, and he records them. All the transgressions of your past life are in the book of record, from which they never can be blotted except by one gracious hand. Would to God that you would accept pardon from that pierced hand! But, apart from that, your iniquities are engraved as in eternal brass, and in that day when the forgotten things shall be brought to light, all the sins that now lie at the bottom of the sea of time shall be cast up upon the shore, and all shall be seen, and every secret thing shall be set in the light of day, and every transgression and iniquity shall be revealed by the light of the great white throne, and the ungodly shall be punished for all their ungodly words and ungodly deeds and ungodly thoughts according to the rules of equity in that last day of assize. O sirs, God will mark iniquity, and then, who that is out of Christ shall be able to stand? Who that has never hidden in the riven Rock of Ages shall find any shelter then?

That third verse makes an appropriate preface to my text; it is the black thunder-cloud which I see written, as with the finger of God and with a lightning flash, the wonderful words we are now to consider, "But there is forgiveness with thee, that thou mayest be feared."

My first head is taken from the first word of the text: "But." Here is A WHISPER OF HOPE. "If thou, Lord, shouldest mark iniquities, O Lord, who shall stand? *But*"—Oh, the sweet music of that little word! It seems to come in when the terrible drum of alarm is being beaten, and the dreadful clarion of judgment is sounding forth. There is a pause with this word, "*But* there is forgiveness." It is a soft and gentle whisper from the lips of love: "*But* there is forgiveness."

This comes into the soul *after a full confession of sin*. When thou hast knelt down before God, and acknowledged thy transgressions and thy shortcomings, and thy heart is heavy, and thy soul is ready to burst with inward anguish, then mayest thou hear this gracious word, "But there is forgiveness." When, under a sense of sin, it seems as if the very fiends of hell were shrieking in thine ears because of the awful doom which is drawing near, when thou shalt be driven from hope and from the presence of God, then, when thou fallest on thy face, in the terror of thy soul because of thy iniquity, then comes this sweet word, "*But* there is forgiveness." It is all true which thy conscience tells thee, it is all true which the Word of God threatens concerning thee; then acknowledge that it is true, and bow thyself in the dust before God, and then thou shalt hear in thy soul, not only in thine ear but in thy heart, this blessed word, "But there is forgiveness."

Some of us remember when we first heard this word. When it came, it was to us like the clear shining after rain: "But there is forgiveness." Some of us were perhaps for weeks and months without any knowledge of this blessed truth, pining for it, hungering for it; and when the Lord brought it home with power into our hearts by the Holy Ghost, oh, there was no music like it! Angels could not sing any tune so sweet as these words spoken to our hearts by the Holy Ghost, "But there is forgiveness." Go thy way, my hearer, and confess before God all thy sin. I will not say what it has been. Peradventure, thou hast lived for many years in the pursuit of sinful pleasures; thou hast been dominated by thine own will, thou hast tried to be lord and master, or queen and mistress, of thine own wicked spirit, and thou hast done evil even as they couldst, and thou art sensible of thy sin, and thy wounds bleed before God because of it. Well, then, in comes this whisper of hope: "But there is forgiveness." God make it as sweet to thee to hear it as it is to me to tell of it!

This whisper of hope sometimes comes to the soul by the Spirit of God *as the result of observation.* A man, full of sin, thinks to himself, "Well, but others also have been full of sin, yet they have been forgiven. What if I have been a blasphemer and injurious? Yet so was Saul of Tarsus, and he had forgiveness from the Lord. What if I have been a thief? Yet so was he who hung upon the cross, and that day was with his Lord in Paradise. What if I have been a fallen woman, and have been defiled with sin? Yet there is forgiveness, for she was forgiven who was a sinner, and came and washed Christ's feet with her tears, and wiped them with the hairs of her head, loving much because she had much forgiven. What, even if I have been an adulterer? Yet such as David. What if I have been a

persecutor? Yet such was Manasseh. Into whatsoever sin I may
have fallen, I observe that others like me have been snatched
from these horrible pits, and why should not I be?" I would
whisper this message into the ear of anybody here who is
conscious of sin. If thou wilt but look about thee, thou wilt see
others like thyself who have been washed, and cleansed, and
sanctified. Some of them are on earth, and many more of them
are in heaven, who have washed their robes, and made them
white in the blood of the Lamb. Sweet, then, is this whisper of
hope arising out of observation of others: "But there is forgiveness."

This whisper comes also *in opposition to the voice of despair*,
for despair says to a soul under a sense of sin, "There is no
mercy for you; you have sinned beyond all limits, your death-
warrant is signed, the verdict has been given against you, there
remains nothing for you but everlasting burnings." Nay, soul,
God's Word against thy word any day! God's Word says,
"There is forgiveness." Nothing can destroy despair except a
message from God himself, and this passage is like a huge hammer to break in sunder the gates of brass and dash in pieces the
bars of iron: "There is forgiveness." "All manner of blasphemy
shall be forgiven unto men." In the greatness of his heart,
Jehovah declares that he delighteth in mercy, and this is the
song which went up to him in the old Jewish Church with many
a repetition, and is just as true to-day,—

> " *He his chosen race did bless*
> *In the wasteful wilderness:*
> *For his mercies shall endure,*
> *Ever faithful, ever sure,*

> " *He hath, with a piteous eye,*
> *Look'd upon our misery:*
> *For his mercies shall endure,*
> *Ever faithful, ever sure.*"

Thou hast not gone beyond his mercy; thou canst not go beyond
his mercy if thou wilt trust his Son. "There is forgiveness."
Let this whisper drive away despair. What a blessed whisper
it is! "There is forgiveness." "There is forgiveness." Let it
enter thy soul, and drive those grim ogres and hobgoblins of

despair away into the sea of forgetfulness. "There is forgiveness."

This whisper of hope is, further, *the answer even to conscience.*
When Mr. Conscience is really at work, he has a very terrible
voice. There is no lion in the thicket that roars like a truly
awakened conscience. Conscience says, "Thou didst know thy
duty, but thou didst not do it." Thou hast sinned away many
a day of grace, thou hast refused Gospel invitations, thou hast
striven against the light of nature and the light of God, thou
wilt go down to hell well deserving thy doom. When the millstone is about thy neck, to sink thee into the abyss, thou wilt
deserve to have it so, for thou hast earned all this for thyself
by thy iniquities. I will not seek to stifle conscience, nor ask
you to shut your ear to his voice. Let him speak; but still, dost
thou not hear between his roarings this sweet note as of a silver
harp, "But—but—but—but there is forgiveness?" O conscience, there is forgiveness! I am as guilty as thou sayest I am,
and much more guilty, for thou canst not see all the sin that I
have committed; "but there is forgiveness."

Let me go still further, and say that this whisper of hope is
an answer even to the law of God. The Ten Commandments are
like ten great cannons fully charged, and if we were, like the
rebels in India, tied to the muzzles of them, and blown to
pieces, it would be only what we well deserve; but just when
the fuse is lighted, and about to be applied, there rings out this
blessed word, "There is forgiveness. There is forgiveness."
The law says, "The soul that sinneth, it shall die;" and the
law knows no mercy, it cannot know any mercy. Sinai has never
yet yielded one drop of water to cool the parched tongue of a
guilty sinner. Never did a shower reach its craggy peaks; it is a
fire-mountain, and the thunder rolls over its summit, with the
sound of a trumpet exceeding loud and long, making all who
hear it to tremble. God, when he comes to judgment, must
judge according to justice; "but—but—but—but there is
forgiveness." There is another mountain beside Sinai. Ye have
not come unto Mount Sinai; but ye have come unto Mount
Zion. There is another Law-giver besides Moses; there is Jesus
the Son of God. There is another covenant besides the covenant
of works, there is a covenant of rich, free, sovereign grace, and
this is the essence of it, "There is forgiveness." Oh, that I could

convey that whisper into the ear of every sinner who is here! I can do that; but oh, that God the Holy Ghost would put it into his heart, that he might never forget, "There is forgiveness"!

Now I advance to my second division. In our text I see, besides the whisper of hope, AN ASSURANCE OF THE WORD OF GOD: "There is forgiveness with thee."

Dear friends, "there is forgiveness." Nature could never tell you this great truth. You may walk the cornfields at this moment, and see the bounty of God in the waving grain; but you cannot read forgiveness there. You may climb the hills, and see the beauty of the landscape; you may look upon silver streams that make glad the fields; but you cannot read forgiveness there. You can see the goodness of God to man, but not the mercy of God to sinners. But if you come to this Book, you can read it here.

Turn to the Old Testament, and you will see that *it reveals sacrifice,*—lambs, and bullocks, and goats. What did they all mean? They meant that there was a way of pardon through the shedding of blood; they taught men this, that God would accept of certain sacrifices on their behalf. Then turn to the New Testament, and there you will see it revealed more clearly still that God has accepted a sacrifice, the sacrifice which he himself gave, for "he spared not his own Son, but delivered him up for us all." In this Book you read how he can be "just, and the Justifier of him that believeth;" how he can be a just God and yet a Saviour; how he can forgive, and yet be just as righteous as if he punished and showed no mercy. This, in fact, is the revelation of the Gospel; this is what this Book was written to teach, to tell you that "God was in Christ reconciling the world unto himself, not imputing their trespasses unto them." Therefore we come to you, not merely with a hopeful whisper, but with a full, distinct, emphatic, unquestionable assurance, "There is forgiveness." "There is forgiveness."

Turn to this Word of God, and you will find *the certainty of forgiveness.* "I believe in the forgiveness of sins." What a grand article of the creed that is! Dost thou believe it? Then do not doubt, do not hesitate. "There is forgiveness." Thou must know that there is such a thing, or else thou wilt not be eager to seek for it. It is in vain to go in quest of a myth or a

peradventure; but here is a certainty for thee. "There is forgiveness." Doubt not of it; believe it to be so, and then seek
thou after it with all thy heart. "There is forgiveness." That
is a matter of certainty.

Notice, if you please, *the broad indefiniteness of the text:* "There
is forgiveness." It does not say, "There is forgiveness for this
sin or for that," but, "There is forgiveness." Where God draws
no limit, do not you draw any. If God sets the door wide open,
and says, "There is forgiveness," then come along, you sinners,
whoever you may be, from gaols and penitentiaries, come along
from your Pharisaic places of boasting and self-righteousness,
come along with you, for there is forgiveness even for you.
Ye rich, ye poor, ye learned, ye ignorant, ye that know nothing,
know at least this, "There is forgiveness." This text shuts out
nobody.

Notice, too, *the immediate presentness of the text.* Our version
has it, "There is forgiveness," but there is not even the verb in
the Hebrew. The translators put in the words, "There is," so
we are to read it, "There was forgiveness;" "There is forgiveness;" "There will be forgiveness as long as life lasts."
But I like it as it stands here. "There is forgiveness" to-night;
"there is forgiveness" now; "there is forgiveness" where thou
sittest, just as thou art, just now. Oh, that I could say it so as
to convince you of the truth of it, and give a grip, a squeeze of
my right hand, to each one of you; I would like to do it! O
do not despair, do not be bowed down any longer, "there is
forgiveness," there is forgiveness now!

And it is intended to have a *personality* about it. It is no use
telling anybody that there is forgiveness for other people, but
none for him. This text is made for you, and the preacher is
sent to proclaim this truth to you, for he is sent to preach as
far as he can to every creature under heaven. "There is forgiveness" for you, though you think there is none. Your
thoughts are not as God's thoughts; neither are your ways as
his ways. There is, there surely is, at this moment, forgiveness.
Oh, that you would prove it by an act of faith! The moment
thou believest in Christ, thy sins are all forgiven thee. Look
thou to him whom I would hold up before thee, as Moses held
up the brazen serpent on the pole, look, for there is life in a
look to him that died for guilty men.

Now I must go a little farther, and notice, in the text, A
DIRECTION OF WISDOM: "There is forgiveness with thee."
"With thee."

Hearest thou this, dear heart? Thou art shrinking from thy
God; thou art anxious to run away from him; *that is where the
forgiveness is*, with God. Where the offence went, from that
very place the forgiveness comes: "There is forgiveness with
thee." "Against thee, thee only, have I sinned," but, "there
is forgiveness with thee;" with the very God whom you have
offended. It is with God in such a way that *it is part of his
nature.* "He delighteth in mercy." "God is love." He glorifies
himself by passing by transgression, iniquity, and sin. There is
forgiveness with God; it is in God's very nature that it lies.
Fly not away, then, from the very place where forgiveness
awaits thee.

"There is forgiveness with thee." Some read the passage,
"There is a propitiation with thee." Now, *the Lord Jesus Christ
is that propitiation*, and he is with God. He has gone up into the
glory, and he is at the right hand of the Father even now.
Make thou thy way to God, for the propitiation is there before
thee. Meet thy God at the mercy-seat lest thou have to meet
him at the judgment-seat. There is forgiveness always with
God, for Jesus is always there. Therefore, go thou to him, and
find it.

"There is forgiveness with thee," that is to say, *God has it in
his immediate gift;* he will not have to hunt for it, for it is with
him, he has it ready to bestow. He will not need thee to plead
for it with so many sighs, and cries, and tears, but he has it
waiting for thee. The writ by which thou shalt be set free is
made out already. "There is forgiveness with thee." The
Lord Jehovah has signed thy free pardon, it lies before him
now; go thou and take it. "There is forgiveness with thee,"
immediately, and if thou dost but believe in Jesus, thou shalt
receive it from his hand.

"There is forgiveness with thee." Then, depend upon it,
there is a way for forgiveness to get to me; for if God has it, he can
get to me with it somehow. I may be far off from hope; I may
be surrounded, as it were, with brick walls, shut in like a man
in one of the *oubliettes* of the Bastille, where men lay till they
were forgotten, and the very gaoler did not know who they

were, nor when they came there. If thou art even in such a sad state as that, God can get at thee; there is forgiveness with him, and he can get it to thee.

And if it be with God, then *there is a way for thee to get to it*, for there is One come who stands between thee and God. There is a Mediator between God and men, the man Christ Jesus; but you do not need a mediator between Christ and yourself, you can come to him just as you are. You do need a Mediator with God, and there is Jesus Christ, who is God and man, able to lay his hand both on thee and on thy gracious God, and to bring thee into his presence.

I feel somehow certain that I am going to have some souls to-night to be my reward. I love to ring those charming bells, "free grace and dying love." A great part of the pleasure of preaching is derived from the fact that I know that God's Word will not return unto him void, but that some who hear the Gospel message will receive it, and be saved. Listen to this word, thou doubting, trembling, despairing sinner, "there is forgiveness," and that forgiveness is with God. If I told you that it was with myself, and that I was the priest, perhaps you would be foolish enough to believe me; but I will tell you no such lie. It is not with any priest on earth, it is with the Lord. "There is forgiveness with thee;" and thou mayest go to God just as thou art, with nothing in thy hand, and cast thyself at his feet, quoting the name of his dear Son. Rest there, and the work is done; for, as God liveth, it is true, that there is forgiveness with him that he may be feared.

The last part of the text shows A DESIGN OF LOVE; "There is forgiveness with thee, that thou mayest be feared."

Somebody said, "I should have thought that it would have read, 'that thou mayest *be loved*'." Yes, so I should have thought; but then, you see, fear, especially in the Old Testament, includes love. It includes every holy feeling of reverence, and worship, and obedience towards God. That is the Old Testament name for true religion—"the fear of God." So I might say that the text declares, "There is forgiveness with thee, that thou mayest be loved, and worshipped, and served." Still, even in the sense of fear, it is a most blessed fact that they who fear the Lord are delightful to him. "The Lord taketh pleasure in them that fear him, in those that hope in his mercy."

Do you not see how it is, that men fear the Lord because he forgives their sins? It must be so, because, first, if he did not forgive their sins, *there would be nobody left to fear him,* for they would all die. If he were to deal with men after their sins, he must sweep the whole race of mankind off the face of the earth ; but there is forgiveness with him, that he may be feared.

Next, if it were certain that God did not pardon sin, *everybody would despair,* and so again there would be nobody to fear him, for a despairing heart grows hard like the nether millstone. Because they have no hope, men go on to sin worse and worse ; but there is forgiveness with God that he may be feared. The devils never repent, for there is no pardon for them. There is no Gospel preached in hell, and consequently there is no relenting, no repenting, no turning towards God among lost spirits. But there is forgiveness with him that he may be feared by you.

What a wonderful effect pardon has upon a man! What a wonderful effect it has upon a man to know that he is pardoned, to be sure that he is forgiven! *He begins to tremble all over.* Remember how it is written, ''And I will cause the captivity of Judah and the captivity of Israel to return, and will build them, as at the first. And I will cleanse them from all their iniquity, whereby they have sinned against me ; and I will pardon all their iniquities, whereby they have sinned, and whereby they have transgressed against me. And it shall be to me a name of joy, a praise and an honour before all the nations of the earth, which shall hear all the good that I do unto them ; and they shall fear and tremble for all the goodness and for all the prosperity that I procure unto it.''

A man who has been forgiven is afraid that he should go and sin again after such love and such mercy. He is melted down by the goodness of the Lord, he does not know what to make of it. For a time, he can hardly believe that it is true. I know that, when I was converted, I felt at first like Peter when the great iron gate was opened, and the angel brought him out of prison, he wist not what was done unto him of the angel, and he thought he saw a vision ; he could not believe it to be true that he was really released. So is it with the saved sinner ; you are so amazed, you are so overwhelmed, that you are even filled with fear at the intense delight of pardon, being half afraid that it cannot really be true that such a wretch as you can have been pardoned, and that all your iniquities are blotted out for ever.

Are there any of God's people here who are afraid that they do not fear God enough? If you want to revive your fear of God, and have it deepened, believe in your pardon. Look! it is a singular way to come to fear God, but believe that you are forgiven, prize your forgiveness, know that your sins are blotted out, cling to the cross, and so all that sweet fear of God, by which is meant the whole of piety, will abound in your soul.

Some think that it will be a good way of deepening their graces to begin to question whether they are Christians. That is the wrong way altogether. Unbelief does not heal anybody; it is faith that heals. Believe thou up to the hilt; believe thou, come what may to thee; believe thou in Christ, though thy sins rage and rave and roar. Believe thou in Christ, though the devil tell thee thou art damned. Should hell seem to open at thy feet, believe thou in thy pardon through the precious blood, and do not stagger at the promise of God through unbelief; and thou shalt feel thyself filled with a holy fear, and joy, and peace, and love, and zeal, and burning desire to serve him who has done all this for thee. "There is forgiveness with thee, that thou mayest be feared."

If any of you poor people here, who have not yet found the Saviour, are saying, "We wish that we could feel our sin more; we wish that we could fear the Lord more;" let me tell you that this fear is to come to you afterwards. There is forgiveness first, and then the fear comes afterwards. All the fear in the world that is worth having is the result of pardoned sin. The fear that is not to be cast out, the fear that hath no torment in it, is that fear which comes of a sense of every iniquity being blotted out. I charge you, believe in Jesus Christ. In the name of Jesus of Nazareth I say to you unbelieving ones,—Believe in him now. Rise, take up your bed, and walk. I, who have no power whatever of myself, yet speaking in my Master's name, know that his power will go with his Gospel, and that his word shall not return unto him void. Believe and live.

XVIII

GOD'S KING MAGNIFIED

"His enemies will I clothe with shame: but upon himself
shall his crown flourish."—Psalm 132: 18.

THE Lord Jesus Christ communicates much to men with
whom he comes in contact, and has a mighty influence
upon them. *He* is blessed, and he is made a blessing. To those
who love him, Jesus Christ becomes a savour of life unto life.
To those who are rebellious and continue to despise him he
becomes a savour of death unto death. Our Saviour, then, has
an influence upon all those with whom he comes in contact and
association. If I compare his human nature with clay, I must
compare it with the scented clay, which yields a perfume on all
sides. You cannot hear of Jesus Christ without either getting
a blessing or involving the responsibility of rejecting a blessing.
I repeat it,—he becomes a blessing to all those who are round
about him, or else, if that blessing be not received, it brings
guilt upon the souls of those who reject him. He is either the
stone on which we build our hope and our trust, or else he
becomes a stone of stumbling and a rock of offence to those who
stumble at his word, being disobedient.

You see, the text teaches very definitely this truth, for it not
only speaks of Christ himself, but of what will become of those
who are his enemies. No doubt we may also very properly
draw from the text what shall become of his friends, for that
same hand which is sure to clothe his enemies with confusion,
will be certain yet to clothe his friends with honour and with
glory. He who uses the left hand so powerfully to smite his
foes, uses his right hand with equal force to bless his friends.

The text, therefore, divides itself very easily and naturally
into the two great declarations, and we see the clothing of the
enemies of the Lord Jesus Christ with divine shame, and then
again, the crowning of the Lord with a flourishing diadem of
eternal glory.

First, then, we look at THE ENEMIES OF CHRIST WHOM GOD
SAYS HE WILL "CLOTHE WITH SHAME."

Who are these enemies of Christ? In the days of his flesh, you
could very easily have discovered them. Some slandered him,
calling him friend of sinners, gluttonous and a wine-bibber,
having a devil, and being even a blasphemer. Some took up
stones to kill him. Some cried, "Crucify him! Crucify him!"
And others bribed the multitude that they might thus hound
him to his shameful and cruel death. Enemies he had on all
sides. But there are many who think to-day that had they
lived in that age they would have been numbered with his
friends. If it be so, is it not strange that they are not among his
friends now? If they would have behaved so well 1800 years
ago, it is singular they should behave so ill now. Our belief is,
and the common actions of mankind justify it, that had the
sinners of this present day who pretended to have so much
affection for the person of Christ, lived in that age, they, too,
alas! would have helped to crucify the Lord of life and glory,
for they do in effect crucify him now.

Who are his enemies, then, to-day? We will not think about
those Scribes and Pharisees, and so on, who are all dead and
gone, but let us ask who are his enemies now? Of course,
everybody says that open sinners *are the enemies of Christ*. Do
they not by their actions say, "We will not have this man to
reign over us"? His Book they will not read. His day of rest
they do not care to keep. To the messages of his ministers they
will not listen. His word, "Believe and live," they cast behind
their backs, and having done this they destroy their own souls,
and do everything that must grieve his Holy Spirit. Are there
none such here now—lovers of pleasure more than lovers of
God—some who would even use the word of blasphemy and
indulge in the sins of the flesh? We are not harsh if we put you
down among the enemies of Christ. You are evidently not with
him, and he himself has said, "He that is not with me is against
me." You are not on the Lord's side, and—there can be no
"betweenites"—you are on the side of his enemies. He himself
declares that it must be so. "If God be God," said Elijah,
"serve him, but if Baal be God, serve him." You do in effect
say, "The world is my god; myself, my own soul, my own
pleasure, my own opinions—these be my gods; as for Jehovah

and his Christ, I know nothing concerning them." Well, you must be put among his enemies, and I would ask you, then, just to take this text, and taste the bitterness of it, and that may save you from knowing its bitterness in another world.

But Christ has other enemies, namely, *those who are outwardly moral and excellent in conversation and conduct, but who deny the Lord Jesus Christ.* There are some very excellent people in all other respects, who doubt his Deity, or say they do : who will even say hard things of him as the Son of God. They say they much revere his character as a man, and conceive him to be, in fact, a very model of what manhood should be, but they will not accept him in his true character as the anointed Son of God and the Saviour of the world. Now, the Lord Jesus Christ will most certainly consider such to be his enemies.

It is no use for a man to say concerning a monarch, "I have a great respect for the monarch in his private character ; I would not do anything to injure him ; I would even hold him up to respect in his private character ; but as a king I will never yield him loyal homage, I will never obey him. Indeed, I will do all I can to pluck the crown from off his head." Could the king do otherwise than reckon such a person to be his enemy? It would be in vain for the man to say, "I am privately your friend." The king would say, "Oh, but I esteem my crown to be as precious as my life." So the Lord Jesus Christ cannot have the crown-rights of his true Deity touched. He "counts it not robbery to be equal with God," and he is called, "God over all, blessed for evermore." He who trod the waves of Galilee's lake, whose voice death heard and gave up its prey, he who opened the gates of Paradise to the dying robber, claims to be none other than equal with the Eternal Father, and like him "God over all," and it is in vain for you to say you respect his character as a man, if you do not accept him in his Deity, and accept him in his official character as the Saviour of sinners, you cannot be otherwise than numbered amongst his enemies. Well, now, if this should seem to be uncharitable, let me say that I cannot help telling you what I solemnly believe to be the truth, and I must therefore, my friend, leave with you this text, "His enemies will I clothe with shame."

But, again ; there are other persons who are sound enough in their doctrinal views concerning Christ, and who are excellent in their moral character, too, but *who are trusting in themselves that they are righteous.* You will, perhaps, be startled when I class you among the enemies of Christ. My dear friend, Christ is the King of Grace. He is in this world to vindicate the plan of salvation by grace. You, you see, instead of accepting this plan of salvation by grace, set up the opposite principle of salvation by merit. Merit is anti-Christ. The very essence of Popery, that which is so hateful in it to us, and we believe so obnoxious to the Lord, is not so much its outward rites and ceremonies, as its inward spirit of setting up human merit.

There are two merits—your own merit, and the merit of Christ. If you trust your own merit, you do in fact proclaim that you are opposed to Christ's way of saving by his merits. Christ claims to be the author and finisher of our faith, the Alpha and the Omega, but if you come in and say, "No, I will do this myself; my moral character, my private devotions, my outward attendance at the house of God, will serve me in good stead as a righteousness," you touch Christ in his tenderest point, for he claims among all his glories this first and chief, that he is the Saviour of sinners, and if you say that you can do without him, and if you profess to be your own saviour, you shall most certainly, however excellent your life may be, be numbered with his enemies. Oh, it will be a sad case for you respectable people, you good, excellent people, when this text shall be fulfilled in you, "His enemies will I clothe with shame."

There is one other class I would fain speak to, and I think they are the worst of all—those who acknowledge that salvation is by grace, and profess to be saved by the blood and righteousness of Christ, who unite themselves with Christ's Church, but *whose lives are so unhallowed as to dishonour him.* You know how the Apostle, half-choked with his sobs as he speaks, says, as he gazes upon such, "There be some of whom I have told you often, and now tell you even with weeping, that they are the enemies of the cross of Christ." What a terribly sad reflection! A member of a Christian church, and yet an enemy of the cross of Christ. I can suggest no better question for each and all of us than this, "Lord, is it I? Lord, is it I?" Why may it not be you? The preacher may ask himself why may it not be he? But whosoever it may be among us, this is certain, that our church standing will, so far from excusing us, only increase our guilt, and so it shall be tragically and sadly true, "His enemies will I clothe with shame."

Having thus given you, then, a brief list of who are Christ's enemies, and being anxious that you should ask yourselves, my dear hearers, whether you are among them, I want now to call your attention to the particular phraseology of the text in order to make out *what is meant by this being clothed with shame.* Do you see it? Shame! Nothing makes a man feel so cowardly and so mean as shame. There have been persons who would sooner die than be put to shame. Many a man would have been able to burn at the stake who has not been able to face public shame. It is a thing which cuts man's nature to the very quick. Now, if you and I have done anything that makes us ashamed do you know what we do? Why, we put our shame into the hollow of our hand, and we keep it there. We do not tell our wife, our children, our neighbours, but if we can, we go and hide our shame, and put it away. Now, God seems to say to you and to me, "You have been hiding that shame of yours; you have been wearing the garb of an outward righteousness; come here; you must put this shame on." "Nay, Lord," say you, "but I want to hide it." "No," saith he, "but you shall put it where it must be seen; where nobody shall be able to see you without seeing it; I will clothe you with it; it shall be all over you; you shall put it on as your outward array; you shall be wrapped in it; you shall sleep in it, awake in it, and walk abroad in it; you shall be clothed with shame!"

And it strikes me that the text may also bear this meaning: that when God comes to fulfil this threat, shame will be the sinner's only garment. He had the garment of a profession once: that is to be torn sharply from him, and he is to be arrayed only with his scarlet, blushing shame. Once his filthy rags, bad as they were in the sight of God, gave him a sort of covering, but now they shall all be stripped from him, and he will have nothing remaining but his shame. Shame shall be his garb from head to foot, nothing but shame in which to wrap himself.

Well, *this threat is sometimes very graciously turned into a promise.* I cannot wish for some of you a better wish than that you may in the first sense in which I am going to explain it, be clothed with shame, for when the Lord comes to a soul and says to it with a voice of love, "Thou hast been mine enemy, but I have loved thee with an everlasting love, therefore with lovingkindness have I drawn thee," then the soul is covered with shame. It cries out, "How could I be an enemy to so dear and true a friend?" I recollect one being converted to God by reading the hymn "Jesu, lover of my soul." "Oh," said the man, "is he the lover of my soul? Then how is it that I have been an enemy to him? Did he love me when on the tree of shame and death? Did he love me so as to pour out his heart's blood to redeem me? How can I have lived without honouring him?" And the man was clothed with shame!

Some of us have felt what it is to be thus clothed, so that when we went into the house of God we felt almost ashamed to sit with God's people; they did not know anything about what we were feeling, but we thought they did; and when we went to pray, we felt ashamed to pray, as though our sins would hide God from us, and we could not expect to obtain a blessing. We were so clothed with shame that we could not get it away from our eyes. Our whole soul seemed covered with it. No pride, no self-righteousness was left. We could not say, "Lord, I thank thee I am not as other men," but we began to cry, "God be merciful to me a sinner!" Oh, it is a mercy when, in a gracious sense, the soul is thus covered with shame, a hallowed shame on account of its many sins!

But alas! this text bears on its front a very much more terrible meaning than this. *There are some persons who are clothed with shame in this world through disappointment.* There are some who think they should put an end to Christianity. They get a notion into their heads, for instance, that if the wife is converted they will break her of it, or if a child shows some sign of grace the man says, "I will laugh it out of him." Or perhaps they do it on a large scale. Like Voltaire, they boast that within another twenty years there will not be a Christian to be found anywhere; they say that the thing is absurd, and is dying out. It is very strange that the very press with which Voltaire printed his works, is now used in Geneva to print the Bible, and that whilst Voltaire himself is only remembered to be execrated, Christianity seems never to have been so strong as it is at the present day.

If all those men who have risen up one after the other to

injure Christ's kingdom, could just now be called back to life and see what has happened, they would look at their predictions and be clothed with shame to see how mistaken they have all been. Their theories have been exploded. They had their little day, and have died out and are generally utterly forgotten. And so will all theories that oppose Christ to-day die out, and their systems of denial will be all clothed with shame.

In the case of those persecutors who have tried to drive religion out of individuals, they have always been disappointed. They have not succeeded, for the poor, trampled-down one has borne it all with supernatural patience, and triumphed by endurance; for the grace of God is not to be expelled from the heart. You know what stout old Martin Luther said. He declared that grace was like leaven; you put it into the meal, and then you may boil it or bake it, fry it or freeze it, but you can never get out the leaven. Once the meal is leaven, nothing can unleaven it. And so is it with the grace of God. You may do what you will with a man who possesses it. Put him into a mortar and pound him with a pestle until there are not two atoms of him left together, and yet the immortal spirit leaving the anatomy and all its weaknesses behind it, would but the more clearly lay hold on Christ, and more fully rejoice in him, and so, when the disappointment which this brings comes upon them, then Christ's enemies are clothed with shame.

Sometimes, again, in this world *the enemies of Christ are clothed with the shame of remorse.* Look at Judas Iscariot when he took the pieces of money, and threw them down in the treasury, and went out and hanged himself. There was the covering of shame. And there have been such men since, who, in life and in death, have been clothed with shame because they have apostatized from the faith, and, after making a profession, have, Demas-like, turned back again to the world. It is a blessed thing if that shame leads them to true repentance, but in many cases it is only a repentance that comes from a fear of punishment, and is not the work of the grace of God! Oh, how many have gone down to perdition with its fire burning in their hearts before they got there, feeling the guilt of sin upon them even before God began to handle them.

But the most terrible fulfilment of my text *is left for another world. Then* shall Christ's enemies be clothed with shame.

Servants of Satan, here is your livery! Do you say you will not
put it on? Listen: "His enemies will *I* clothe with shame."
God will put it on you. You would not wear the robe of righteousness; you shall not be able to decline to wear the robe of
shame. God himself here stands, as it were, and declares that
he will dress his creature in the proper garment for him to
wear. You must put it on; there is no escape. You must wear
it. Here is your eternal convict's dress, and, convicted of
being an enemy of God, you must wear it—of all dresses the
most terrible. To be clothed with pain would be far less dreadful
than to be clothed with shame. I would sooner at any time feel
the acutest pain that is possible in the body than feel shame,
for a prick of the conscience is worse than the thrust of the
surgeon's knife. To go crawling about God's world not able to
look one's fellow-creatures in the face! Why, I would sooner
die! And then, in the next world, to be so ashamed that you
will not be able to look even the devil in the face, because he
never had a day of grace as you have had; never a Saviour
preached to him, never made any pretence of being converted
to God, and therefore, though an enemy of Christ, has no such
cause of shame as you will have. Clothed with shame! You
will be like the man of whom we read, that when the king said
to him, "How camest thou in hither, not having a wedding
garment?" he was speechless. Why speechless? Shame made
his tongue refuse to do its office; and so will shame do with you.

Shall I tell you why when you hear of the cross of Christ
and yet reject it, you will be ashamed? You will be ashamed
then of your sins. You are not able, perhaps, to boast of them
now, but you will be ashamed to think then that they shall be
published. Men are afraid now to have some things put in the
newspaper, but what will it be when God will gazette your
private sins, when he shall publish to the whole assembled
world of every age, to heaven, and earth, and hell, the sins
which you have committed; when they shall be read out so
that all shall hear, and all your filth be discovered? What shame
will this revelation of secret things produce! And what will be
your shame when the hypocritical profession which you have
made shall also be laid bare? Then shall those who were open
sinners laugh you to scorn, and say of you, as the prophet
pictures the kings saying of the great monarch of Babylon,

"Art thou become like unto one of us? Art thou also become weak as we, and covered with shame?"

Most of all, perhaps, you will be ashamed when you see the very people you despised reigning in triumph—when you see the saints whom you laughed at sitting at the right hand of the Judge—those fools who disdain this world's pleasures now entering into everlasting pleasure—and you, the wise man, who took the bird in the hand and would not wait for the bird in the bush,—now rewarded for it all by receiving the very worst things, inasmuch as you had your best things first, and must now have your worst things last.

It is a sad, sad text I have to preach upon. I would to God it would go into your souls, that you may turn unto the King, and be no more his enemies. God himself hath said it—it is no word of mine, "His enemies will I clothe with shame." He himself, who can do it, who can make you ashamed, however proud you are, who knows how to put his hand inside your heart and touch the strings thereof, and loosen them, so that your pride can no longer help you to brazen it out with him—he has said it, "His enemies will I clothe with shame." I pray you, "Kiss the Son lest he be angry, and ye perish from the way, when his wrath is kindled but a little; blessed are all they that put their trust in him."

Now, we take the second part of our subject: "Upon himself shall his crown flourish." We are here very clearly taught that THE SAVIOUR WILL WEAR A CROWN, THAT THE CROWN WILL FLOURISH, THAT IT WILL FLOURISH UPON HIM.

Brethren, I need not detain you long by mentioning to you the crowns which Jesus wears. He has the crowns-royal of the kingdoms of heaven, and earth, and hell; for "the government is upon his shoulder, and his name shall be called Wonderful, the Counsellor, the Mighty God, the Everlasting Father, the Prince of Peace."

He is the King of kings and the Lord of lords. But he has a crown which he specially now wears as head of the Church, and in this he takes great delight—the crown which is called in the matchless song, "The crown wherewith his mother crowned him in the day of his espousals." That is the crown which the Church has put upon him, and which she still delights to put upon his head. Do you not all delight to crown the Saviour, my brethren and sisters in Christ? What song wakes up your heart more completely than the one—

> *"All hail the power of Jesus' name!*
> *Let angels prostrate fall;*
> *Bring forth the royal diadem,*
> *And crown him Lord of all."*

Have we not sometimes seemed to make these walls echo again and again as we sang—

> *"Crown him, crown him,*
> *Crowns become the Victor's brow"*?

Crowned once with the thorn for us, he ought now to be crowned with the royal diadem. Every one of us must seek to spend and to be spent that we may add to the lustre of that tiara, that he may be exalted above all principalities and powers in the estimation of men, and that he may have a kingdom in all men's hearts.

Christ is thus said to have a crown, and it is added *that his crown shall flourish.* There are some crowns that are gradually diminishing in lustre, "but upon himself shall his crown flourish." When does a crown flourish? You understand that the very term is metaphorical. It is a metaphor expressive of joy, comfort, tranquillity in a kingdom. Now, when does a crown flourish? Does it not flourish *when the sovereign is beloved by his subjects?* The foundations of a throne are always to be found in the love of the people. Christ's crown, then, flourishes indeed, for the upright love him. His name is as ointment poured forth; therefore the virgins love him. We can truly sing, " Jesus, the very thought of thee With sweetness fills my breast."

A crown flourishes when the power of the monarch is *victorious in war, and acknowledged in peace.* It is so with Christ. Oh, that it were more publicly so! We are praying for Revivals, and may God send them! Oh, that Jesus Christ's crown may flourish in the conquest of innumerable hearts who shall add fresh territories to the dominion of the Saviour, for a crown flourishes when a king's subjects increase and his numbers are multiplied.

It shall be so with Christ. Until the sun has gone down with age, and the moon has quenched her nightly lamp, and every star has, like a withered fig-leaf, fallen from the sky, Christ's Kingdom shall go on and on. As a brook at first, it seemed to leap down Calvary's side. It has swollen to a river now. Still it deepens, and widens. It becomes an ocean which shall cover the earth as the waters cover the sea. Christ rose and it was twilight, now he begins to climb the steep, and the day is coming but the full noon-tide draweth nigh, when he shall flood the whole earth with the splendour of his light and his glory, and when it shall be found that its going forth is from one end of the heavens to the other. May the long-expected day fully come! May the realms of woe, of sin, and death, be filled with this great light! His crown shall flourish.

It is remarkable that while all sorts of dynasties have come and gone the dynasty of Christ still exists! How many mighty monarchs have climbed, with great slaughter, to their thrones, and where are they now? Rome has gone, but the Man of Nazareth is King still! And, besides Rome, how many empires have arisen? Earth has been shaken with the tramping of their legions, but where are their thrones and the men who filled them? They are gone, gone to the dust from which they came! But the name of Jesus shall endure for ever; always shall men be blessed in him, and all generations shall call him blessed. The day shall come, unless the Lord himself appears, when the moss shall grow in the halls of the greatest kings, when the marts of commerce shall have shifted from their places. Perhaps the day may come when this modern Babylon, this emporium of all the riches of the earth, shall cease from her glory. Perhaps to Western climes—for everything moves Westward—the greatness may yet go. We do not know. "Thy throne, O God, is for ever and ever; a sceptre of righteousness is thy sceptre; thou lovest righteousness and hatest wickedness, and therefore God, even thy God, hath anointed thee with the oil of gladness above thy fellows."

Do notice, once more, it is said, "*But upon himself* shall his crown flourish." Does it mean that the crown shall always be seen to have reference to himself? Does it also mean that it shall be by his own power and his own person that he shall sustain the dignity of his crown? Sometimes the crowns of monarchs seem to flourish upon the heads of their prime ministers or privy councillors. It seems as if the empire flourishes because of some admirable person at its back. But it is not so with Christ. *"Upon himself* shall his crown flourish." He won it; he wears it; he sustains it. He throws down the gauntlet to every foe who would rob him of it. Now, this seems to say to us when we preach his Gospel, we must preach Christ, because it is upon truth concerning him that his crown shall flourish. If we do not, therefore, preach up Christ himself, if he be not the great subject of our discourse, if he be not held up manifestly crucified among the people, we have kept back the mightiest theme. It is upon himself that his crown must flourish. Preach Christ, make him first and make him last, and there will be souls won, and saints comforted; for "upon himself shall his crown flourish."

What is wanted in the midst of his Church, then, is that the King himself should appear in his glory; that he should once again make bare his arm, and use that mighty sword of his, which cuts through coats of mail, and pierces to the dividing asunder of soul and spirit, joints and marrow, and when he comes, oh, when he comes, his crown flourishes indeed! We must pray for him to be constantly with us by his Spirit. We must watch, also, for his personal Advent, for he whom the disciples saw go up to heaven shall in like manner appear again. Then the glory! Then the manifestation of the hidden ones! Then the declaration of the love of God towards those who have been under reproach and under adversity! Be of good courage, brethren, for he cometh, he cometh, and then "upon himself shall his crown flourish."

I have thus tried to preach both to saint and sinner. Oh, that he would bring the sinner to himself to-night! Oh, dear hearer, I cannot bear the thought that you should have to wear shame as your everlasting covering! "His enemies will I clothe with shame." See what your livery is to be for ever and ever! See what your everlasting garment is to be! God grant that you may, instead of being clothed with shame, breathe the prayer "Lord, clothe me with thy righteousness: wash me in thy precious blood: make me thy friend, and suffer me no longer to be amongst those of whom it is written, 'Shame shall be the promotion of fools.'"

XIX

DAVID'S FIVE-STRINGED HARP

"I said unto the LORD, Thou art my God: hear the voice of
my supplications, O LORD. O GOD, the Lord, the strength of
my salvation, thou has covered my head in the day of battle.
. . . I know that the LORD will maintain the cause of the
afflicted, and the right of the poor. Surely the righteous shall
give thanks unto thy name: the upright shall dwell in thy
presence."—Psalm 140: 6, 7, 12, 13.

THIS Psalm was written by David when he was sorely
vexed by many adversaries. These adversaries were bent
upon his destruction; they could not bear that the son of Jesse
should be favoured of God, and that he should come to the
throne; so they set their wits to work to invent all manner of
slanders against him. They misconstrued his actions, they
misrepresented his motives; they spat the very venom of asps
from their mouths against him; and, at the same time, they
said one to another, "If we can lead him to do wrong, if we can,
somehow or other, entrap him, either in his speech, or in his
private character, or in his public actions, then we shall have
a weapon wherewith we can smite him." The ungodly are fully
aware that slander is, after all, a very dangerous weapon to
handle, and, like the Australian boomerang, it is very apt to
come back to the man who throws it. Stones, hurled into the
air, often fall upon the head of the thrower; and slander often
recoils upon those who utter it. So, if they can but get a truthful accusation against a man of God, then they are exceeding
glad. Slander is like shooting at a man with powder only, or
with very small shot, that can sting, but cannot kill; but, oh,
if they can discover some questionable action of the man, or
some decided wrong-doing, then they can load their rifles with
bullets, and have something deadly to fire at the righteous!

I want you to notice how this man of God acted in this
trying time. He betook himself to his knees; he began to pray,
"Deliver me, O Lord, from the evil man: preserve me from the

violent man." And again, in the next Psalm, he said, "Lord, I cry unto thee: make haste unto me; give ear unto my voice, when I cry unto thee." He found his remedy for all the stings of falsehood in drawing near to the living God. He was a wise man thus to bathe his wounds in that bath which alone could take the venom out of them, by a prayerful drawing nigh to the Most High, and he mingled great faith with his prayer.

When trying to expound this Psalm, I was much struck with the positive way in which David speaks all through it. Notice that sixth verse: "I said unto the Lord, Thou art my God." That is a grand way to talk. And then, further on, in the twelfth verse: "I know that the Lord will maintain the cause of the afflicted." He has no question about the matter, no hesitation; he does not say, "I hope he will;" but, "I know he will, I am confident of it." And that makes him say, in the last verse, "Surely,"—he felt so certain about it that he could say, "Surely the righteous shall give thanks unto thy name." It is a blessed thing when faith rises as tribulations increase. A little faith may do for a skirmish with the enemy but you want the full assurance of faith for a pitched battle. When the waters are up to the ankles, a little faith may enable you to stand; but when you get to "waters to swim in," then you need, in childlike confidence, to cast yourself entirely upon the stream of divine love, or else, assuredly, you will sink.

May God be pleased to increase the faith of all of us who do believe in Jesus! If we are tempted and tried very sorely, may the great High Priest, whom we cannot see, but who always sees us, and foresees every danger to which we are exposed, pray for us till he can say to each one of us, as he did to Peter, "Satan hath desired to have you, that he may sift you as wheat: but I have prayed for thee, that thy faith fail not:" for, if faith keeps her proper place, and prayer does her duty, there will be a way for the child of God to escape from every trial.

There are five things in my text to which I want especially to draw the attention of any who are in sore trouble, and particularly those who are in trouble from enemies who are seeking to ruin them. That which occupied and satisfied David's mind may wisely occupy and satisfy ours when we are in a similar condition to his. Flowers from which this bee has sucked some honey are the kind of flowers for us to alight upon, with the expectation that in them we shall find honey, too. The first thing I see here is, *possession asserted*: "I said unto the Lord, Thou art my God." The second is, *a petition presented*: "Hear the voice of my supplications, O Lord." The third is, *preservation experienced*: "O God the Lord, the strength of my salvation, thou hast covered my head in the day of battle." The fourth is, *protection expected*: "I know that the Lord will maintain the cause of the afflicted, and the right of the poor." The last is, *praise predicted*: "Surely the righteous shall give thanks unto thy name: the upright shall dwell in thy presence." I can only speak very briefly upon each head.

The first is very precious; I pray that every child of God may realize and experience it. It is POSSESSION ASSERTED: "I said unto the Lord, Thou art my God."

What was *the possession*? It was the Lord himself: "I said unto the Lord, Thou art my God." The word "LORD" here means Jehovah; you see that it is in capital letters, and whenever our translators print the word "LORD" thus, they mean Jehovah. "I said unto Jehovah, the only living and true God, Thou art my God." This is a wonderful speech for David to make: "'Thou art my God,' in opposition to the gods of the heathen. They may worship Baal and Ashtaroth, but 'thou art my God.' I count other gods to be idols, the works of men's hands, and I despise them; all other confidences, all other grounds of trust, are to me but as broken cisterns that can hold no water. 'I said unto Jehovah, the only living God, Thou art my God,' in opposition to every other who is called God."

"'I said unto Jehovah, Thou art *my* God.' I have taken thee unto myself as much as if no other man ever trusted thee. I feel that I could stand alone, and acknowledge thee to be the God of the whole earth; I said to my heart, 'All that God is, is henceforth mine.' He has given himself to me in the covenant wherein he said, 'I will be their God;' and he is as much mine as if he belonged to nobody else; yea, as fully, as completely, and as entirely mine, if I am a believer in him, as if I were his only child, his only chosen, his only redeemed one." Oh, but this is a wonderful thing, to put the lines of possession round the Infinite, to lay the grasp of faith upon the Incomprehensible, and to say, "Jehovah, thou art my God."

Your possessions are very large. "How say you so?" asks one; "my garments are wearing out, and I am sure I do not know how I shall ever renew them. My cupboard is very bare, and my purse is empty." My dear brother in Christ, you are a very rich man after all, for all these treasures that may be eaten up with moth, or cankered and corrupted, what are they? But if God be your God, all things are yours, for all things are in God, and the God who has given himself to us cannot deny us anything. Nay, he has already by that very act given everything to us. So I pray that every child of God may know that he has this possession, and be able to say without any hesitancy, "O Jehovah, thou art my God."

Observe in the text, not only mention made of the possession, but of *the claim to it.* "I said unto Jehovah, Thou art my God." David exhibited his title-deeds; he did not say to himself, "That possession is mine, but I will leave it unrecognized and unclaimed," but he declared his right to it: "I said unto Jehovah, Thou art my God." Oh, if the children of God would sometimes be silent instead of speaking, they would be wise; but if, on the other hand, they would sometimes speak instead of remaining silent, they might be equally wise. Have *you* ever *said* to the Lord, "Thou art my God;" have you said it? "Well, I have hoped it," says one. Oh, but I want you to get much beyond that, till, with full assurance, helped of the Holy Spirit, you can say, "It *is* so; my faith has grasped my God, and I have dared to say it, say it at the mercy-seat, to say it when I stood at the foot of the cross, and I expect to say it, before long, when I stand before Jehovah's throne above, 'Thou art my God.' I put in my claim. I dare do no otherwise. I could not let thee go without claiming thee as my own. O Lord, thou hast been my dwelling place in all generations. I have said unto thee, Thou art my God."

Notice also where this claim was made, in whose presence, and who was *the attesting Witness* to it: "I said unto Jehovah, Thou art my God." It is a very easy thing to say to the minister, "The Lord is my God;" or to say it to some Christian friend by way of profession; but it may not be true. It is a very solemn thing to be able to say to Jehovah, "Thou art my God." True believers have dialogues with their God; they are accustomed to speak with the Most High. They may say some good things to men, but they say their best things to God: "I said unto Jehovah, Thou art my God." Can you stand, at this moment, as in the dreadful presence of the Eternal? Can you realize to yourself that he sees and hears you, that he is all around you, that he is in you, can you think of his infinite holiness and his inflexible justice, and yet say to him, "Thou art my God; thou art a consuming fire, but thou art my God"? Even our God, the God of those who believe, is a consuming fire, yet we call him ours. It is a grand thing, in time of trouble, in time of slander, in time of temptation, if you can just turn your back on it all, and say, "I look to God, and I say, 'O Jehovah, thou art my God. I say it even in thy presence.'" If you can truly say this, it will spread over your spirit a delightful calm, it will encase you as in armour of proof, it will make your bleeding wounds to be stanched, and your broken heart to rejoice, if you can say it.

And, once more, it seems to me to be a grand point in this text to note *the occasion chosen* by David to say, "Thou art my God." It was in the time of his trouble that he repeated to himself the fact that he had made this declaration: "'I said unto Jehovah, Thou art my God.' Men said that I had a devil; but I said, 'Thou art my God.' They said I was a castaway: but I said, 'Thou art my God.' They said I was without a friend; but I said unto Jehovah, 'Thou art my God.' They said of me everything they could think of that was bad, and they would have said worse things if they could have thought of them; and after they had done their worst, and said all they could say, I said unto Jehovah, 'Thou art my God.'"

Sometimes, in the court, a judge stops a witness, and says, "I do not want to know what you said, and what the other man said; I want to know what you saw." But in this case, we do not wish to stop the good man, we wish him to go on, and tell us more of what he said when he was in the very midst of his trouble. "'I said unto Jehovah, Thou art my God;' and my enemies may say what they like after that. Now, open your mouths, let your venom come forth; ye who are like adders and asps, sting as sharply as you may, you can do me no hurt, for 'I said unto Jehovah, Thou art my God.'"

The next thing I see is, A PETITION PRESENTED. It ran in this fashion,—"Hear the voice of my supplications, O Lord,"

from which I gather that *his prayers were frequent.* He puts
the word in the plural: "Hear the voice of my *supplications.*"
He did not, in those days of trouble, pray once, and have done
with praying; but he prayed again, and again, and again, and
again, and again, and again. When you have double trouble,
take care that you have double prayer. When men speak worst
against you, then speak most with your God. Multiply your
supplications as God multiplies your tribulations. "Hear the
voice of my supplications, O Lord." Importunate prayers will
prevail.

Next, I gather that *David's prayers were full of meaning,*
"Hear the *voice* of my supplications." There are some people's
prayers that are dumb prayers. They just offer so many words,
and yet there is no voice in them. It is a grand thing to have a
voiceful prayer. We cannot always tell what is the "voice" of
a man's prayer, especially when that prayer is full of moans,
and tears, and sobs, and sighs; but God hears a peculiar "voice"
in every true supplication. If there were a houseful of children,
and they were all to cry, yet a mother would distinguish her
baby's supplication from all the other cries; and when she
went to the child, she would find out what the little one wanted.
You and I would not know, perhaps, but she does. "Poor
darling" she says, and she puts herself into such sympathy
and union with her baby that she soon spells out the child's
meaning. What the babe cannot express, the mother can hear
and discern; and when you cannot pray as you would, God can
hear the voice of your supplications just as if you had said what
you wanted to say. He takes the meaning out of our hearts,
for our thoughts are like words to God. Remember that, to
speak into a man's ear, you must make a sound, else he cannot
distinguish your voice, but in God's ear there need be no sound
whatever, for he can hear the voice of your tears, the voice of
your silent supplication.

> "*To him there's music in a groan,*
> *And beauty in a tear.*"

Is it not a blessed thing that God understands the meaning of
our prayers? "Hear the voice of my supplications."

We learn also that David's prayers were *meant for God:* "I
said unto Jehovah, Thou art my God. Hear the voice of my

supplications, *O Jehovah.*" Some men's prayers are meant for themselves, just to quiet their consciences. Other men's prayers are meant for their friends, that they may see what pious people they are. But the true suppliant's prayer is meant for God; when he directs the envelope that contains his supplications, he addresses it to the God of heaven, for the prayer is meant for him.

And, once more, David's prayers were of such a kind that *he could not rest unless he had the Lord's attention.* This was his great cry, "Hear the voice of my supplications, O Jehovah." He could not bear to hear his own voice, unless God heard that voice. I do urge every troubled child of God to go straight away to his own God, and cry unto him. You thought of going down the street, and calling on Mrs. So-and-So, and telling her your sorrow. Yes, very well; you may do so if you like; but it is a shorter road to go to God with your trouble. Straightforward makes the best runner; and there is no door that has such an inviting knocker, and that opens so easily, as the door of God. Go you to the Lord with your trouble, ask him to hear you, for assuredly he will.

Now David, to encourage himself, mentions PRESERVATION EXPERIENCED: "O God, the Lord, the strength of my salvation, thou hast covered my head in the day of battle;" as much as to say, "Thou hast done this for me before, wilt thou not do the same again? As thou hast begun with me, do not leave off with me till thou hast taken me to the country where there are no more battles, and where my head shall be covered with a crown of glory, and need not be covered with a helmet to ward off the enemy's sword."

You remember that, when David went out to meet Goliath, two warriors came towards him, for Goliath came out with his armour-bearer: "the man that bore the shield went before him." Poor little David! He had no armour-bearer, had he? Saul had offered him armour that he might wear in the fight, but it did not fit him. He had never tried and proved such a protection as that, so he laid it aside. But was David without armour? No; the Hebrew of our text runs, "Thou hast covered my head in the day of armour." That is to say, *God had been David's Armour-bearer.* The Lord had borne a shield before him; instead of the harness in which warriors put their confidence, God had covered David with a coat of mail through which no sword of the enemy could possibly cut its way. Has it not been so with us in days past? Have we not had our heads covered when God held his shield above us? Have we not been guarded from all hurt by the providence and by the grace of the Most High? I know it is so. Well, then, the God that delivered us out of the jaw of the lion, and the paw of the bear, will deliver us from the uncircumcised Philistine; and the God that in our youth taught our hands to war, and our fingers to fight, so that the bow of steel was broken by our arms, will not leave us, and forsake us now that we have grown older and feebler; but even to the end will he preserve and protect us. Wherefore, let us be of good cheer, and let our past experience encourage us still to trust in the Lord.

"Thou hast covered my head in the day of battle," said David; that is, *God had guarded his most vital part.* "Lord, I have a cut or two here and there; I have scars upon my right arm, my foot has been injured, but 'Thou hast covered my head.' The adversaries could not give me such a blow as would lay bare my brain, and spill my soul upon the field, for 'Thou hast covered my head.'" Flesh wounds there may be, and deep bleeding gashes that cause pain and sickness of heart, but the essential part has been guarded, and we may rest contented that it shall be protected unto the end.

Moreover, David adds here that *God had been the strength of his salvation.* The power that had saved him had been God's power, and it is so with all of us who have been brought into the way of life.

Now, if the Lord had meant to destroy us, would he have done so much for us as he has done? I feel, when I think of some of my present troubles, very much like Admiral Drake, who had sailed round the world, and been here and there fighting the Spaniards on the great ocean, and when he came back to the Thames, it blew a gale, and his ship was likely to be driven ashore. He said, "No, no, no; we have not gone round the world, and now come home to be drowned in a ditch." So let us say, "No, no, no; we have not experienced so much of the goodness of God to be drowned in a paltry ditch like this." So let us still rejoice in the God who has preserved us until now, and who will preserve us until the day of Jesus Christ.

But I hasten on to notice the fourth thing in our text, that is, PROTECTION EXPECTED: "I know that the Lord will maintain the cause of the afflicted, and the right of the poor."

If a man is oppressed, if he is slandered, if he is evil spoken of, let him just say to himself, "God will see to this. *He is the Judge of all the earth,* and shall not he do right?" Do not meddle with the case yourself; leave it in the Lord's hands. Our proverb says, "If you want a thing done well, do it yourself;" but, if it is anything which has to do with your own character, let me tell you that this is the worst proverb that ever was invented. If you want a blot that you have made, or that somebody else has made, multiplied into two, try and rub it out with your finger while it is wet; but if you are wise, you will leave it alone. All the dirt that ever comes on a man's coat will brush off when it is dry. I do believe that, sometimes, holy characters shine all the brighter because they have been tarnished for a while by the filth cast upon them by ungodly men. If men cast mud at you, leave it alone. "But," says one, "this slander affects my character." Oh, yes! I know; but who are you that your character should not be assailed? "But it is the only one I have," say you. Well, that is quite right; and mind that you do not get another, and a worse one, by making a fool of yourself. Leave it alone, and be wise. The God who gave you the grace to have a good character will take care of what he has given you, and you need not be afraid, for God is a righteous Judge.

Moreover, beside that, *God is a compassionate Friend* and when he sees any of his dear saints very poor and afflicted, do you not think that, when they cannot take care of themselves, he will take care of them? David thought so, for he said, "I know that the Lord will maintain the cause of the afflicted, and the right of the poor." The rich man can take care of his own rights, but the poor man cannot; so God will take care that the poor man shall not lose his rights, or if he does, God will avenge him of his adversary. Trust thou thy cause with God; thou canst not have a better Advocate or a better Helper. Put not forth thy hand unto unrighteousness, neither speak thou on thine own behalf. Thou wilt be wise if thou wilt do as thy Master did, "who, when he was reviled, reviled not again," who was led as a lamb to the slaughter, and, as a sheep before her shearers is dumb, so opened he not his mouth.

Now, lastly, here is PRAISE PREDICTED : "Surely the righteous shall give thanks unto thy name."

They are down in the dumps to-day, they are troubled and burdened, despised and made to cry; but, says David, "Surely they shall give thanks unto thy name." *Praise is assured by gratitude.* There shall come a day when their gratitude shall be so great that they shall be obliged to give thanks unto God on account of all that he has done for them. "Surely" they shall; God will so astound them by his delivering mercy that they shall be compelled to speak up, and to speak out, and give thanks unto the name of the Lord.

Aye, and they shall do more than that, for they shall not only express their thanks, but *they shall praise God by their holy confidence*: "The upright shall dwell in thy presence." They shall be drawn nearer to God, and be peaceful, and happy, and quiet, and at ease. This is a beautiful and comforting promise : "The upright shall dwell in thy presence." All the world is up in arms against them, and there is a great uproar ; but what do they say? "Surely goodness and mercy shall follow us all the days of our life : and we will dwell in the house of the Lord for ever." One of the grandest ways of praising God is not by singing psalms and hymns—that is a very sweet way of praising him—but a grander way is by being quite calm in the time of trouble, quite happy in the hour of distress, just dwelling with God, and finding all your griefs assuaged in his blessed presence. How really and truly a child praises his father when he just bears anything from him! "It must be right," says he, "for my father does it;" and I believe that, when a child of God says, "It is the Lord; let him do what seemeth him good," he is praising God more than he could ever do with the cornet or the high-sounding cymbals.

And, once more, we can equally praise God by *abiding in fellowship with him.* "The upright shall sit in thy presence." So it may be rendered. How can I explain it? If you could look within the veil up yonder, in the glory country, you would see a Lamb in the midst of the throne, and round about him all those redeemed by blood, who have entered into their felicity; and you down here, in your time of trouble, can just go to your Father's table, and take your seat as one of his children, or go to your dear Saviour's feet, and take your place with Mary, and so you will be praising the Lord Jesus Christ in the most effectual manner. I know that your temptation will be to be buzzing about the kitchen there with Martha, fretting and worrying over what has happened, and what has not happened; but all that the Lord Jesus Christ will say to you will be, "Martha, Martha, Martha, Martha, thou art cumbered about many things."

I know men who ought to be called Martha, for they are as much cumbered as ever the women are, and just as ready to fret and to worry, so that the Saviour might say to them, "You are cumbered about many things; but if you want to praise me, come and sit here; come and learn of me, for that is the good part, which shall not be taken away from you; come and listen to me, give up your whole heart to drinking in my Word, and I will bless you. You come and mind my business, and I will stay and mind your business. Come and try me, and I will give you proof that trusting in me is the safest and best way of living in this world."

All this I have spoken to the people of God. I would you were all such, and, if you are not, I pray the Lord to bring you into the bonds of the covenant. It is a very blessed thing to come to Christ, and when you do come to him, all these precious things are yours. Trust in what Christ has done for sinners, trust in the promise of the faithful God to save all who believe in Jesus; and when you have trusted, you shall never be confounded, sinner though you be.